9 CHEMICAL PATTERNS

There are millions of different chemicals and it would be a huge task to remember the properties of each of them. Luckily no-one has to – scientists have identified **patterns** among elements and compounds which help us to be able to **predict** the properties of chemicals. This module shows you how to explain and predict such properties and how we make use of this knowledge in bleaches, food preservatives and fertilisers.

Relevant National Curriculum Attainment Targets: Old ATs (6), (7), (8) New AT (4)

9.1 The chemist's map

Decision time

You make decisions all the time. You make simple decisions such as what time to get up on a Saturday morning and important ones such as what to do when you leave school.

To help you make the right decisions about your career you'll probably try to get information from experts – the Careers Service, etc. You need to know whether the information is reliable before using it to make your choice.

Capricorn

(23 December–20 January)

Venus in Capricorn means you're going on a long journey. Some good news on the 15th means money isn't as tight as you expected. Forget spending wisely – buy something luxurious to cheer yourself up.

Would you buy a hifi and pack your suitcase on the basis of this information?

Finding patterns

If you're going somewhere new you may use a map to help you get to your destination. A road map shows an overall pattern between main roads and motorways. Once you understand this overall pattern you can use it to plan your route.

You may choose the quickest or the most scenic route or the one that avoids most of the traffic. As you get near your destination you can use a more detailed street map. You can see how the smaller streets fit into the larger pattern.

You'll find it easy to plan your route when you can follow an overall pattern in a map.

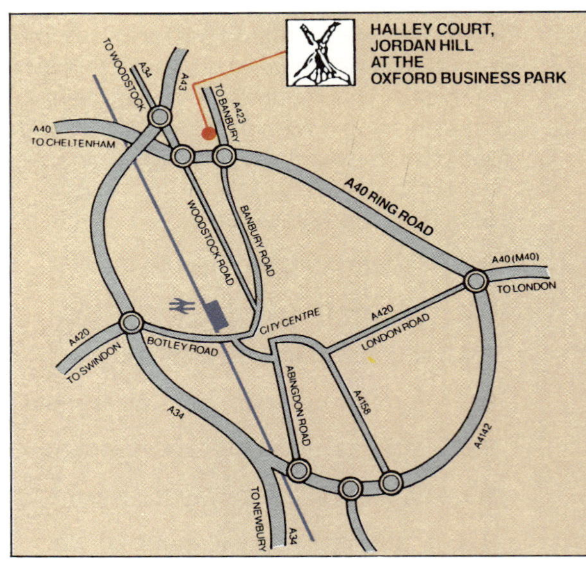

A chemical map

Scientists look for maps and patterns in the world so that they can make predictions.

Nearly 200 years ago, with the discovery of many chemical **elements**, chemists needed a map of the elements so that they could begin to find an overall pattern among them. However, it took chemists about 100 years before they found a pattern that was reliable enough to use.

Like the large road map you use to plan your travels, it contains more detailed patterns within it. And like using a road map, before you can begin to use the **Periodic Table** you need to understand what the patterns mean.

Potassium and copper are elements. As you will see later, they are both metals – but as you can see here, they react very differently with water. The Periodic Table helps you to make sense of the differing reactions of the elements.

The Periodic Table of Elements

TRANSITION METALS (columns between Group 2 and Group 3)

Period	GROUP 1 ALKALI METALS	GROUP 2 ALKALINE EARTH METALS											GROUP 3	GROUP 4	GROUP 5	GROUP 6	GROUP 7 HALOGENS	GROUP 8 INERT GASES
1								1 1 H hydrogen										4 2 He helium
2	7 3 Li lithium	9 4 Be beryllium											11 5 B boron	12 6 C carbon	14 7 N nitrogen	16 8 O oxygen	19 9 F fluorine	20 10 Ne neon
3	23 11 Na sodium	24 12 Mg magnesium											27 13 Al aluminium	28 14 Si silicon	31 15 P phosphorus	32 16 S sulphur	35.5 17 Cl chlorine	40 18 Ar argon
4	39 19 K potassium	40 20 Ca calcium	*	*	*	52 24 Cr chromium	55 25 Mn manganese	56 26 Fe iron	59 27 Co cobalt	59 28 Ni nickel	64 29 Cu copper	65 30 Zn zinc	Ga gallium	Ge germanium	As arsenic	Se selenium	80 35 Br bromine	84 36 Kr krypton
5	Rb rubidium	Sr strontium	*	*	*	*	*	*	*	*	108 47 Ag silver	112 48 Cd cadmium	In indium	119 50 Sn tin	Sb antimony	Te tellurium	127 53 I iodine	131 54 Xe xenon
6	Cs caesium	137 56 Ba barium	La lanthanium	*	*	*	*	*	*	195 78 Pt platinum	197 79 Au gold	201 80 Hg mercury	Tl thallium	207 82 Pb lead	Bi bismuth	Po polonium	At astatine	Rn radon
7	Fr francium	Ra radium	Ac actinium															

A range of elements called the lanthanides fit here

Another range of elements called the actinides fit here

KEYS

12	Relative Atomic Mass (common elements only)
C	Symbol
6	Mass Number (common elements only)
Carbon	name

* these represent various other elements not as common in everyday life

Blue: metallic elements

Green: non-metallic elements

Pink: non-metallic elements that rarely take part in chemical reactions

9.2 Patterns between elements

Elements and compounds

The world you live in is made of simple building blocks of substances called **elements**. Each element has its own special properties.

A few elements are found naturally on their own in the Earth or in the air. The element oxygen, for example, is a colourless gas which makes up about 20% of the air. Other elements occur in combination with each other, in the form of **compounds**. The properties of elements are different to those of their compounds.

Formation of oxides

There are 92 elements found naturally on Earth. All these different elements have different chemical properties. Many compounds can be formed by the different combinations of all these elements. Chemists look for patterns in the chemical properties of the elements so that they can make predictions about new compounds and about the properties of compounds.

When another element combines with oxygen it forms an **oxide**. Some oxides dissolve in water to form solutions which are either acidic, alkaline or neutral. The elements can be grouped together depending on the properties of their oxides.

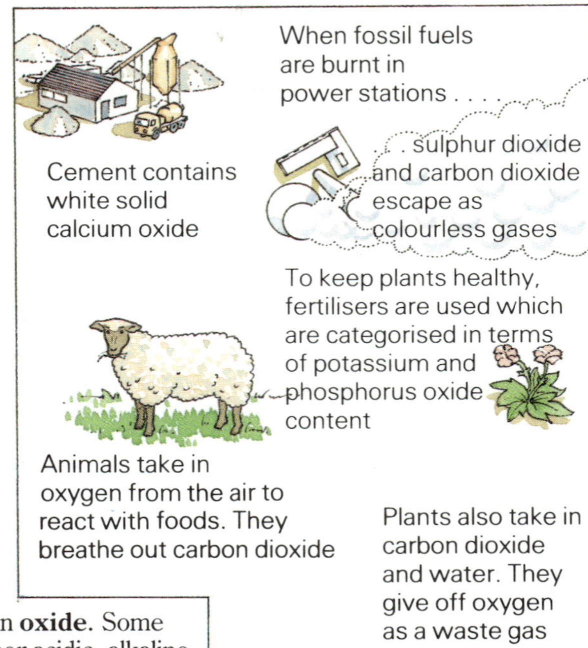

*Oxygen combines with other elements to form compounds called **oxides**.*

You can measure the acidity or alkalinity of a solution by using a scale called the **pH scale**. **Acids** such as vinegar have a *pH less than 7*, while **alkalis** like ammonia have a *pH greater than 7*. Distilled water is not acidic or alkaline – it is **neutral**. Its pH is 7.

Elements which form soluble oxides can be divided into three types depending on the pH value of their oxide solution. One type dissolves in water to form alkaline or **basic** solutions. They are called *basic oxides*. Why are phosphorus oxide and sulphur dioxide called *acidic oxides*? What type of oxide do you think water is?

You can test the pH value of a solution by adding universal indicator. It will turn a particular colour depending on the pH value of the solution.

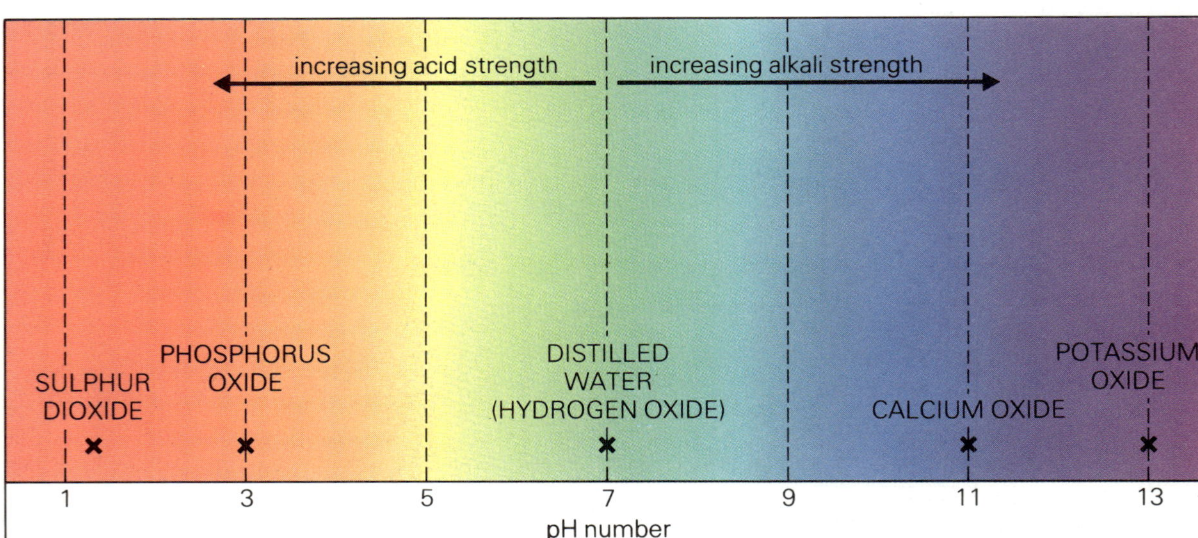

Metals and non-metals

You can see that the *chemical* properties of some of the elements, such as the properties of their oxides, are beginning to fall into a pattern.

Sulphur and phosphorus form acidic oxides whilst potassium and calcium form basic oxides. But do the same groups of elements have *physical* properties in common? Look at the data on some physical properties of the elements.

Elements which are good conductors of heat and electricity, and have a shiny appearance are called **metals**. Elements which are poor conductors of heat and electricity are called **non-metals**. You should now begin to see a pattern emerging. What type of elements do you think form basic oxides – metals or non-metals?

Element	Appear-ance	Good conductor of electricity	Good conductor of heat
Sulphur	yellow solid	No	No
Potassium	shiny metal	Yes	Yes
Phosphorus	orange solid	No	No
Calcium	shiny metal	Yes	Yes

The physical properties of metals are different to those of non-metals.

A special case

The element carbon is mostly found occurring in the Earth as a black, shiny solid called graphite. It is a good conductor of heat but a poor conductor of electricity. Why do its physical properties suggest it might be a metal?

If carbon is burnt in oxygen it forms a colourless gas called carbon dioxide which is slightly soluble in water. You can test the acidity or alkalinity of the solution with different indicators. Look at what happens to the colour of the solution when three different indicators are used to test it.

Use the charts, showing the colour of the indicators at different pH's, to decide whether this oxide of carbon is acidic or alkaline.

Universal indicator *Litmus solution* *Phenolphthalein*

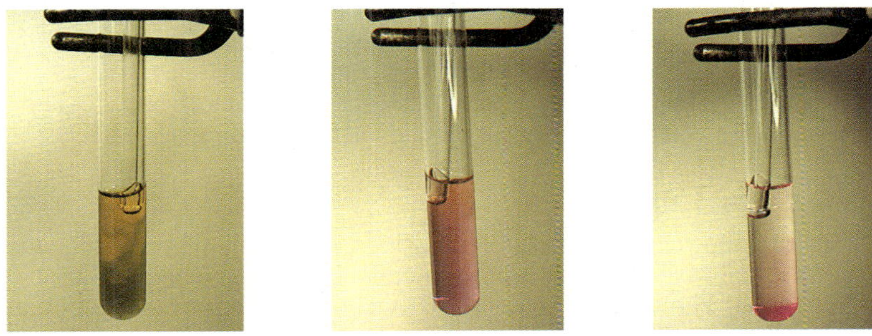

Carbon dioxide solution turns different indicators different colours . . . . is it acidic or alkaline?

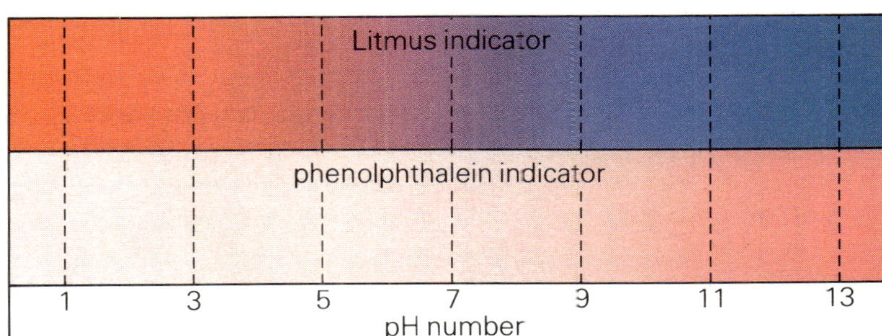

Indicators change colour at different pH's. Different indicators have different colour changes.

1 Look at the first picture. Name all the oxides taken in by the plant.

2 Choose *two* examples to show that elements and compounds have different properties.

3 Give *one* example to show that in reactions elements in one compound can transfer to become part of another compound.

4 What colour would a solution, formed by dissolving sulphur dioxide in water, be if:
a litmus indicator was added?
b phenolphthalein indicator was added?

5 The oxide of an unknown element dissolves in water to form a solution which turns phenolphthalein indicator pink. Predict *three* physical properties of the element.

6 If a solution turns litmus blue and universal indicator green, what colour would it turn phenolphthalein? What would be the pH range of the solution?

7 State two ways that carbon dioxide can enter the atmosphere. Why is rainwater naturally acidic? Why does the burning of fossil fuels increase its acidity?

YOU CAN READ MORE ABOUT CHEMICAL AND PHYSICAL PROPERTIES ON SPREAD 2.1.

Looking for patterns in elements

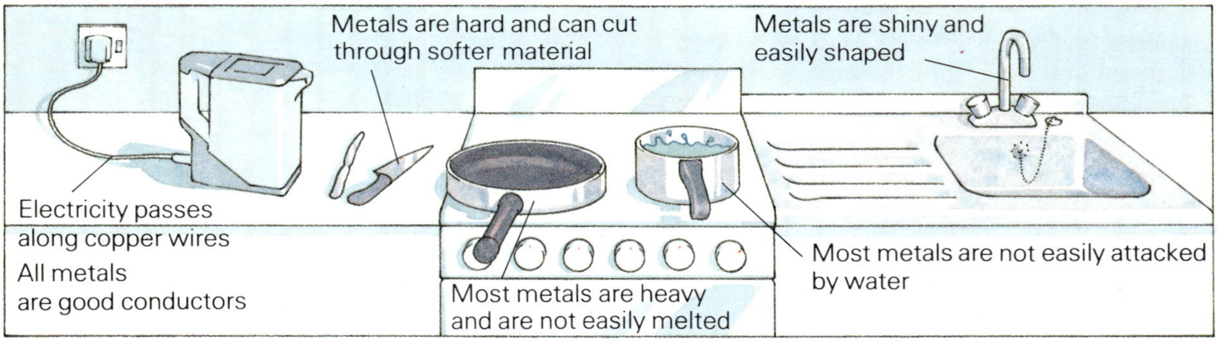

Most metals have several properties which are very similar.

Patterns in metallic elements

About 150 years ago chemists knew of the existence of about 60 elements. They tried to classify them by looking for patterns in their properties and the properties of their compounds. They knew that elements could be sub-divided into metals and non-metals (*see 9.2*). The picture shows you some typical properties of fairly common metals.

Some unusual metals

By investigating the properties of metallic elements chemists found some that did not always behave like other metals. One of these metals is sodium (Na). The pictures below show you how it differs from most other metals.

Two other metals, lithium (Li) and potassium (K), have very similar properties to those of sodium. So metals are not *all* alike and a small group of three metals has been found with properties different from other metals but similar to each other.

Sodium floats on water and reacts violently with it.

Sodium has a dull appearance because it reacts quickly with oxygen from the air but you can cut it easily to show a shiny inside.

Some non-metals can change the colour of universal indicator solution. Can you see any patterns?

A group of non-metals

If there are groups of metals that have similar chemical properties, can other patterns be found in the non-metals? This picture shows you what happens to the colour of universal indicator solution when you add to it the four non-metals chlorine (Cl_2), carbon (C), bromine (Br_2) and sulphur (S). Which of these non-metals would you group together?

Making sense of the patterns

Are you beginning to see a pattern between the chemical properties of different metals and non-metals? The key to understanding this pattern lies in the structure of elements and compounds. In 1808, John Dalton, an English chemist, published his **atomic theory**. In this theory he proposed that elements are made up of tiny particles called **atoms** and that atoms of different elements can join together to form compounds.

Copper is made up of copper atoms . . .

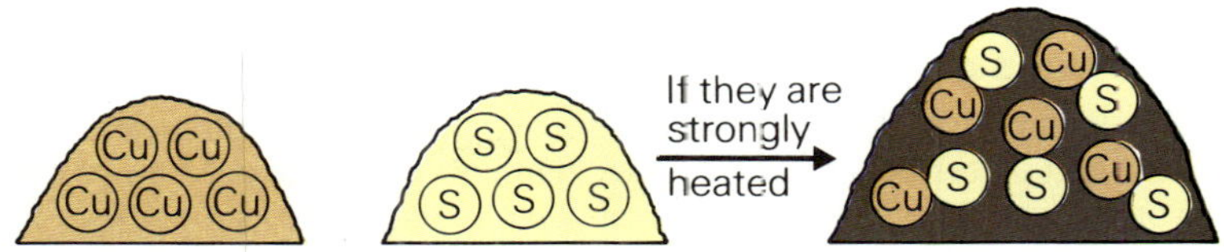

. . . sulphur is made up of sulphur atoms.

1 copper atom joins to 1 sulphur atom to form copper sulphide

Dalton and other chemists studied the *masses* of different elements needed to form compounds. The masses of copper and sulphur that react together are shown in the table. What does it show you about the ratios of the masses of copper and sulphur needed to make copper sulphide?

Mass of Cu (g)	8	32	64
Mass of S (g)	4	16	32

Since 1 atom of copper combines with 1 atom of sulphur to form copper sulphide, a copper atom must be twice as heavy as a sulphur atom. By looking at many reactions between elements, chemists were able to compare the **relative masses** of atoms of different elements. Then these masses were compared to the masses of a hydrogen atom, which was used as a standard. This gave the **relative atomic mass** (RAM) of the element.

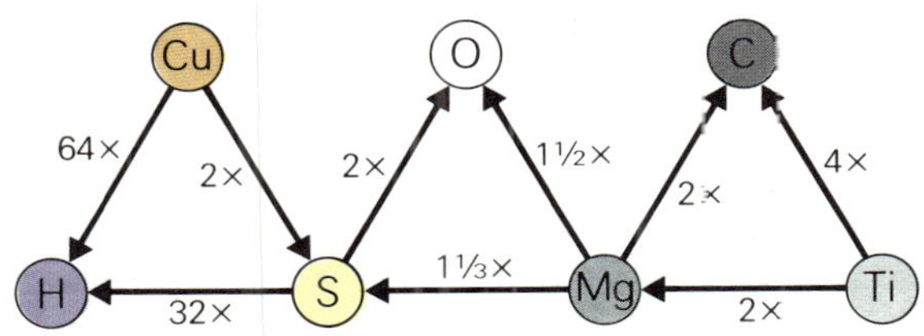

C = carbon
O = oxygen
Mg = magnesium
Ti = titanium
Cu = copper
H = hydrogen
S = sulphur

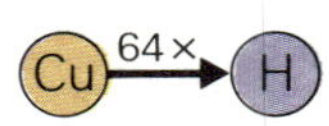

Copper is 64 × *heavier than* hydrogen.

So the RAM of copper is 64.

Finding a pattern in the RAM's

In 1817 a German chemist called Dobereiner found a pattern in the RAM's of the elements. He noticed that when three elements with similar chemical properties were grouped together, the RAM of the middle element was almost or exactly the average of the other two. Although there were only a few such groups, his discovery provided a link between the RAM of an element and its properties.

Element	Relative atomic mass (RAM)
Li	7
Na	23
K	39

What do you notice about the RAM of Na compared to those of Li and K?

1 State *three* ways in which potassium behaves as **a** a typical metal **b** an unusual metal

2 What evidence do you have that chlorine can be used as a household bleach?

3 The table below shows some masses of iron and sulphur that react to form iron sulphide. Assuming 1 atom of iron reacts with 1 atom of sulphur
a Fill in the gaps
b What is the RAM of iron?

Mass of Fe (g)	14	?	560
Mass of S (g)	?	64	320

4 Use the information in the figure above to find out the RAM of oxygen, titanium, magnesium and carbon.

5 The elements S, Se and Te follow Dobereiner's pattern for RAM's. The RAM of S is 32 and the RAM of Te is 128. What is the approximate RAM of Se?

6 Below is a list of elements and their respective RAM's. Which three do you predict would have the same properties?

Element	Si	Ca	Cu	Sr	Ba
RAM	28	40	64	88	137

9.4 Understanding the patterns

Mendeleev's periodic table

At the beginning of the nineteenth century, chemists had already established patterns between certain elements. You can read more about this on 9.2 and 9.3. The search for new patterns continued for the next fifty years. In 1869 a Russian chemist, called Mendeleev, arranged all the elements which were known in order of increasing relative atomic masses. The table below shows you how he did this. He arranged the elements in horizontal **periods** and eight columns called **groups**. Mendeleev found that elements in the *same group* had similar chemical properties. This repetition of properties is called *periodic* and so the table became known as the **Periodic Table**.

Dimitri Ivanovitch Mendeleev (1834–1907) was the founder of the modern Periodic Table.

Part of Mendeleev's Periodic Table. Elements with similar properties occur at regular intervals in the table when arranged in order of increasing RAM's.

← GROUP →

PERIOD ↓	1	2	3	4	5	6	7	8
1	1 H							
2	7 Li	13 Be	11 B	12 C	14 N	16 O	19 F	
3	23 Na	24 Mg	27 Al	28 Si	31 P	32 S	35 Cl	
4	39 K	40 Ca						56 Fe 39 Ni 59 Co
5				*			80 Bı	
6								
7				118 Sn		128 Te	127 I	
8								
9								
10								
11				207 Pb				
12								

The proof of the pudding . . .

Mendeleev's table contained a separate group – Group 8 – for elements that did not fit into his arrangement. He also left gaps – indicated by * – if no known element fitted the space. He realised that if the table was to be of value, he should be able to predict some of the properties of these missing elements. Look at the graph which shows you how the density of two metallic elements in Group 4 changes with their RAM. If you assume that the missing element in Group 4 together with Sn (tin) and Pb (lead) form one of Dobereiner's three-element groups (*see 9.3*), what would you predict the RAM and density of the missing element to be?

Mendeleev called this missing Group 4 element ekasilicon but it is now called germanium. When it was eventually discovered it was found to have a RAM of 73 and density of 5.3 g/cm^3. Does it fit the graphical relationship?

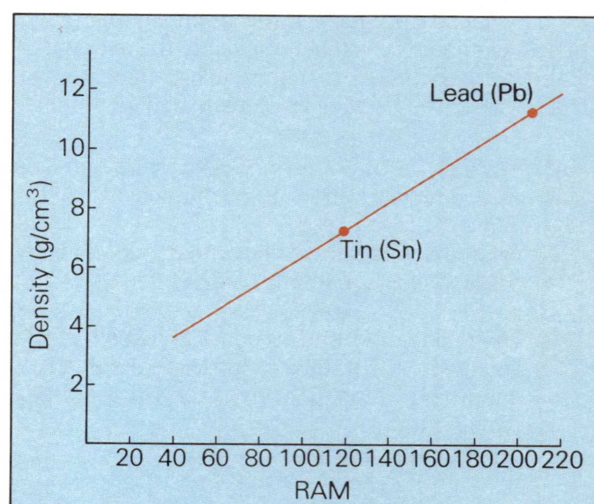

The graph shows the change in density with RAM of the metallic elements Sn and Pb in Group 4.

... is in the atomic numbers

Although Mendeleev's table proved very useful in predicting properties, there were problems. Elements with RAM's that did not fit were being forced into wrong positions. Look at Groups 6 and 7 in Mendeleev's table. He placed iodine after tellurium because its properties were similar to the other elements in that group. Also no place could be found for the noble gases argon, helium, neon, krypton and xenon, when they were discovered in the 1890s. Mendeleev and other scientists needed new knowledge to sort out these problems. The puzzle was solved by the discovery of the sub-atomic particle – the **electron** – at the beginning of this century.

← GROUP →

PERIOD ↓	6	7	8
1			$_{2}$He
2	$_{8}$O	$_{9}$F	$_{10}$Ne
3	$_{16}$S	$_{19}$Cl	
4		$_{35}$Br	
5			
6			
7	$_{52}$Te	$_{53}$I	

Iodine comes after *tellurium when Mendeleev's table is rearranged in order of atomic number instead of RAM's. Where have the noble gases been found to fit?*

The atom was found to consist of a central core or **nucleus** surrounded by particles called electrons. Atoms of different elements contain different numbers of electrons. The number of electrons in the atom of an element is the same as its **atomic number.** By rearranging the Periodic Table in order of *increasing atomic number* instead of RAM's, the problems of elements in wrong positions and where to put the noble gases were solved.

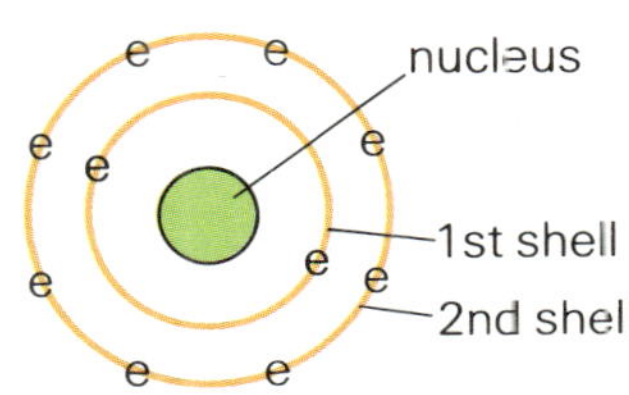

$_{10}$Ne

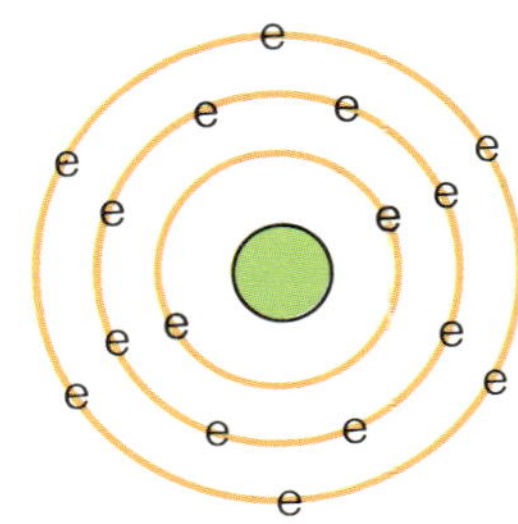

$_{16}$S

The noble gases were found to be very unreactive. Neon, with an atomic number of 10, has 10 electrons surrounding the nucleus. The first shell contains 2 electrons and the second shell 8 electrons. Both shells are full. An electronic structure with only full shells is said to be stable.

Most atoms are like sulphur with only partly filled outer shells. Sulphur has 16 electrons and an electronic structure 2,8,6. This means it has 2 electrons in the first shell (full), 8 in its second shell (full) and 6 in its third (not full). Oxygen has an electronic structure 2,6. It is in the same group as sulphur.

The key – outer shell electrons

Although the arrangement of elements in order of increasing atomic number put elements in their correct places, it did not explain why they should be in particular groups. But this *is* explained by the arrangement of the electrons in energy levels or **shells** around the nucleus of an atom. Each shell can only hold a definite number of electrons [1st shell: 2, 2nd shell: 8, 3rd shell: 8 . . .] but the outer shell isn't always full. Elements in the same group have the same *number of electrons* in their outer shell.

1 Look at Mendeleev's table. Which other element besides iodine is out of place?

2 Below are some properties of three elements in Group 4. Use this information to predict the corresponding properties of germanium.

Element	Appearance	Appearance of oxide
Carbon	dark grey	colourless gas
Silicon	dark grey	white powder
Tin	light grey	white powder

3 What do you think happened to the elements Fe, Co and Ni in Group 8 of Mendeleev's table?

4 The noble gas after He and Ne is argon (Ar). What do you think its atomic number and electronic structure are?

5 Use the figure above to work out the electronic structures of fluorine (F) and chlorine (Cl). What is the relationship between the number of outer shell electrons and the group to which an element belongs?

6 In what ways is the modern Periodic Table *different to* and *the same as* Mendeleev's? Look back to 9.1.

YOU CAN READ MORE ABOUT ATOMIC NUMBER AND STRUCTURE ON SPREAD 8.9.

9.5 Patterns in Group 1: the alkali metals

GROUP 1

3	Li
11	Na
19	K
37	Rb
55	Cs
87	Fr

Physical patterns

Like all metals, the elements in Group 1 are good conductors of heat and electricity. However, they are not typical metals (*see 9.3*). Look at the table opposite. Which metal in the group would you predict to have the lowest melting point?

Element	RAM	Melting Point (°C)	Size of atom (nm)
Li	7	180	0.133
K	39	64	0.203
Na	23	98	0.157

Some physical properties of the three most common elements in Group 1.

Chemical patterns – reactions with oxygen and chlorine . . .

Group 1 contains the most reactive metals in the Periodic Table. These alkali metals are dull in appearance because their shiny surfaces react quickly with oxygen from the air. When one of these metals reacts with oxygen a metal oxide is formed which has the general formula M_2O – M stands for any alkali metal. For example, sodium (Na) combines with oxygen to form sodium oxide, Na_2O.

Sodium + oxygen → sodium oxide

$$4Na + O_2 \rightarrow 2Na_2O$$

There is a fairly energetic reaction between lithium and chlorine to form a white solid Li Cl.

Chlorine reacts with the Group 1 metals to form metal chlorides with the general formula MCl. For example, potassium combines with chlorine to form potassium chloride, KCl.

Potassium + chlorine → potassium chloride

$$2K + Cl_2 \rightarrow 2KCl$$

The pictures show you the reaction of some Group 1 metals with chlorine. What do they show you about the reactivity of the metals as you go down Group 1?

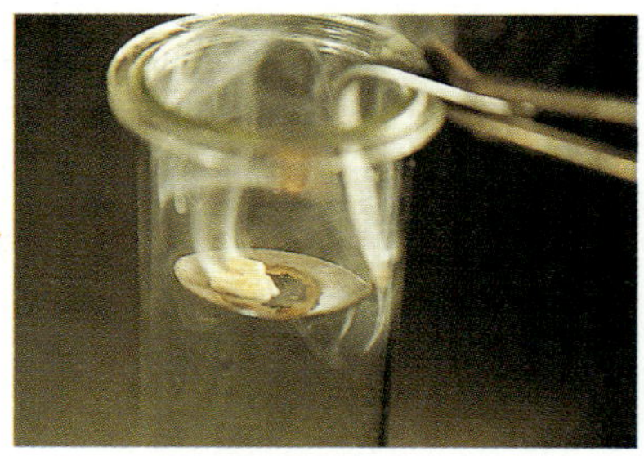

Sodium reacts energetically with Cl_2 to produce white NaCl.

. . . with water

Lithium, sodium and potassium all react similarly with cold water. They skim across its surface and react vigorously, producing hydrogen gas. The metals eventually dissolve to produce an alkaline solution – this is why they are often referred to as the alkali metals – containing the metal hydroxide, MOH.

Sodium reacts with water releasing hydrogen gas and producing an alkaline solution containing sodium hydroxide, NaOH.

Sodium + water → sodium hydroxide + hydrogen

$$2Na + 2H_2O \rightarrow 2NaOH + H_2$$

The reaction of different alkali metals with water is very similar but the reactivity depends on the particular metal. These three pictures show lithium, sodium and potassium reacting with cold water. Which is which?

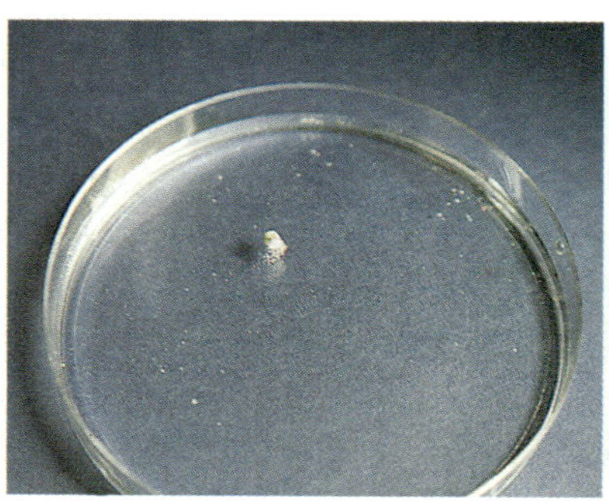

Explaining the patterns

Size

Each atom has a nucleus containing positive particles called **protons**. Surrounding the nucleus are negatively charged particles called **electrons** (*see 9.4*). In any atom there are *the same number* of protons and electrons. Its overall charge is balanced. The electrons are arranged around the nucleus in energy levels or shells (*see 9.4*). Look at the diagrams of the lithium and sodium atoms. Can you explain why the size of the atoms increases as you go down the group?

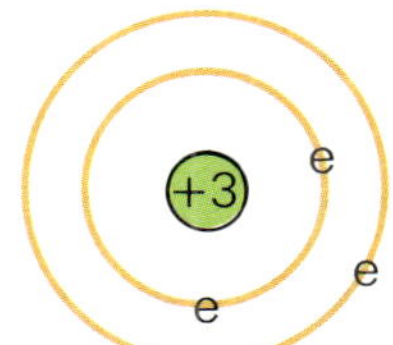

The Li atom has 3 protons in the nucleus and 3 electrons which are in two shells. It has the electronic structure 2,1.

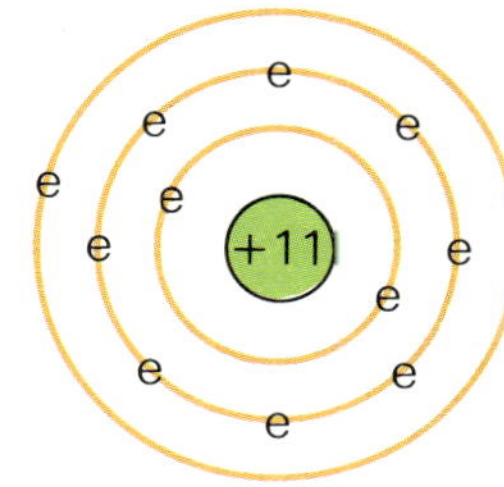

The Na atom has 11 protons in the nucleus and 11 electrons which are in three shells. It has the electronic structure 2,8,1.

Reactions

When atoms of some elements are involved in chemical reactions, they obtain **stable** electronic structures like those of the noble gases (*see 9.4*) – all their electron shells are full. Since alkali metals all have one electron in their outer shell, they obtain full shells in the same way as each other – so they have similar chemical reactions.

Reactivity

The reactivity of an alkali metal is a measure of how easily it loses its 1 outer shell electron. The more easily the electron is lost, the more reactive the alkali metal is. The positively charged protons in the nucleus of the atom attract the negatively charged electrons in the shells, keeping them in their shells. However, the further away the electrons are from the nucleus, the less strongly they are held in attraction to the positive nucleus. Also, the outer shell electrons are shielded from the positive charge in the nucleus by the inner shells of electrons. How do the diagrams explain why sodium is more reactive than lithium?

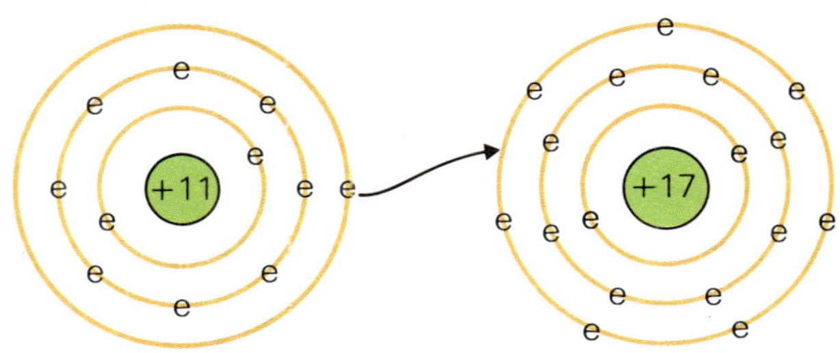

The easiest way for the Na atom to achieve full shells is to lose 1 electron from an outer shell to another atom

The Cl atom has 7 electrons in its outer shell so by gaining the electron from the Na atom it also achieves full shells.

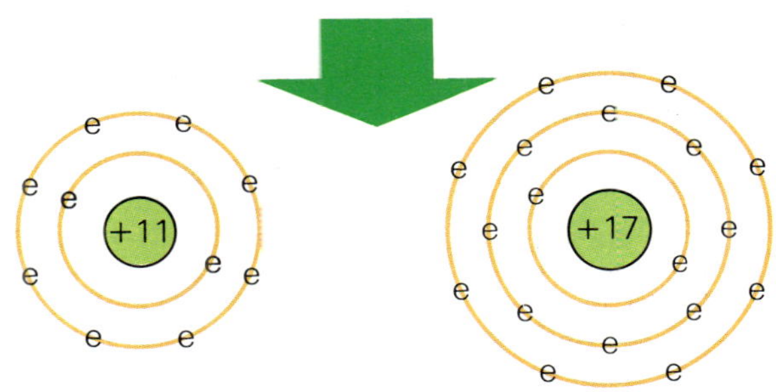

The Na atom now has 11 protons and 10 electrons so it is a positively charged atom or ***ion*** *– the sodium ion, Na^+.*

The chlorine atom now has 17 protons and 18 electrons so it is a negatively charged atom or ***ion*** *– the* chloride *ion, Cl^-.*

1 The force of attraction between metal atoms decreases as their size increases. Explain why the melting point of the metals decreases as you go down the group.

2 Write a symbol equation for the reaction between rubidium and water. Describe what you would expect to observe if you added rubidium to cold water.

3 Write down the symbol and electronic structure of the ion formed when lithium loses 1 electron.

4 What precautions do you think you should take when using an alkali metal?

5 Draw a diagram of the potassium atom. Explain why it is more reactive than sodium but less reactive than caesium.

6 Write down as many similarities as you can find between the chemistry of the elements sodium and potassium and their compounds.

7 Find the metals Be, Mg and Ca in the Periodic Table.

a What group are they in and how many electrons do they have in their outer shells?

b Predict what happens to the size of the atoms and their reactivity as you go down the group.

9.6 Patterns in Group 7: the halogens

GROUP 7

$_9F$
$_{17}Cl$
$_{35}Br$
$_{53}I$

Physical patterns

Most metals are very similar in appearance – not so with non-metals. One of the most striking features of the non-metal halogens in Group 7 is that at room temperature they don't appear to have much in common.

Look at the picture of the three most common halogens – chlorine, bromine and iodine. Would you expect fluorine to be a gas, solid or liquid at room temperature?

At room temperature chlorine is a greenish yellow gas, bromine a reddish brown liquid and iodine a shiny black solid.

Bleaching action

You may know that chlorine and its compounds are used as household bleaches to remove stains and colour from dyes. Other halogens can also be used as bleaches. The pictures show you what happens when you add three halogens to water containing universal indicator. What does this show you about the reactivity of the halogens as you go down the group?

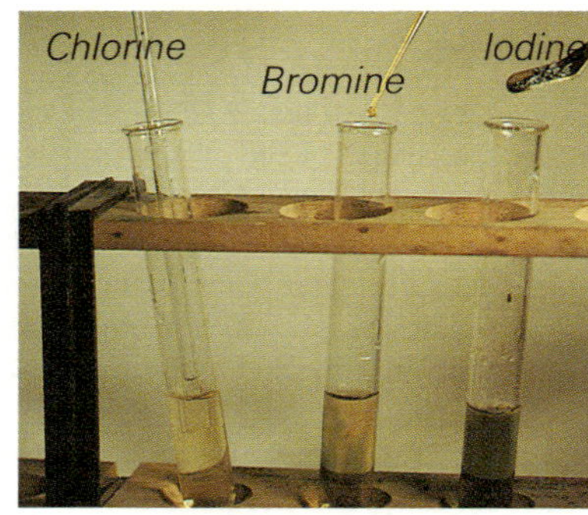

Colour of indicator after 2 minutes.

You can see that the addition of chlorine to the indicator has quickly bleached the indicator. Sometimes you may even see the indicator turn red first, showing that an acidic solution has been formed (*see 9.2*). Chlorine reacts with water to form a solution containing two acids: hydrochloric acid (HCl) and hypochlorous acid (HClO). The red colour of the indicator is quickly lost because HClO is such a good bleaching agent!

Chlorine + water → hydrochloric acid + hypochlorous acid

$$Cl_2 + H_2O \rightarrow HCl + HClO$$

Bromine (Br_2) and iodine (I_2) react with water in a similar way but much more slowly. Fluorine is the most reactive element known but reacts with the water in a different way and does not produce a bleach.

Colour of indicator after 10+ minutes.

Household bleaches

Most household bleaches are made by the reaction between chlorine and sodium hydroxide. This produces a solution containing sodium hypochlorite (NaClO) which is a good bleaching agent.

Chlorine + sodium hydroxide → sodium chloride + sodium hypochlorite + water

$$Cl_2 + 2NaOH \rightarrow NaCl + NaClO + H_2O$$

Halogens are also used as chemical agents to kill germs. This also shows their different reactivities. Chlorine is used as a germicide in swimming baths but it is too reactive to use as a germicide on open skin wounds. People used a mild antiseptic containing iodine dissolved in alcohol – *tincture of iodine* – for this because it is less reactive.

This label shows some of the safety factors you should take note of when you use bleaches for cleaning. What else is this type of bleach used for?

Displacement reactions

You can confirm the order of reactivity of the halogens by looking at their **displacement reactions**. A displacement reaction is one in which the more reactive element 'pushes out' or *displaces* the less reactive element. This means a more reactive halogen such as chlorine should displace a less reactive halogen such as iodine from one of its compounds. You can check the halogen present at the end of the reaction by using a suitable solvent.

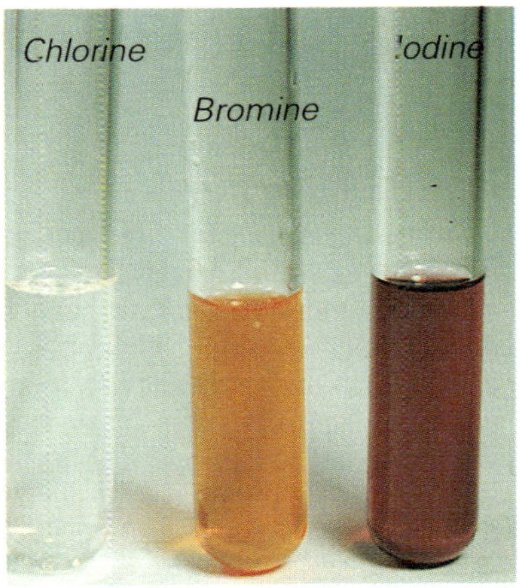

Halogens will dissolve in suitable solvents such as trichloromethane to give characteristic colours.

The pictures below show you what happens when chlorine is added to potassium bromide solution and to potassium iodide solution.

When chlorine is bubbled into potassium bromide solution, the less reactive bromine is displaced by the more reactive chlorine.

$$\text{Potassium bromide} + \text{chlorine} \rightarrow \text{potassium chloride} + \text{bromine}$$
$$2KBr + Cl_2 \rightarrow 2KCl + Br_2$$

However, if iodine is added to potassium bromide solution, the less reactive iodine is *not* able to displace the more reactive bromine.

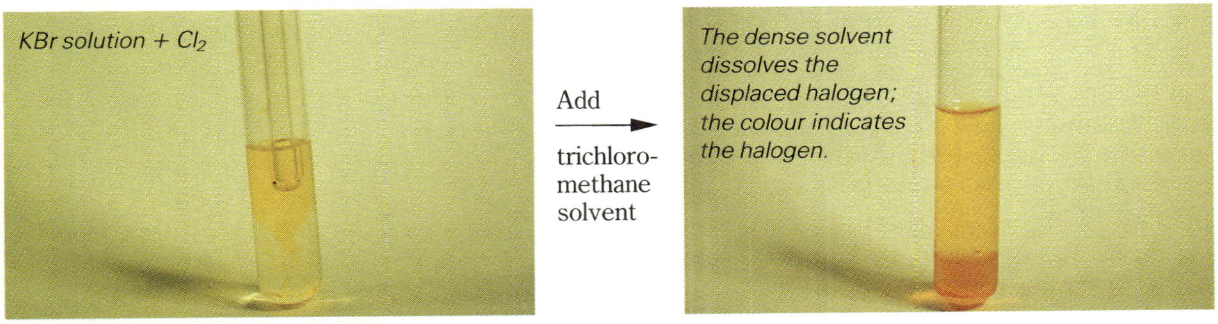

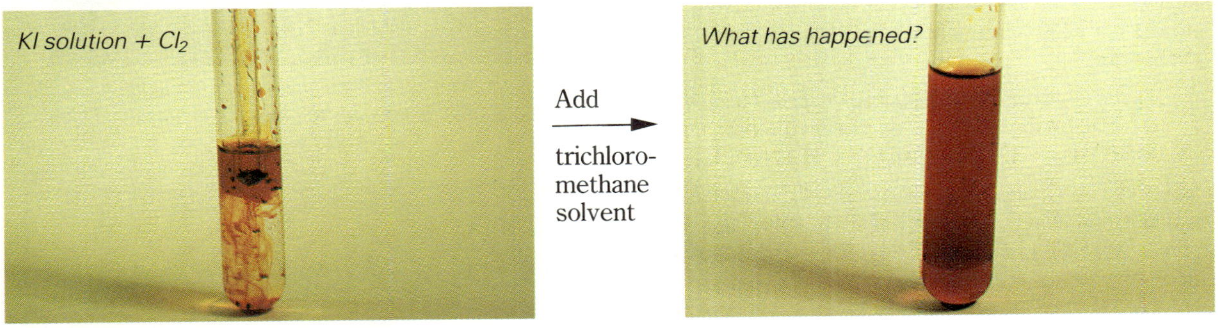

1 Find out what the word 'halogen' means

2 Look at the picture at the top of the opposite page. What does it tell you about the melting points of the halogens as you go down the group?

3 Look at the pictures in the middle of the opposite page. What would you eventually expect to happen to the indicator containing iodine solution?

4 Write equations for the reactions of
- **a** bromine and water
- **b** iodine and sodium hydroxide solution.

5 Why would it be dangerous to flush battery acid down a drain using a household bleach?

6 State what you would observe and write equations for the reactions (if any) if the experiments in the photos above were carried out using
- **a** potassium iodide (KI) and chlorine
- **b** potassium iodide (KI) and bromine
- **c** potassium chloride and bromine

7 Write down as many similarities as you can find between the elements chlorine and bromine.

8 In what ways are the halogens different to the alkali metals?

Patterns in the middle: Group 4

Physical patterns

Group 4 is a 'family' of elements in the middle of the Periodic Table. The first element in the group, carbon, is found naturally in two different forms – diamond and graphite. The table shows that the elements in this group have a mixture of metallic and non-metallic properties. If you look at the position of the group in the Periodic Table this is not as surprising as it might at first seem. Can you suggest a reason for it?

Element	Appearance	Electrical conductivity	Ductility
C Carbon	graphite: shiny black solid	good	poor
	diamond: clear solid		
Si Silicon	shiny grey solid	semi-conductor	poor
Pb Lead	shiny grey-blue solid	good	good

Chemical patterns – the oxides

You have already seen (*9.2*) that you can find out about the chemical nature of an element by looking at the chemical properties of its oxide. Metals form basic oxides and non-metals, such as carbon, form acidic oxides. But elements in Group 4 have more than one oxide. Carbon, for example, forms carbon dioxide, CO_2, *and* (the less stable) carbon monoxide, CO. For simplicity you can study the more representative oxide of each element – which in the case of carbon is carbon dioxide.

The acidic nature of carbon dioxide can be shown by its reaction with the alkaline solutions of metal hydroxides such as calcium hydroxide, $Ca(OH)_2$ – limewater. Carbon dioxide reacts with limewater to produce a white cloudy precipitate of calcium carbonate.

$$\text{Calcium hydroxide} + \text{carbon dioxide} \rightarrow \text{calcium carbonate} + \text{water} + \text{carbon dioxide}$$

$$Ca(OH)_2 + CO_2 \rightarrow CaCO_3 + H_2O + CO_2$$

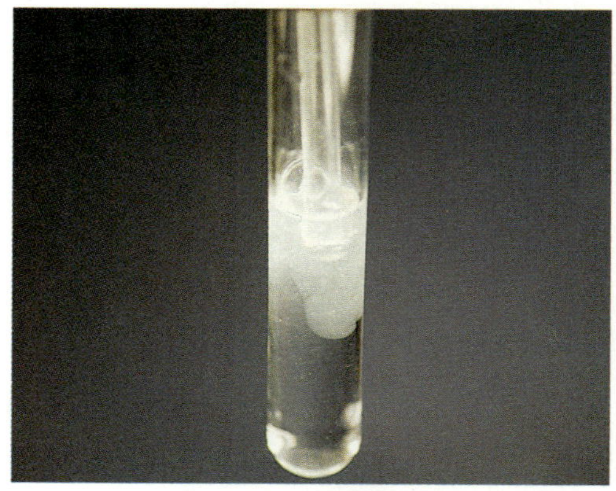

The reaction of CO_2 with limewater (calcium hydroxide solution) produces a white cloudy precipitate. This reaction is used as a test for CO_2.

Many of the Group 4 oxides are insoluble in water so it is not possible to find out if they form acidic or basic solutions. Silicon dioxide, SiO_2, for example, is the main ingredient of sand – and you know that sand isn't soluble! However, some acidic oxides will react with some basic oxides. Sodium is a metallic element from Group 1 and sodium oxide, Na_2O, is therefore a basic oxide. This reacts with SiO_2 to form sodium silicate, Na_2SiO_3.

$$Na_2O + SiO_2 \rightarrow Na_2SiO_3$$

This shows that SiO_2 is an acidic oxide – so silicon behaves chemically as a non-metal like carbon.

SiO_2 reacts with lead oxide, PbO, to form lead silicate which is used in cut glass. What type of oxide is PbO?

Although lead oxide, PbO, is a basic oxide when it reacts with SiO_2, it also reacts with a metal hydroxide such as sodium hydroxide. This shows it can also react as an acidic oxide, like carbon dioxide. Metal oxides like lead oxide which have the properties of both basic and acidic oxides are called **amphoteric oxides**.

Sodium silicate or water glass is used to make crystal gardens.

Metallic versus non-metallic character

When atoms of elements in Groups 1 to 8 are involved in chemical reactions they try to obtain noble gas electronic structures (*see 9.4 and 9.5*) They try to fill their shells – the first shell can hold 2 electrons and the other shells 8 electrons each. The way each atom does this depends on the number of electrons in its outer shell.

Atoms with less than 4 electrons in their outer shell *lose* these electrons. This is a characteristic reaction of a *metal*. Atoms with more than 4 electrons in their outer shell *gain* the electrons from metal atoms they are reacting with. This is a characteristic reaction of a *non-metal*. Look at what happens to metallic magnesium atoms and non-metallic oxygen atoms when they combine to form magnesium oxide.

Atoms of non-metals can also achieve full shells in another way. They can *share* electrons with other non-metal atoms. The diagram shows you how nitrogen and chlorine atoms share electrons to form nitrogen chloride.

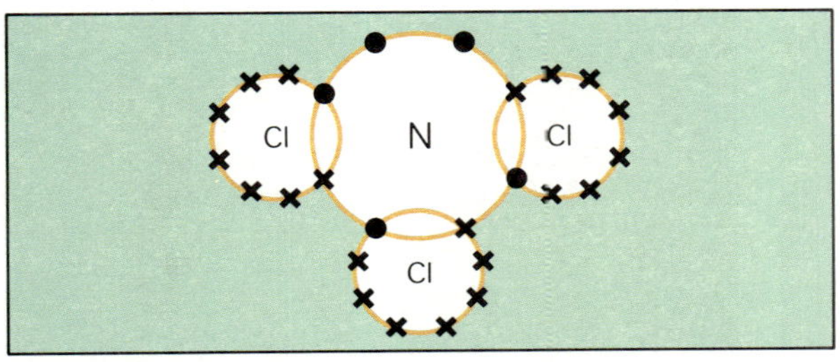

By sharing electrons (● and X), nitrogen and chlorine can achieve 8 electrons in their outer shells.

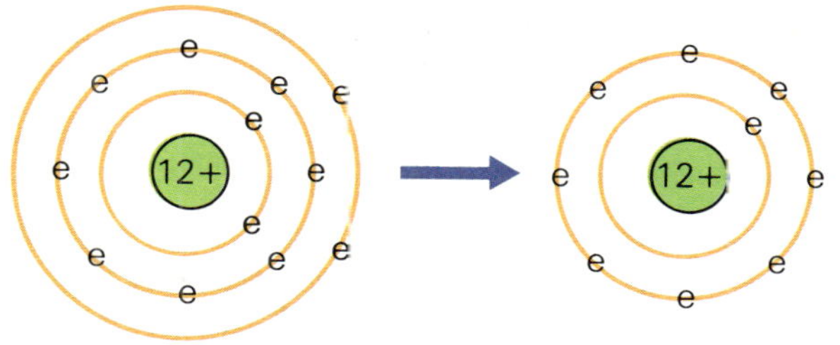

The Mg atom, electronic structure 2,8,2 loses 2 electrons . . .

. . . to form the positive ion Mg^{2+} 2,8. Metals lose electrons to form positive ions.

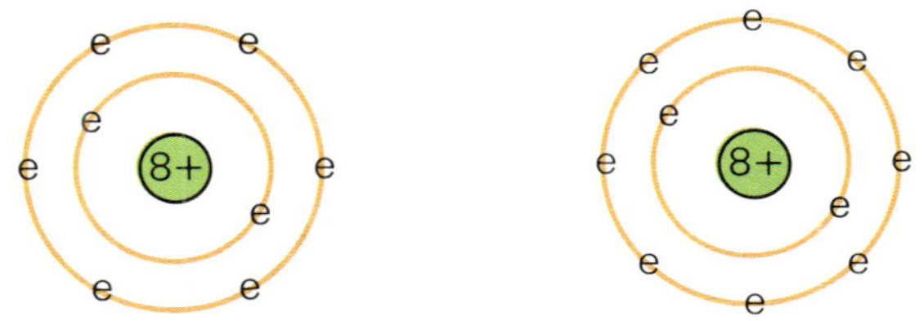

The O atom, electronic structure 2,6 gains the 2 electrons lost by the Mg atom . . .

. . . to form the negative ion O^{2-} 2,8. Non-metals gain electrons to form negative ions.

Changes in Group 4

The position of an element in the Periodic Table is given by its number of electrons – its **atomic number**. The group shows the number of electrons in the outer shell of each element. So all elements in Group 4 have 4 electrons in their outer shell. Because of this you might think these elements could equally lose, gain or share their 4 outer electrons to get full shells. However, they rarely gain electrons and other factors such as the size of atoms make a difference as to whether they lose or share (*see 9.5*).

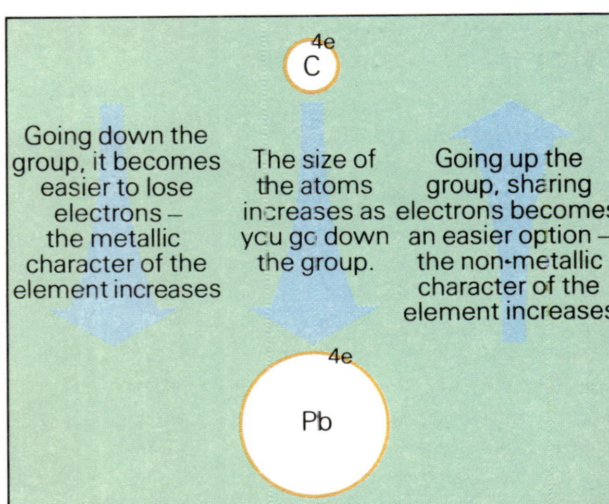

The chemical nature of the elements in Group 4 changes as you go up and down the group.

1 Look at the table on the opposite page. What physical properties of graphite suggest it is **a** a metal **b** a non-metal?

2 Why would you expect the chemical properties of diamond and graphite to be identical even though their physical properties are different?

3 What do the chemical properties of the oxides show you about the metallic character of the elements as you go down Group 4?

4 Look at the elements in the table below.

Element	Li	S	F	Ca	Al
Atomic number	3	16	9	20	13

Which would you expect to behave as metals and which as non-metals?

5 The **valency** of an element is the number of electrons lost, gained or shared when it reacts with other elements. What is the valency of each of the elements in question 4?

6 Which element would you expect to be more metallic – nitrogen or antimony? Give a reason for your answer.

9.8 Patterns in the reactions of metals

Reactions with water

The majority of elements in the Periodic Table are metals. You have already seen patterns in the family of metallic elements in Group 1 (*see 9.5*). You can build up a general pattern for other metals in the same way by looking at different reactions. The picture shows you the reactions of three different metals with cold water.

There is a large difference in the reactivity of these metals with water. Which metal is the most reactive?

When calcium reacts with cold water an alkaline solution containing calcium hydroxide is formed and hydrogen gas is released.

$$Ca + 2H_2O \rightarrow Ca\,(OH)_2 + H_2$$

How does this reaction compare with the reactions of the Group 1 metals with water?

Reaction with acids

Some metals react with acids such as hydrochloric (HCl) and sulphuric (H_2SO_4). The reaction produces hydrogen and a solution containing a **salt.** The salt formed depends on the type of acid. Hydrochloric acid produces salts called *chlorides* and sulphuric acid produces salts called *sulphates*. For example, magnesium forms magnesium chloride when reacting with hydrochloric acid but magnesium sulphate when reacting with sulphuric acid. The equations for the reactions are:

$$Mg + 2HCl \rightarrow MgCl_2 + H_2$$
$$Mg + H_2SO_4 \rightarrow MgSO_4 + H_2$$

The equations for the reactions of iron with the two acids are very similar except that the salts formed are iron chloride ($FeCl_2$) and iron sulphate ($FeSO_4$).

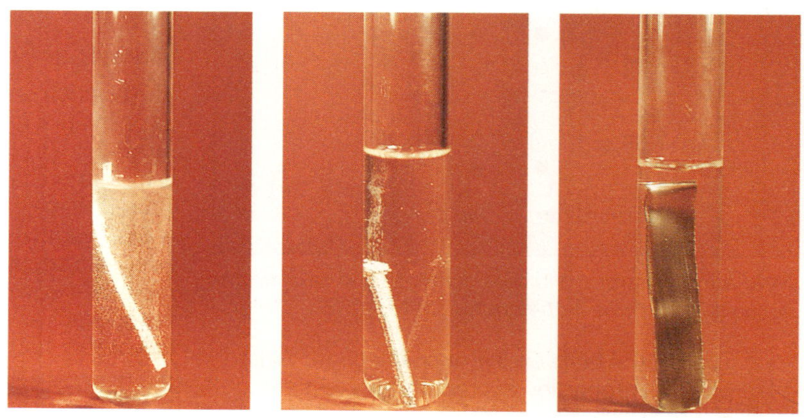

You can also obtain an order of reactivity by reacting metals with acids.

Displacement reactions

A more reactive metal will displace a less reactive metal from a solution of its salt. For example, if a piece of magnesium is placed in copper sulphate solution it will displace copper from the solution because magnesium is more reactive than copper. The surface of the more reactive metal (magnesium) becomes coated in the less reactive metal (copper):

$$Mg + CuSO_4 \rightarrow MgSO_4 + Cu$$

It's easy to coat some metals with copper using displacement reactions, but electroplating like this gives longer lasting coatings.

Simple cells

A battery or simple cell contains two metals of different reactivity in a conducting solution – an **electrolyte**. You can measure the energy output of the cell by a voltmeter connected to the two metal plates or electrodes, as shown here. The difference in reactivity between the magnesium and copper is much greater than the difference in reactivity between the iron and the copper.

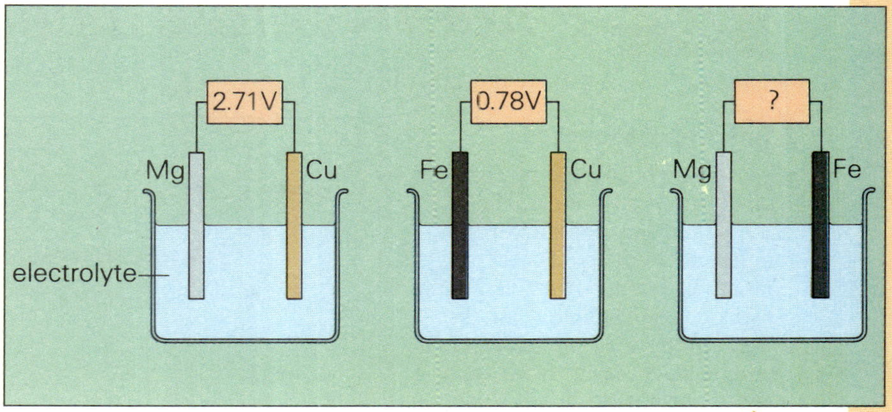

What does this show you about the difference in reactivity between two metals and the size of the voltmeter reading?

The reactivity series

You can order metals in a 'league table' of reactivity called the reactivity series. This is based on their reactions with other chemicals such as water and acids as well as their displacement reactions and the energy output of simple cells. The higher a metal's position in the league table, the more reactive it is. The diagram shows you the position of some metals in the table. It can also help you to predict the voltage output of a simple cell. What do you think the voltmeter reading will be in the cell in the diagram above using magnesium (Mg) and iron (Fe) electrodes?

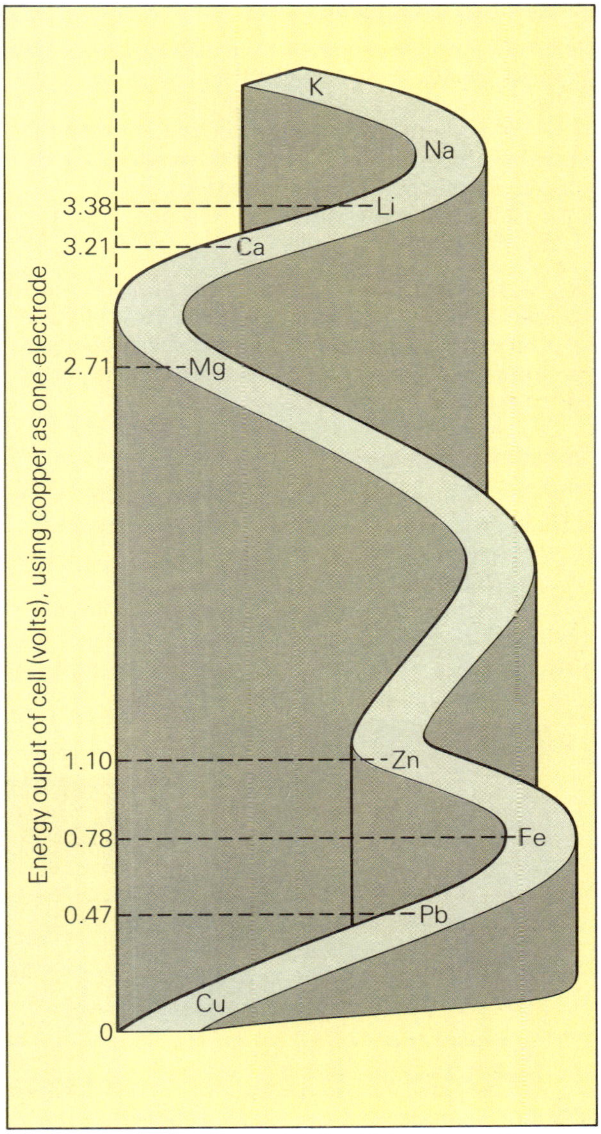

The more reactive the metal, the higher its position up the slope.

1 Why do you think lithium batteries do not use electrolytes containing water?

2 Look at the first picture. What do you notice about the reactivity of the Group 2 metals (Mg and Ca) as you go down the group?
Is this similar to the pattern found in Group 1?

3 Write equations for the reaction of iron with hydrochloric and sulphuric acids.

4 Which metals in the reactivity series on the right will react with acids but not displace magnesium from magnesium sulphate solution?

5 Why do you think copper is an ideal metal to use in making coins?

6 **a** A simple cell gives a voltage output of 0.32 volts. What two metals could have been used as electrodes?
b What would be the voltage output of a simple cell that used the same metal as both electrodes?

7 Chemical reactions involve transfer of electrons. Why do you think alkali metals like lithium give high readings of voltage compared with other metals?

YOU CAN READ MORE ABOUT REACTIVITY SERIES ON SPREADS 2.14 AND 8.13.

Patterns across a period

A physical changeover

A period is a horizontal row of elements in the Periodic Table. Each period contains a different number of elements. The 1st period only contains two elements – hydrogen and helium – and the 2nd and 3rd periods contain eight elements each. Apart from the first and last periods, each one starts with an alkali metal and finishes with a noble gas.

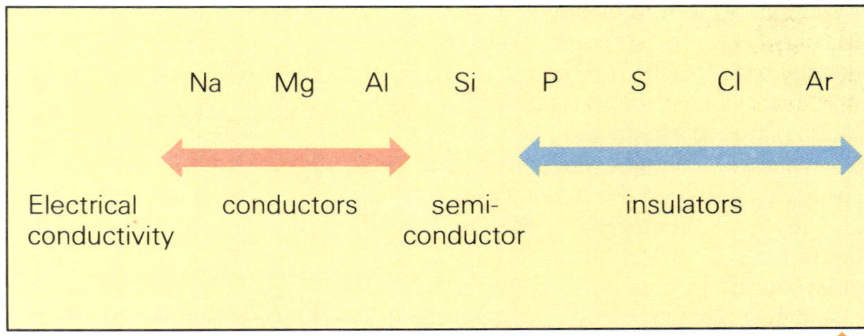

As you go from Group 1 to Group 8 across the Periodic Table there is a changeover from metallic to non-metallic properties. Where does the changeover occur in the 3rd period, shown here?

A chemical changeover

There seems to be a change in the physical properties of the elements at silicon – elements before this behave as metals and after as non-metals. You can determine whether there is also a change in their chemical properties by looking at the reactions of the oxides. Remember metals form oxides and hydroxides that react with acids. Non-metals form oxides that react with alkalis.

Aluminium is coated with a thin layer of aluminium oxide, Al_2O_3. Look at the pictures. How do they show that the changeover in chemical properties from metals to non-metals in this period occurs at aluminium?

If you cook rhubarb or make jam in an aluminium pan, the surface layer is removed. The acids released by cooking react with the Al_2O_3 as well as attacking the metal.

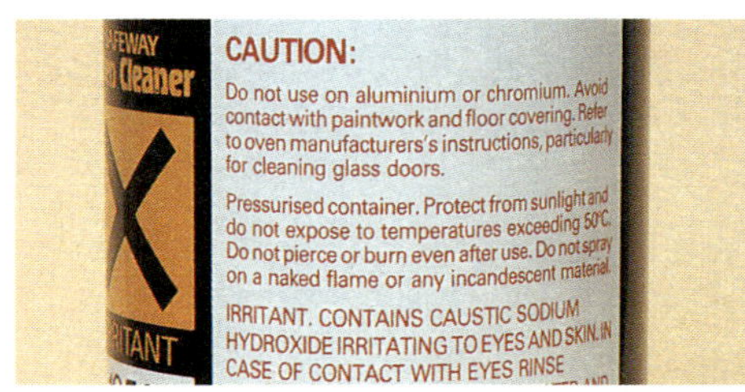

Many kitchen cleaners are not suitable for cleaning aluminium. The alkalis in the cleaners react with the Al_2O_3 before reacting with the metal.

Reactivity with water

The first element in the period, sodium, reacts violently with cold water, whilst the last element, argon, is completely unreactive with water – and with all other substances! Although this might seem to indicate that the reactivity decreases as you go from Na to Ar, the pictures show you that there is no clear pattern across the whole period. Can you suggest why this is not entirely unexpected?

Magnesium reacts with steam to produce magnesium oxide, MgO, and hydrogen.

Phosphorus can set fire spontaneously in air but can safely be stored in water.

Chlorine reacts with water forming a germicide used in swimming baths.

Formula of hydride	NaH	MgH_2	AlH_3	SiH_4	PH_3	H_2S	HCl
Common name	sodium hydride	magnesium hydride	alane	silane	phosphine	hydrogen sulphide	hydrogen chloride
Valency (V) of element in the period	1	2	3	4	3	2	1

The formula of the hydrides depends on the valencies of the elements

V = 2 V = 1
Mg H , crossing over the valencies gives the simplest formula MgH_2 (the number 1 is omitted). When valencies are greater than 1, you might have to divide by the smallest valency to find the simplest formula which is based on whole numbers.

V = 2 V = 2
Mg O , crossing over the valencies and dividing by 2 gives the simplest formula MgO.

V = 3 V = 2
B O , crossing over the valencies gives B_2O_3. You don't divide by the smallest valency, 2, since this doesn't give whole numbers.

Patterns in the formulae of hydrides

When an element combines with hydrogen, it forms a hydride. Look at the table, showing you the formulae of the hydrides across the 3rd short period. You can see that the number of atoms of hydrogen joining with one atom of Mg and S is the same. In each case 2 atoms of hydrogen join with 1 atom of either Mg or S. These numbers give us information about the **valency** of an atom (*see 9.7*). In this example, the valency of hydrogen is 1; the valency of magnesium and sulphur is 2. Valencies are useful in helping you to work out the simplest formula of a compound. If you look at magnesium hydride to see how its formula has been worked out, you will see that the valencies of magnesium and hydrogen have been *crossed over*. Has the same method been used to obtain the formula of hydrogen sulphide?

Valency and atomic structure

As you go along the period from Na to Ar, the atomic number and hence the number of electrons increases by one. The electronic structure of the atoms shows that the number of electrons in the outer shell also increases by one. When atoms of elements react they achieve full electronic structures by gaining, losing or sharing electrons (*see 9.7*). The diagram below shows how the atoms of elements in the 3rd period do this.

Atomic number	Na 11	Mg 12	Al 13	Si 14	P 15	S 16	Cl 17	Ar 18
Electronic structure	2,8,1	2,8,2	2,8,3	2,8,4	2,8,5	2,8,6	2,8,7	2,8,8
Atom achieves noble gas electronic structure by . . .	losing electrons (Al sometimes shares)			sharing electrons		gaining or sharing electrons		
No. of electrons lost, gained or shared	1	2	3	4	3	2	1	

Can you see a connection between the valency and the number of electrons lost, gained or shared?

1 Look at the Periodic Table on 9.1.
- **a** How many elements are there in the 4th, 5th and 6th periods?
- **b** How many elements will have to be made in the 7th period before a noble gas is made?

2 Why is the valency of argon zero? What do you think is the main chemical characteristic of the noble gas elements?

3 Use the valencies above to deduce the formulae of sodium oxide, aluminium oxide and silicon oxide.

4 Use the Periodic Table to deduce the valencies of nitrogen and fluorine. What is the formula of the compound formed by the combination of these elements?

5 Element X reacts with element Y to form XY_3. Element Z reacts with Y to form ZY_2. What is the formula of the compound formed between X and Z?

6 Why does the way in which atoms achieve a noble gas electronic structure match the finding that the metallic character of elements decreases across the 3rd short period?

Patterns in forming salts

Acids

Acids are a very important group of chemicals. The vinegar that you may put on your fish and chips contains ethanoic acid. Hydrochloric acid is used in your stomach to help you digest your food. Hydrochloric acid is also used by chemists as an acid in the laboratory along with sulphuric and nitric acids. Like all acids, their dilute solutions in water have a pH less than 7 and they have the same effect on indicators such as turning blue litmus paper red (*see 9.2*). They also react with compounds called bases.

Name of acid	Formula of acid
hydrochloric	HCl
sulphuric	H_2SO_4
nitric	HNO_3
ethanoic	$HOOCCH_3$

The table shows you the formulae of the common laboratory acids. What element is common to all the acids?

Bases

Bases are substances that cancel out or neutralise acids. This means the base reacts with the acid and removes its acidic properties. The diagrams show you examples of acids being neutralised by bases. Bases which dissolve in water are given a special name – **alkalis**. Alkalis have a pH greater than 7 and turn red litmus paper blue.

What happens on neutralisation?

When an **acid** reacts with a **base**, a **salt** and **other products** are formed.

Bases determine the other products . . .
The picture below shows you what is formed when the *same* acid is added to *different* bases. Note that the type of salt is the *same* but the other products are *different*.

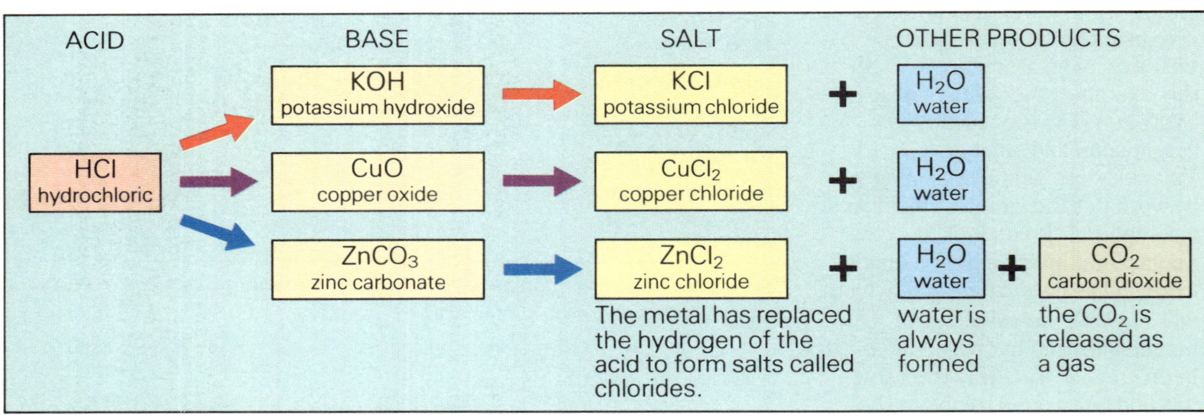

. . . and acids determine the type of salt
When the *same* base is added to *different* acids, note how the type of salt is *different* but the other product of the reaction is the *same*.

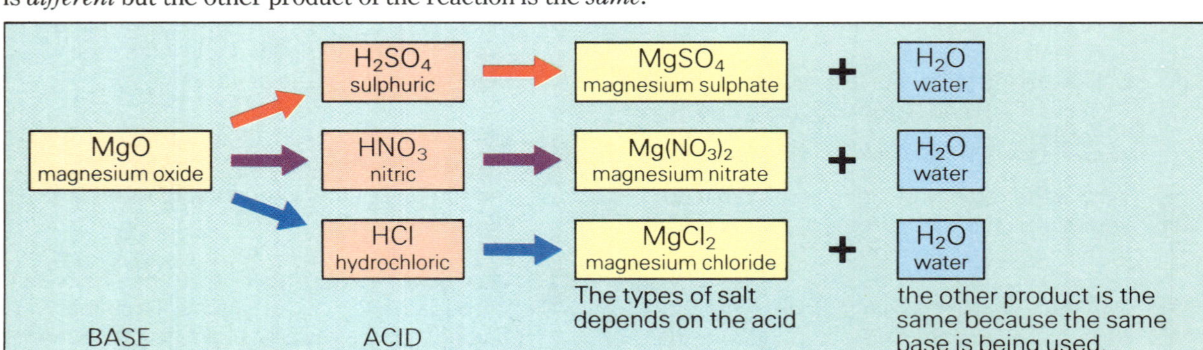

Making salts

When a salt is made from an acid and a base it is important to make sure that all the acid has been neutralised by the base. The method you should use to prepare the base depends on the solubility of the base in water.

Insoluble base: The only way to be sure that all the acid has been neutralised is to use more base than is needed. This is called using *excess base.*

Excess of an insoluble base such as copper carbonate ($CuCO_3$) is added to neutralise all the sulphuric acid . . .

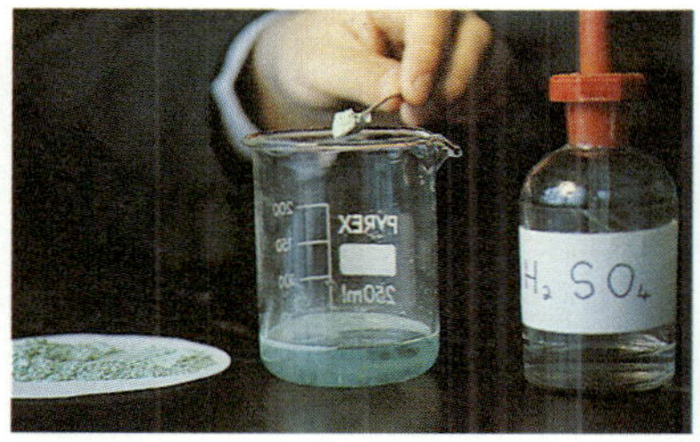

. . . The excess base is filtered off and the copper sulphate solution collected in an evaporating basin . . .

*. . . **Some** of the water is slowly evaporated. Copper sulphate crystals are formed when the remaining solution is left to cool. This can be collected and dried on filter paper.*

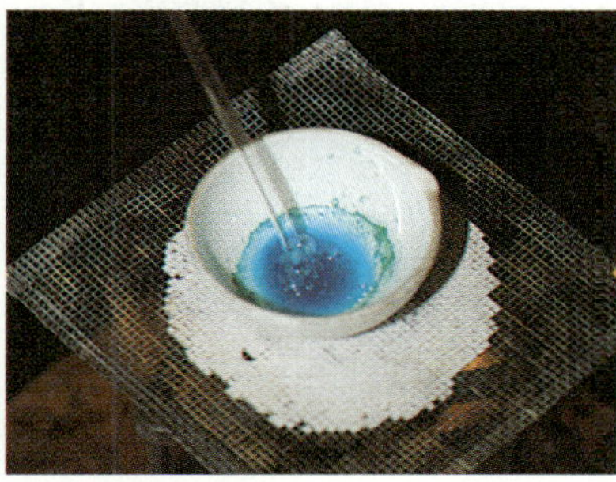

Alkali (soluble base): It is not possible to filter off an excess of a soluble base, so another way has to be found! The only way to be sure that all the acid has been used up is to use *exactly* the right amount of base. At this point the mixture will be neutral – so a suitable indicator can be used.

An indicator such as phenolphthalein is added to the acid to show when it has been neutralised.

1 Magnesium hydroxide is used to cure acid indigestion. What salt does it produce in your stomach?

2 Acid rain contains a mixture of nitric and sulphuric acids. What is formed when it corrodes buildings or statues made of limestone (calcium carbonate)?

3 Hydrogencarbonates give the same 'other products' as carbonates. What is formed when sodium hydrogencarbonate reacts with nitric acid?

4 Potassium nitrate is used to make fireworks. Suggest a suitable acid and base from which it can be made. Why should the potassium nitrate solution produced not be evaporated to dryness to obtain crystals?

5 Look at the preparation of copper sulphate.
- **a** How would you know when all the acid had been used up?
- **b** Why is it better to stir the mixture of acid and base?

6 Look at the preparation of sodium chloride.
- **a** What colour is the phenolphthalein in the acid?
- **b** What colour would it turn if one drop of excess alkali were added?
- **c** Why is the maximum yield of sodium chloride not obtained by evaporating part of the water?

7 Which of the two methods for preparing salt would you use to prepare
- **a** KNO_3 from KOH and HNO_3
- **b** $ZnCl_2$ from ZnO and HCl?

Looking at neutralisation

That effervescent feeling

Many people prefer to take tablets such as aspirin or paracetamol in soluble form rather than having to swallow them. Manufacturers add an 'effervescent base' to make these soluble tablets. This means they add a base which reacts with an acid to produce a gas. The tablet also contains an acid in solid form such as ascorbic acid (Vitamin C) or citric acid found in citric fruits. When the tablet is added to water, carbon dioxide is produced. This disperses the less soluble particles evenly throughout the water.

Soluble tablets like soluble aspirin contain an acid and an 'effervescent base' such as sodium carbonate or sodium hydrogencarbonate.

Products when bases react with acids

Base	'Active' part	Water H_2O	Carbon dioxide CO_2
metal oxide	oxide ion O^{2-}	✓	✗
metal	hydroxide OH^-	✓	✗
metal carbonate	carbonate ion CO_3^{2-}	✓	✓
metal hydrogen-carbonate	hydrogen-carbonate HCO_3^-	✓	✓

The basic ingredient

When deciding which base to use, the manufacturers of soluble tablets use the fact that *any* metal carbonate or hydrogencarbonate will react with *any* acid to produce water and carbon dioxide. The active part of the base is the carbonate ion, CO_3^{2-}, or hydrogencarbonate ion, HCO_3^-. Other bases such as metal oxides and hydroxides have active parts as the table shows. The fact that the product depends on the 'active' part of the bases and not the acid suggests that in *all* acids the same particle is reacting with the base.

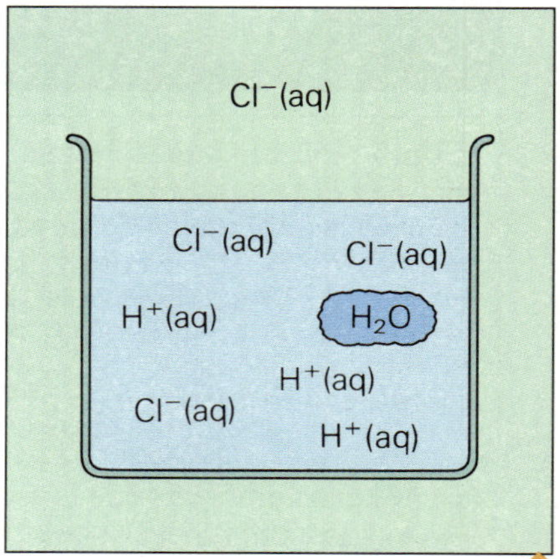

Hydrochloric acid is fully dissociated into H^+ (aq) ions and chloride ions, Cl^- (aq) in water.

The active ingredient in acids

In a tablet containing an acid and a base such as a metal carbonate, the acid and base don't react until they have been added to water. The particle in the acid responsible for its properties only exists when the acid has been dissolved in water. When an acid molecule is added to water, it breaks up or *dissociates* into ions. The two diagrams show you what happens when hydrochloric acid (HCl) and ethanoic acid (CH_3COOH) are added to water. The (aq) after each ion means **aqueous**. This tells you the ion is surrounded by a number of water molecules (think of *aquatic, aquarium*!). The ion is said to be **hydrated**. The particle common to both acids is the hydrated hydrogen ion, H^+ (aq). The strength of the acid depends on the concentration of H^+ (aq) ions in the solution.

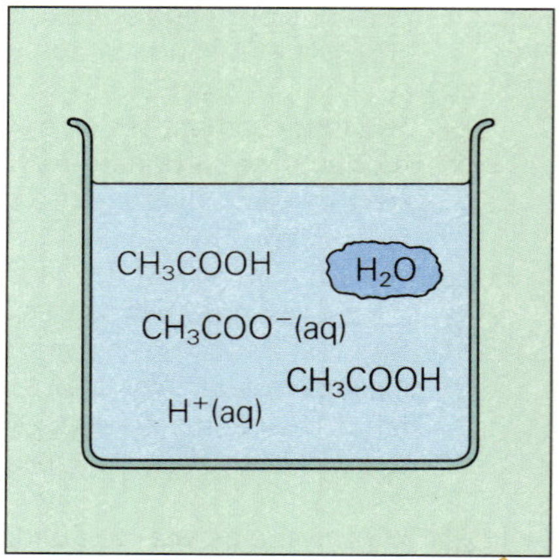

Ethanoic acid, CH_3COOH, is only partly dissociated into H^+ (aq) ions and ethanoate ions, CH_3COO^- (aq) in water.

How do the diagrams explain why hydrochloric acid is a strong acid but ethanoic acid is weak?

Neutralisation

Sodium hydroxide solution is fully dissociated into positive sodium ions, Na^+ (aq) and negative hydroxide ions, OH^- (aq).

If a soluble base or alkali such as a Group 1 metal hydroxide, MOH, is dissolved in water it dissociates into positive ions, M^+ (aq), and negative hydroxide ions, OH^- (aq). The diagram below shows what happens when hydrochloric acid is added to sodium hydroxide solution.

The reaction between the sodium hydroxide and the hydrochloric acid can be represented by the 'active' part of the acid and the 'active' part of the base. The 'active' part of the acid is *always* H^+ (aq) and in this example the 'active' part of the base is OH^- (aq). The equation representing this reaction now becomes:

hydrated hydrogen ions + hydrated hydroxide ions → water
or $H^+ (aq) + OH^- (aq) \rightarrow H_2O$.

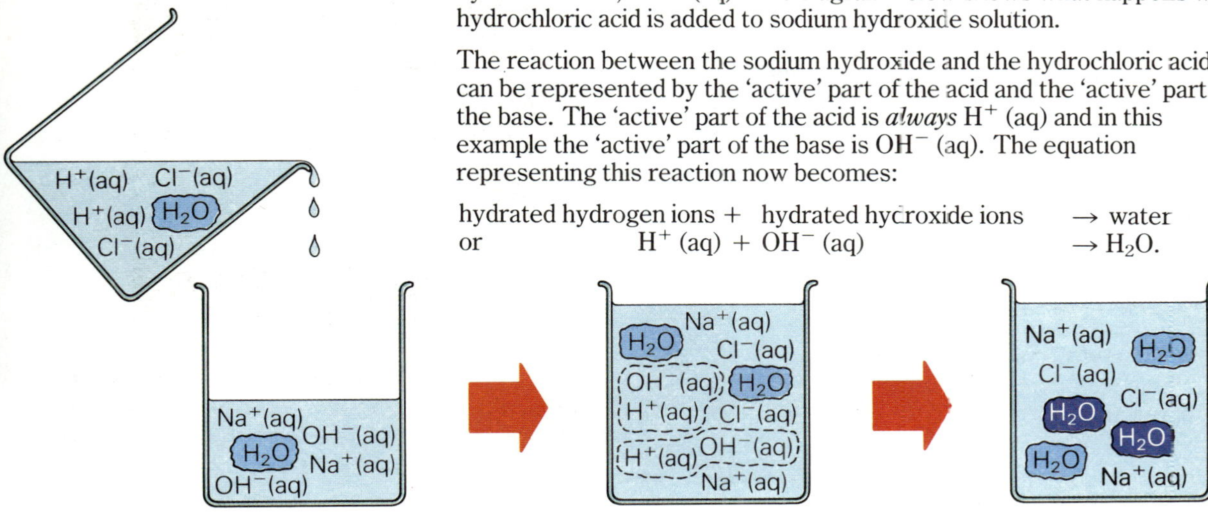

When hydrochloric acid is added, the H^+ (aq) ions and OH^-(aq) ions react to form . . .

. . . water. The Na^+ (aq) and Cl^- (aq) ions remain as a solution of sodium chloride. The salt has not taken part in the reaction – it is a chemical 'leftover'.

This is called an *ionic* equation. Note that the product is the same as that in the table opposite. For an insoluble base some of the base, however small, will actually dissolve in the water. This means an insoluble metal carbonate will always have a small part of the 'active' carbonate ion in solution as CO_3^{2-} (aq). This will react with any H^+ (aq) ions in solution to give the products shown in the table opposite. As it reacts, more carbonate dissolves.

$$CO_3^{2-} (aq) + 2H^+ (aq) \rightarrow H_2O + CO_2.$$

Proton donors and acceptors

The hydrogen ion, H^+, is formed by a hydrogen atom losing an electron.

$$H - e \rightarrow H^+$$

The diagram shows that a hydrogen ion is a proton.

When a hydrogen atom loses an electron, it forms a proton.

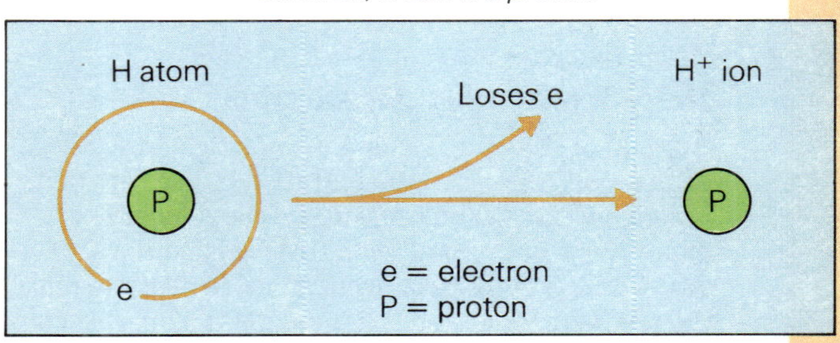

Since all acids give their protons to bases when they are neutralised by them, they are called **proton donors.** Why do you think bases are called **proton acceptors**?

1 Why do you think Vitamin C and citric acid are commonly used in soluble medicine tablets?

2 What other factors does a manufacturer need to consider when choosing a metal carbonate for a soluble tablet?

3 Nitric acid produces the nitrate ion, NO_3^-, and sulphuric acid the sulphate ion, SO_4^{2-}, when dissolved in water. They are both strong acids. Draw models to show what happens when they dissolve in water.

4 Draw a model similar to the one at the top of the page to explain what happens when sulphuric acid is added to copper carbonate ($Cu^{2+}CO_3^{2-}$).

5 Write an ionic equation for the reaction between
a potassium hydrogencarbonate and nitric acid
b magnesium oxide and hydrochloric acid.

6 Ammonia (NH_3) is a base and reacts with an acid to form the ammonium ion (NH_4^+). Write an ionic equation for its reaction with an acid.

9.12 Rates of reaction

Same reaction, different rates

Some chemical reactions such as those in a firework are very fast and spectacular yet others, for example the rusting of iron, are much slower. The *rate of reaction* is a measure of how fast the reaction can take place. The pictures show what happens when acids react with limestone and marble chips (both different forms of calcium carbonate). Does the reaction always occur at the same rate? What factors might alter the rate of reaction?

Acid rain can eat away at limestone figures over years but . . . .

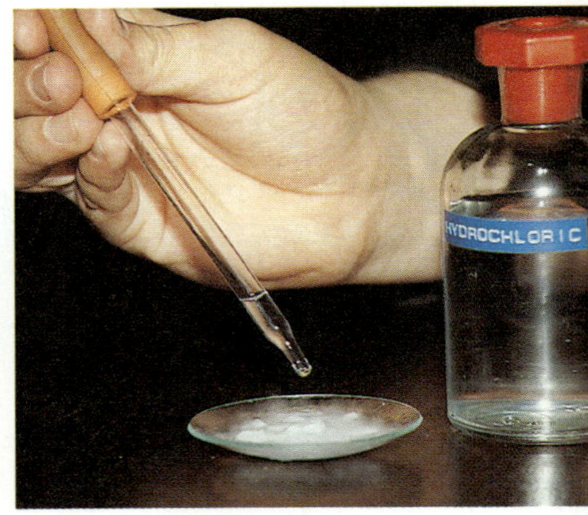

. . . . the reaction between marble chips and acid in the laboratory can be over in a couple of minutes.

Measuring rates

You can investigate the factors that change the rate of reaction between calcium carbonate and an acid in the laboratory. If the acid used is hydrochloric, then the products of the reaction are calcium carbonate, water and carbon dioxide:

$$CaCO_3 + 2HCl \rightarrow CaCl_2 + H_2O + CO_2$$

In order to find out the rate of reaction, you need to *measure* something in the reaction that changes with *time*. One of the things you could measure is the mass of material in the flask. This is decreasing all the time because carbon dioxide is escaping into the air during the reaction. Alternatively you could collect the carbon dioxide and record the amount of gas collected every minute using an apparatus like this.

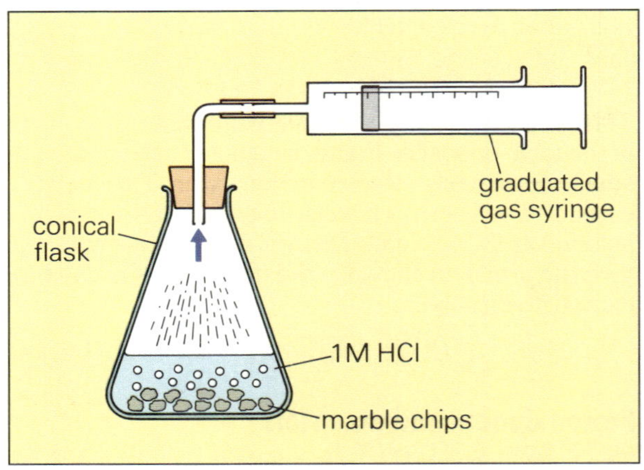

You can measure the volume of CO_2 collected at regular intervals using a gas syringe like this.

Effect of increasing concentration

A group of students decided to investigate the effect of increasing the acid concentration on the rate of its reaction with calcium carbonate. They did the experiment twice, first using 1M acid and then 2M acid which is twice as concentrated. In order to make the test fair, they used the same mass of marble chips and the chips were all about the same size in both cases. What else did they need to do in order to make the test fair?

They compared the results of both experiments by recording their results on a graph. The steeper the slope of the graph, the faster the rate of the reaction. What does the graph of their results show you about the effect of the concentration of the acid on the rate of the reaction as it proceeds?

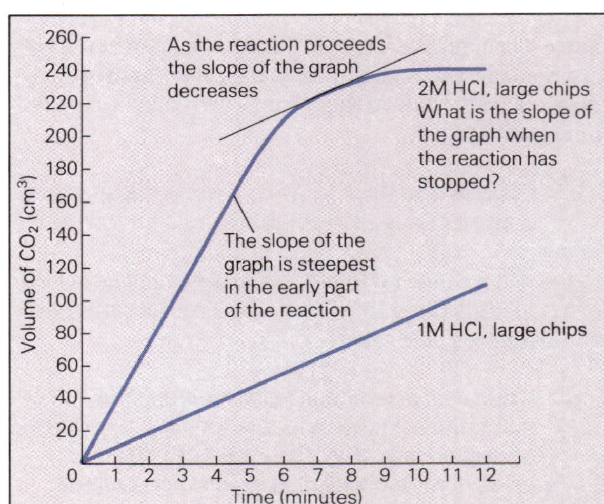

How much faster is the reaction using 2M HCl compared to 1M HCl?

Effect of changing particle size

Another group of students decided to investigate the effect of changing the size of the marble chips. The conditions they used are shown in this picture. Their teacher looked at the experiment and noticed some errors. Can you see what they were?

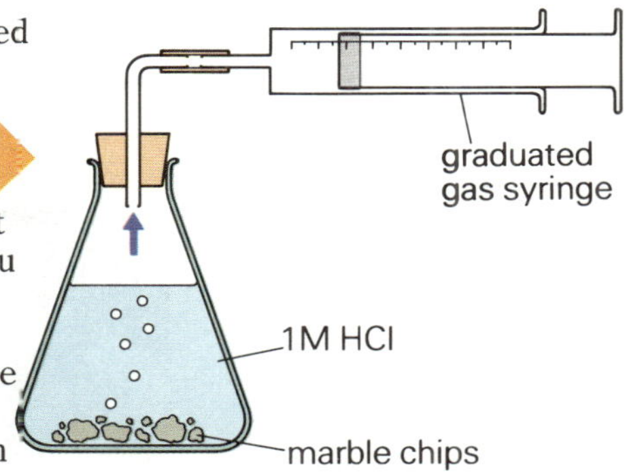

Time (mins)	Volume of CO_2 (cm^3) ① 1M HCl Large chips	② 1M HCl Smaller chips
2	18	54
4	36	108
6	54	162
8	72	206
10	90	230
12	108	240

After correcting these errors, the students recorded two sets of results using large chips and then small chips with 1M acid in each case. Their results are shown in the table. What do they show you about the effect of *decreasing* the particle size on the rate of reaction?

Explaining reaction rates

For a chemical reaction to take place the particles of each element must collide. Not all collisions between particles will lead to a chemical reaction since some will not have enough energy. For reactions carried out at the same temperature, if you can increase the chance of a collision then a reaction is more likely – the rate of reaction will be greater.

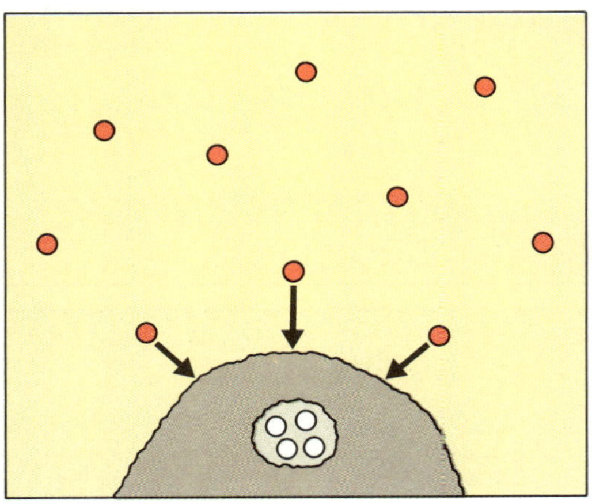

Only those ○ particles on the surface of the large solid can collide with ● particles.

By increasing the concentration of ● particles, there is a greater chance of collisions with the ○ particles.

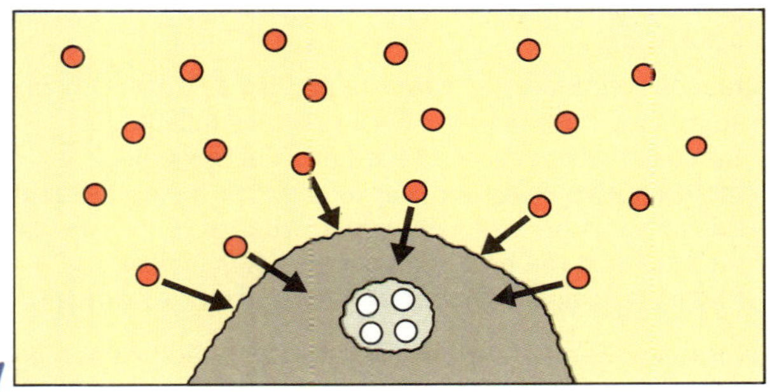

By breaking the larger solid into smaller pieces, you can increase its surface area so there is more chance of ● colliding with the ○ particles.

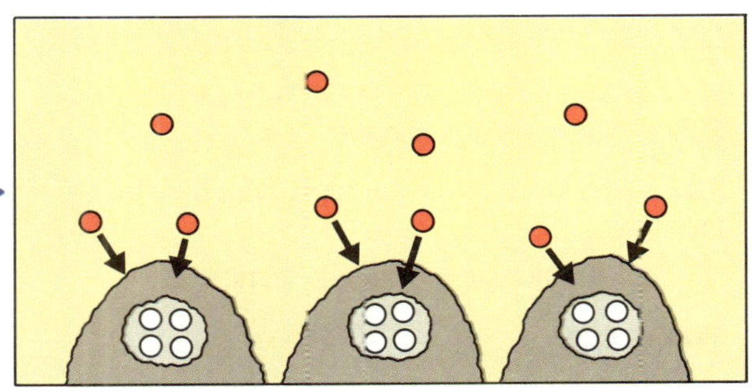

Can you see why increasing the concentration of the acid (increasing the number of particles) or breaking up the marble chips into smaller pieces will increase the rate of reaction?

1 Look at the pictures at the beginning of the spread. Suggest two reasons why the laboratory reaction is faster.

2 What other method(s) could the students have used to measure the volume of carbon dioxide?

3 Describe how you would measure the rate of reaction between acid and marble chips by following the change of mass of the chips with time. What precaution would you have to take to ensure the accuracy of your results?

4 Plot a graph of the results in the table above. Use the graph to predict when the first experiment will be complete. Draw on the graph the shape of the curve you would predict for
a twice the mass of the smaller chips
b half the mass of powdered marble.

5 How could a group of students modify the experiment to investigate the effect of temperature on the rate of reaction?

6 Flour dust can react explosively with air. Why isn't this a problem with wheat grain?

Food deterioration

Rotten food

When you buy pre-packed food you'll notice it has a sell-by date. The fresh fruit you buy – fruit, meat veg – will 'go off' after a certain time. All food becomes unsuitable to eat and harmful to health after a certain time. Food deterioration can be caused by microscopic living organisms – **micro-organisms**, such as bacteria. Micro-organisms need food for energy and for growth (increasing their numbers). There are many different types of micro-organisms which thrive on different types of food.

Sour milk

Just as *you* need sugar for energy, so bacteria rely on sugars for their energy. Milk contains milk sugar, **lactose**, which bacteria feed on. The milk sugar is broken down or **hydrolysed** by water molecules and this process provides energy for the bacteria. Certain molecules in the bacteria speed up this process – these are called **biological catalysts** or **enzymes**.

The conversion of lactose in milk to lactic acid depends on the number of bacteria present.

Lactic acid is produced as a waste product of this process and this affects the flavour and the texture of the milk – it makes it taste and look sour. As more lactic acid is produced in the milk, its pH decreases.

Look at the graph. Why does the reaction slow down after about 40 hours?

The overall process can be represented by the equation:

lactose + water → lactic acid

Sour grapes

Not all micro-organisms are harmful to food. The ancient Egyptians, for example, were already brewing alcohol from yeast which feeds on fruit and other plants. Yeast belongs to the class of micro-organisms called fungi and feeds on carbohydrates in plants. Enzymes in the yeast break down the carbohydrates into ethanol (an alcohol) and carbon dioxide. This releases energy. The overall process (called **fermentation**) can be represented by the equation:

carbohydrate → ethanol + carbon dioxide

$C_6H_{12}O_6 \rightarrow 2C_2H_6O + 2CO_2$

You can measure the rate of the reaction by counting the number of bubbles of carbon dioxide produced in a minute. This graph shows that the reaction rate depends on the temperature. What is the best temperature range for getting yeast to make ethanol and carbon dioxide fastest when brewing beer?

The mould growing on this yoghurt belongs to a group of micro-organisms called fungi.

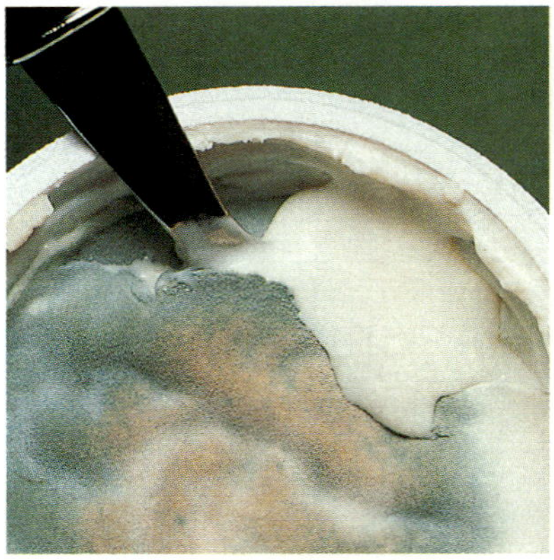

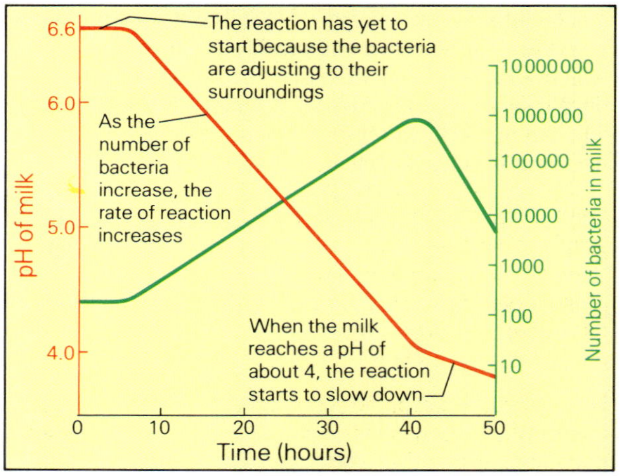

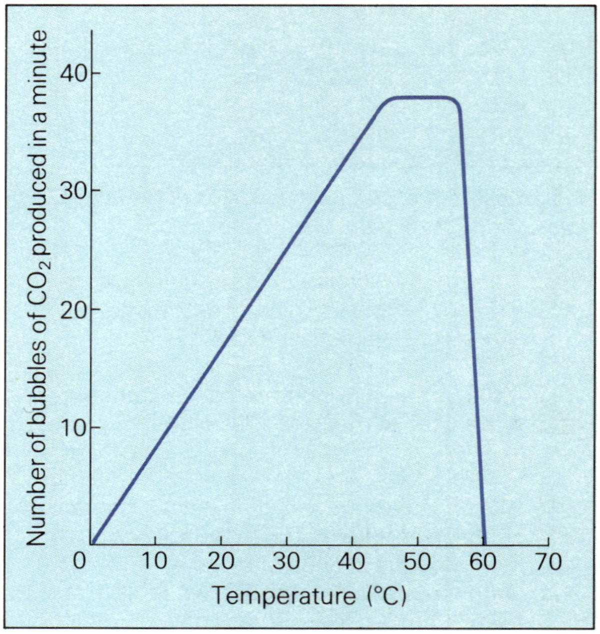

Browned off

Some foods, for example many fruits and vegetables, contain enzymes in their cells. Apples contain an enzyme which speeds up the formation of a brown polymer (a large chain molecule). If the cells are ruptured or broken, this enzyme is exposed and it reacts with the air. This causes the apples to go brown – you've probably seen this many times.

Some students carried out an investigation into the effects of pH and temperature on apple browning. Look at their results. What pH does the enzyme work best in?

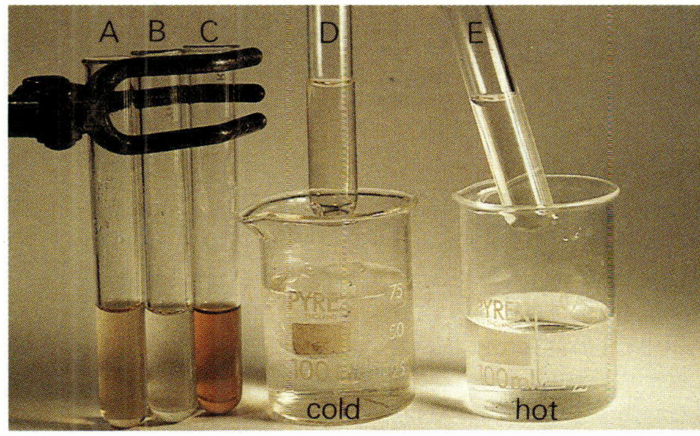

Contents of each tube (cm^3)					
	A	B	C	D	E
Water	5	–	–	5	5
Acid	–	5	–	–	–
Alkali	–	–	5	–	–
Apple juice	3	3	3	3	3

Effect of temperature and catalyst on reaction rate

Molecules at the same temperature don't all have the same energy. Some molecules are moving faster than others. This means their energies are spread over a wide range at a certain temperature. The graph shows you the distribution of energies you would expect to find in a large number of molecules at two different temperatures. As you can see the distribution changes with temperature. For a chemical reaction to take place, the molecules must have a certain minimum energy (E on the graph). Only those molecules with an energy greater than this minimum energy will take part in a chemical reaction. From the graph you can see that more molecules will react at T_2 than T_1. But *without* an increase in temperature, more molecules will still react if a catalyst – or enzyme – is added. A catalyst provides an alternative lower energy pathway for a chemical reaction.

How does the graph help to explain why the rate of a chemical reaction is faster for a catalysed than for an uncatalysed reaction *at the same temperature?*

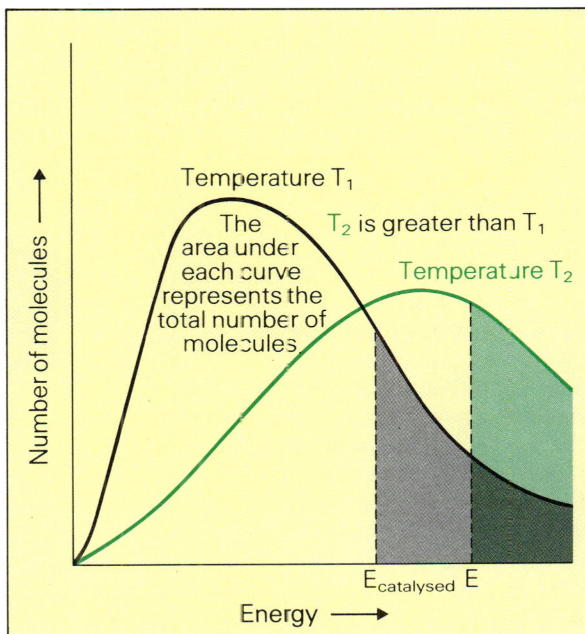

The minimum energy for an uncatalysed reaction is 'E' on the graph. At temperature T_1, molecules react but at the higher temperature, T_2, and molecules react since more molecules have energies greater than the minimum energy needed. The rate of reaction increases at the higher temperature because more molecules are reacting. If a catalyst is added the rate of reaction increases without the need for a higher temperature.

1 Explain how food preservation is helped by
a freezing **b** pickling in vinegar
c cooking then sealing in cans.

2 Draw a graph to predict the growth of yeast cells at different temperatures.

3 A group of students investigating fermentation using yeast noticed that at every temperature the number of bubbles of carbon dioxide was uneven at first then became steady. Explain what was happening.

4 **a** Why do you need to handle apples carefully?
b Look at the picture of the apple browning experiment. Why haven't the apples turned brown at 0°C and 100°C?

5 State two reasons why lemon juice is often added to fruit cocktails.

6 Look at the graph above. What area would you shade to show how many more molecules react in the catalysed reaction at temperature T_2?

YOU CAN READ MORE ABOUT POLYMERS ON SPREADS 2.11 AND 8.3.

9.14 Getting the right recipe

Making cakes

If you want to make a cake, having a list of the ingredients in a recipe book isn't enough. You also need to know the *relative* amounts of each ingredient – what proportions of margarine, flour, eggs etc. you need. If you know these, you can make the cake any size by altering the *amounts* of the ingredients but keeping their *relative* amounts the same. For example if you need 150 g margarine and 200 g of flour to make a smallish cake, you'll need 225 g of margarine and 300 g of flour to make a larger one.

You make a cake by using the correct materials and the right ingredients in the right amounts. A chemist makes metals, plastics, glass and many other useful materials in the same way.

Making materials

When you make a material such as a metal alloy, a new plastic or glass you will also need the list of ingredients. This is contained in the word equation. But although this tells you the ingredients to use, or **reagents** as they are called, it doesn't tell you how much you need nor the amount of products that will be formed.

This word equation tells you the ingredients used and formed when copper oxide and carbon are mixed together then heated.
Copper oxide + carbon → copper + carbon dioxide.
But it doesn't tell you the amount of carbon and copper oxide to use nor how much copper and carbon dioxide will be formed.

The right amount

You can find the relative amounts of each reagent from the equation containing the chemical formulae – the **balanced symbol** equation – for the reaction. This gives you information about the *type* and *number* of atoms of the elements in the reaction. You can also find the relative atomic mass (RAM) of each element from the Periodic Table (*see 9.1 and 9.3*). The relative mass of each compound in the equation is the *sum* of the RAM's of its elements. Once you have calculated the *relative* mass of all the reagents and products you can work out how much of each element or compound to use (assuming you can fix the mass of the substance) since their relative masses will always stay the same. The table shows the relative masses of the products and reagents needed when copper oxide is reduced by carbon to form copper and carbon dioxide is given off. How much carbon do you need to reduce 40 g of copper oxide and how much copper will be formed?

$$2CuO + C \rightarrow 2\,Cu + CO_2$$

	$2CuO$		C	$2\,Cu$	CO_2	
Type of element	Cu	O	C	Cu	C	O
Number of atoms of each element	2	2	1	2	1	2
RAM of each element	64	16	12	64	12	16
Relative mass of compound	2 × 64 + 2 × 16 = 160		+ 1 × 12 = 12	= 2 × 64 = 128	+ 1 × 12 + 2 × 16 = 44	

From the relative masses of the compounds, 160 g of copper oxide are reduced by 12 g of carbon to form 128 g of copper and 44 g of carbon dioxide or 80 g of copper oxide are reduced by 6 g of carbon to form 64 g of copper and 22 g of carbon dioxide. Note that in each case the relative amounts of reagents and products are the same and the mass of reagents = mass of products.

Making plastics

Plastics are large molecules called polymers made by joining together smaller molecules called monomers. Different plastics can be made by joining together different types of monomers. The plastic polytetrafluoroethene (PTFE) is made by joining together tetrafluororethene monomers. Look at the relative mass of the molecules in the equation.

	ethene	+	fluorine	→	tetrafluoroethene	+	hydrogen fluoride
	C_2H_4	+	$4F_2$		C_2F_4	+	4HF
Relative mass of molecule	$2 \times 12 + 4 \times 1 =$ <u>28</u>	+	$8 \times 19 =$ <u>152</u>	=	$2 \times 12 + 4 \times 19 =$ <u>100</u>	+	$4 \times 1 + 4 \times 19 =$ <u>80</u>

How much ethene and fluorine would a chemical factory need to use to produce 25 tonnes of tetrafluoroethene?

Glass is a product of sand, limestone and sodium carbonate.

Making glass

Ordinary glass is a mixture of materials. It is made by heating together silicon oxide, sodium carbonate and calcium carbonate.

How much sand would a glass company need to use to react with 5.03 tonnes of sodium carbonate and 5 tonnes of calcium carbonate?

Look at the Periodic Table on 9.1 to find the RAM's of the elements in the questions.

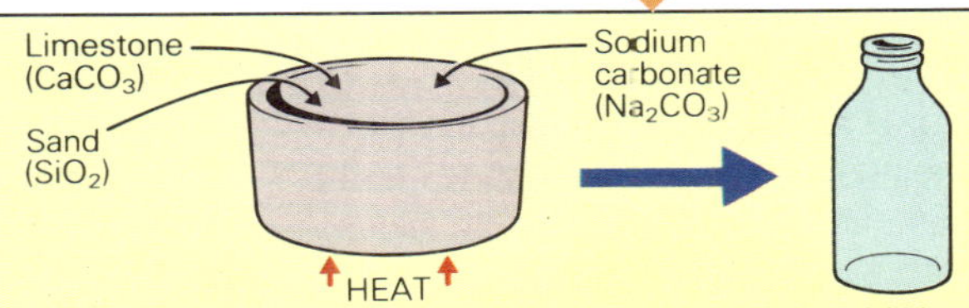

The sand reacts with the sodium carbonate <u>and</u> limestone (RAM Na = 23, C = 12, O = 16, Si = 28, Ca = 40)

Na_2CO_3	+	SiO_2	=	Na_2SiO_3	+	CO_2
2×23+1×12+3×16=		1×28+2×16		2×23+1×28+3×16=		1×12+2×16=
<u>106</u>	+	<u>60</u>	=	<u>122</u>	+	<u>44</u>
$CaCO_3$	+	SiO_2	=	$CaSiO_3$	+	CO_2
1×40+1×12+3×16=				1×40+1×28+3×16=		
<u>100</u>	+	<u>60</u>	=	<u>116</u>	+	<u>44</u>

1 Iron is made in a blast furnace by the reduction of iron oxide, using carbon monoxide.

$$Fe_2O_3 + 3CO \rightarrow 2Fe + 3CO_2$$

How much iron oxide needs to be reduced to obtain 28 tonnes of iron?

2 How much ethanol (C_2H_6O) could be made from the fermentation of 0.5 kg of grape sugar?

$$C_6H_{12}O_6 \rightarrow 2C_2H_6O + 2CO_2$$

3 A limestone company heats limestone ($CaCO_3$) to produce lime (CaO). How much limestone does it need to heat each day to make 112 tonnes of lime?

$$CaCO_3 \rightarrow CaO + CO_2$$

4 The reaction between chlorine and ethene is used to make chloroethene (vinyl chloride), the monomer used to make PVC. How much chloroethene could be made from 142 kg of chlorine?

$$C_2H_4 + Cl_2 \rightarrow C_2H_3Cl + HCl$$

5 Baking powder sodium hydrogencarbonate ($NaHCO_3$), decomposes on heating to produce carbon dioxide (CO_2) which makes cakes rise.

$$2NaHCO_3 \rightarrow Na_2CO_3 + H_2O + CO_2$$

a What mass of carbon dioxide is produced by heating 8.4 g of baking powder?
b If the volume of 44 g of CO_2 is 24 litres at room temperature and pressure, what will be the volume of the CO_2 in **a** at the same temperature and pressure?

YOU CAN READ MORE ABOUT PLASTICS ON SPREAD 2.11.

Chemical processes in nature

A growing problem

Every living organism needs food – the animals and plants that you eat also need food. To produce the large amounts of food needed by humans today, farmers need to make sure that their crops grow well and stay healthy. Plants need essential elements, some of which they take from the soil through their root system. These elements must be put back into the soil or the plants will not continue to grow properly. Nature can do this – but not quickly enough to satisfy the increasing human demand for food. Farmers try to solve the problem by adding artificial fertilisers.

Without the use of fertilisers, you would not have as much food to choose from . . . can you think of any disadvantages to using fertilisers?

Nitrogen – an essential element

Nitrogen is one of the elements that plants need to survive. It is a very common element – it makes up almost four-fifths of the air you breathe! So why do farmers buy nitrogen fertilisers? Why can't all plants take it directly from the air?

Nitrogen, like oxygen and fluorine, exists in nature as nitrogen molecules, N_2. These N_2 molecules are remarkably unreactive. Nitrogen (like phosphorus, the other non-metallic element in the same group) doesn't react with water. It also has a very low solubility in water. This means most plants can't absorb it on its own through their roots. It has to be changed into compounds which are water soluble for plants to take it in.

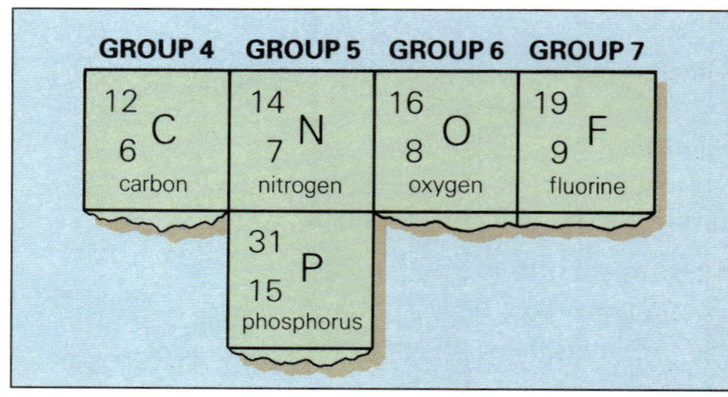

Nitrogen is a non-metallic element. How many electrons does it have in its outer shell and what is its valency?

Soluble compounds of nitrogen

Although nitrogen is a very unreactive gas, it can react with other elements. In nature, the large amount of energy released by lightning helps nitrogen and oxygen in the air to react and form nitrogen monoxide.

$$N_2 + O_2 \rightarrow 2NO$$

The nitrogen monoxide quickly reacts with more oxygen to form nitrogen dioxide.

$$2NO + O_2 \rightarrow 2NO_2$$

Nitrogen dioxide is an oxide of a non-metal and, like other non-metal oxides, it dissolves in water to form an acidic solution. When mixed with air and water, it forms nitric acid.

$$4NO_2 + 2H_2O + O_2 \rightarrow 4HNO_3$$

Like phosphorus, nitrogen also forms a hydride called ammonia, NH_3. It is a colourless gas with a pungent smell and is used in smelling salts . . .

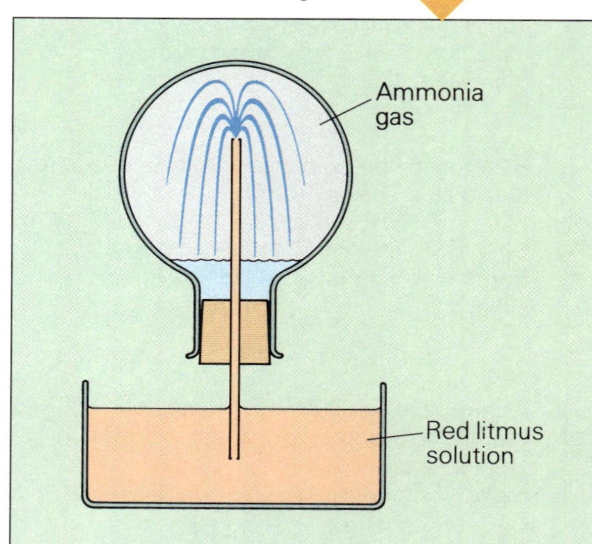

This flask contains ammonia gas. A small amount of water from the middle tube dissolves all the ammonia and a fountain is produced. What does this show you about the solubility of ammonia in water and the pH of the resulting solution?

The Haber process

Ammonia and nitric acid are soluble nitrogen compounds but neither are suitable for adding directly to the soil as fertilisers. Can you suggest why?

Chemists knew how to change both these into compounds which were less soluble in water, had a pH nearer to 7 and could be more easily put on the soil – the problem was how to make them in large quantities. In 1911, Haber, a German chemist, discovered that ammonia could be made directly from nitrogen and hydrogen. Both reagents are available in large quantities – nitrogen from the air and hydrogen from the reaction between water and natural gas. The elements are converted into ammonia using an iron catalyst and suitable conditions of temperature and pressure.

$$N_2 + 3H_2 \rightarrow 2NH_3$$

The gaseous mixture at the end of the reaction contains about 18% ammonia. This is removed by cooling and the unused nitrogen and hydrogen are recycled.

If ammonia is mixed with air and passed over a heated catalyst (platinum/rhodium alloy) at 1000° C it is **oxidised** into nitrogen monoxide which can be converted to nitric acid:

$$4NH_3 + 5O_2 \rightarrow 4NO + 6H_2O$$

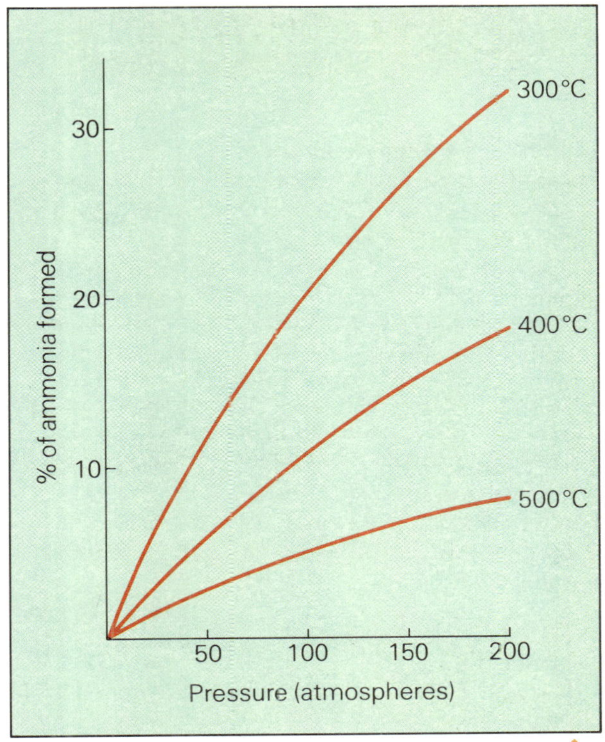

The yield of ammonia depends on the pressure and temperature chosen. Why do you think the reaction is not carried out at room temperature?

Making nitrogen fertiliser

Ammonia is an alkali or soluble base, so a solution of ammonia in water will react with acid to form a salt. Ammonia solution reacts with nitric acid to form ammonium nitrate – a white solid salt.

$$NH_3 + HNO_3 \rightarrow NH_4NO_3$$

Ammonium nitrate is soluble in water but not as soluble as ammonia, its pH is nearer to 7 than either ammonia or nitric acid and it can be made into granules that are easily added to the soil.

Ammonium nitrate is a very common nitrogen fertiliser.

1. Fertilisers can drain into rivers and streams causing pollution. Do you think that only organic farming, which uses manure as a fertiliser, should be allowed?

2. Draw the structure of the ammonia molecule, showing how nitrogen and hydrogen share electrons to achieve full shells.

3. Limestone, calcium carbonate $CaCO_3$, is often added to acidic soil. Write an equation to show how it neutralises nitric acid.

4. Look at the graph showing the different yields of ammonia in the Haber process. If the pressure used was 200 atm., what was the temperature of the reaction and why do you think it was chosen?

5. How does the use of a catalyst help to speed up the production of ammonia?

6. A company produces 1020 tonnes of ammonia every day. How much nitric acid does it have to produce to react with this ammonia and how much fertiliser will it make?

YOU CAN READ ABOUT THE NATURAL CYCLE OF NITROGEN ON SPREAD 4.10.

Index *(refers to spread numbers)*

For additional information, see the following modules:

2 Materials
8 Structure and Bonding

Photo acknowledgements

These refer to the spread number (in italics), and where appropriate, the position on the page (lh = left-hand page, rh = right-hand page).

J Allan Cash *9.9* lh, bottom right; Environmental Picture Library (C. Westwood) *9.12* lh, top left; Sally & Richard Greenhill *9.15* lh; Holt Studios *9.15* rh; John Olive *9.1*lh, *9.3*lh left, *9.8* lh bottom; Ann Ronan Picture Library *9.4*; Science Photo Library *9.13* rh;

All other photos: Clare Hayes (× 33)

Picture Research: Jennifer Johnson, Norman Franks

THE SCIENCES FOR GCSE

10 INHERITANCE AND SELECTION

Living things often share characteristics, but have **variations** which set them apart as individuals or species. Variations may be **inherited** by offspring – and the effect of useful or unhelpful variations may **select** which individuals survive. This module will help you to understand the natural 'code' which controls variation and inheritance – and how scientists use this knowledge both to grow disease-resistant crops, and to catch criminals!

Relevant National Curriculum Attainment Targets: Old AT 4
New AT (2)

10.1 Molecules that make life

You're unique

There may be many people in your school but you can easily be recognised from the rest. In fact, there are over 5 000 million people on the Earth and each one is different. These differences are called **variations**. Your hair colour, eye colour, weight and height are just a few of the **characteristics** that vary – and distinguish you from everyone else.

Family likeness

It is often easy to tell that related people are members of the same family because they have similar characteristics. The similarity between children and parents suggests that some characteristics are *inherited* – passed on from one generation to the next. Investigating family trees is one method that is used to study human **inheritance**.

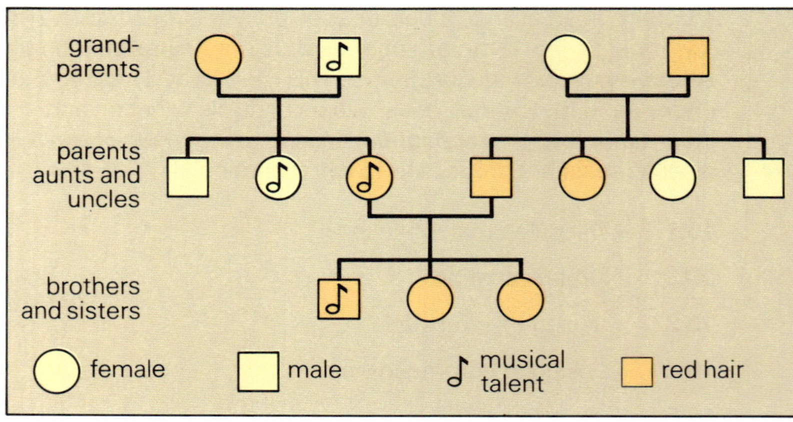

A family tree showing that some members have red hair and some are talented musicians.

Working on your inheritance

Not all characteristics are simply passed on from parents. For example, the strength and ability to become an Olympic athlete are not just inherited – they depend on the right lifestyle, diet and training as well as natural talent. In other words, physical strength and ability are affected by **environmental factors**. Many other human characteristics, such as height and weight, are influenced by environmental as well inherited factors.

You need more than natural talent to reach the top.

What will I become?

What will this baby be – a football star? prime minister? rock guitarist? This will depend on many things but some aspects of the baby's future will have been determined already. Inside each of the millions of cells that make up the baby's body is a chemical called **DNA** (deoxyribonucleic acid) which contains instructions to make an entire human being. DNA is an extremely long spiral molecule divided into regions called **genes**, which provide *coded* instructions for particular characteristics, such as hair colour. Many human features are affected by the DNA that we inherit – intelligence, state of health and even life span.

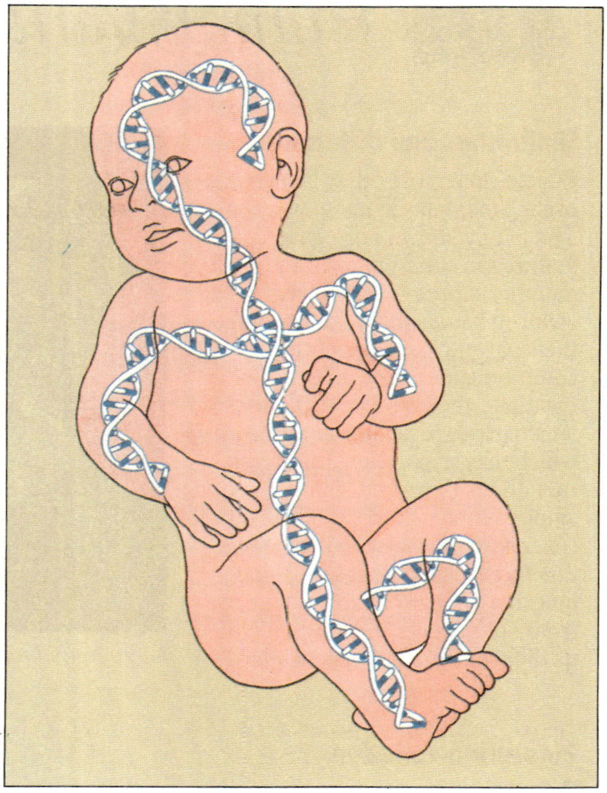

DNA contains the complete code to make an entire human being.

The human code

If the DNA from every cell in your body was unravelled and joined end to end, it would stretch to the Moon and back about 8 000 times! This huge amount of DNA contains millions of individual genes. Techniques have been developed that enable scientists to isolate and analyse the coded instructions in single genes. In 1989, scientists from all over the world became involved in a project to identify every gene in the human body – and reveal the complete human code. At present, only a fraction of the total DNA instructions have been analysed, and it will be many years before this DNA testing works out the complete instructions for making a human being.

Changing inheritance

DNA testing has helped to identify some faulty genes which cause serious illnesses. It might be possible to treat people with such illnesses using **gene therapy** – replacing faulty genes with normal ones. The new techniques for analysing DNA are also probing the mystery of how disorders such as cancer and heart disease develop.

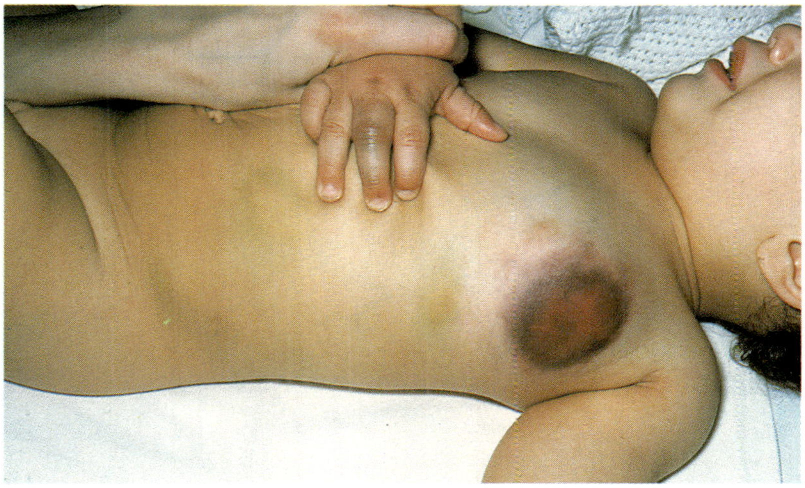

Even a small knock can result in large bruises in this child because he suffers from haemophilia (excessive bleeding) – a disease caused by a faulty gene.

1 When a group of students examined the data in the family tree on the opposite page, they produced the hypothesis that 'red hair and musical talent are inherited characteristics'.

State, giving your reasons, whether you agree or disagree with their hypothesis.

2 Do you think being good at science is an inherited characteristic? Give reasons for your answer.

3 DNA testing will present us with many difficult problems, for example:

- should someone who will develop a deadly disease later in life be told?
- should gene therapy be used only for treating diseases or also for improving other inherited features?

a What other possible problems can you think of?

b Do these problems mean that we should stop this form of testing?

Human variation

Similarities and differences

People, like most other living organisms, vary in many ways. The family shown here have features in common but each member differs from the rest. The children have similar features to their parents because of the common genes they inherit. For example, they may inherit genes which produce curly hair and genes which may make them tall. Even though brothers and sisters have similar features, no two children (except identical twins) will inherit *exactly* the same genes. We each inherit a *different* mixture of genes from our parents, making each of us different from everyone else.

Members of the same family inherit similar features.

Measuring variation

A survey of variation was carried out on 200 first-year pupils in a high school. Two characteristics were measured – pupils' height and their ability to roll their tongue into a U-shape. The results of the survey are shown in these histograms.

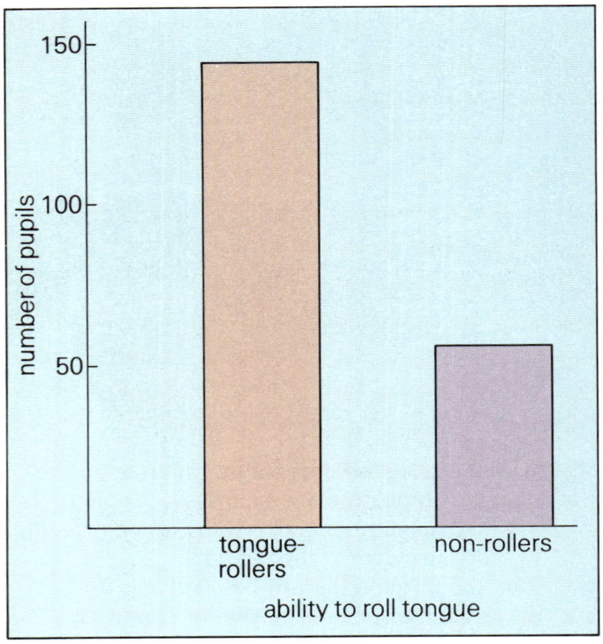

There are no half-way values for tongue rolling – people either can roll their tongue or they cannot. This type of variation is called **discontinuous variation**.

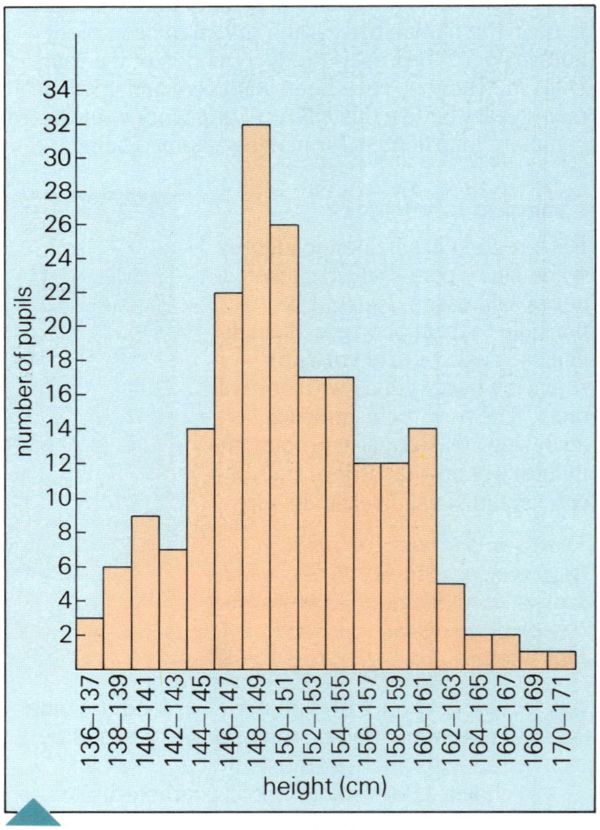

In this histogram there is a *continuous* range of height from the tallest pupils to the smallest. This type of variation is called **continuous variation**.

Effects of the environment

A girl may inherit genes that could make her tall, but if she is undernourished, she will not grow to her full height. All characteristics which show *continuous* variation are *affected by the environment* as well as by inherited factors.

Tongue-rolling is just one example of discontinuous variation. Another example is your blood group. People belong to one of four main blood groups A, B, AB or O. Like all examples of *discontinuous* variation, your blood group is *entirely due to your genes* and is not affected by your environment.

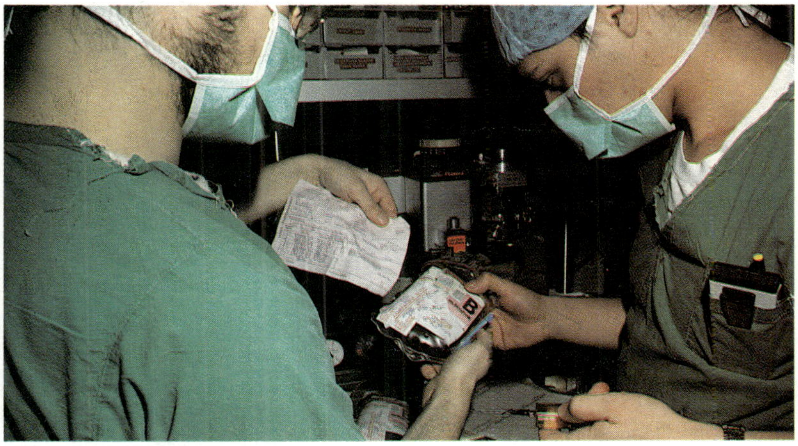

People can become very ill if they are given blood of the wrong group during transfusion.

Investigating variation

Identical twins develop from the same fertilised egg cell. This means that they are born with *identical* genes which control their future growth and development. Investigations involving identical twins can provide valuable information about how characteristics are affected by inherited and environmental factors.

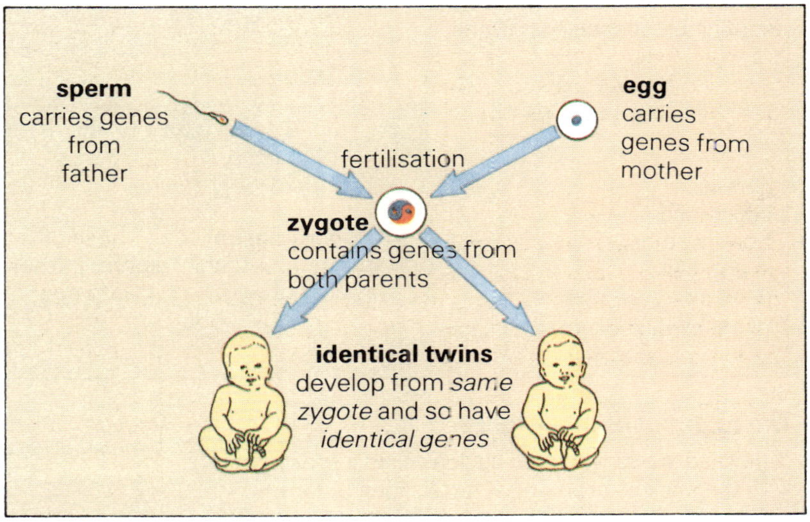

Katie and Rebecca are identical twins who were separated at birth and brought up in different families. When they were 16 years old, the following data was recorded about them:

	Katie	Rebecca
weight	62 kg	51 kg
hair colour	red	red
freckles	present	present
measure of intelligence	134	119

1 Use the evidence in the table about the twins to suggest, with reasons

a which characteristics are controlled by inherited factors only,

b which are influenced by the environment in which the girls were raised,

c which characteristics show continuous variation.

2 Look at the survey of pupils' height on the opposite page.

a What number of pupils were 160 cm or taller?

b Give *two* reasons why the pupils show a large variation in height.

c Name one other human characteristic which shows the same type of variation.

3 In another investigation into variation, the maximum span of the right hand was measured. The results were:

hand span (mm)	number of students
170–179	2
180–189	5
190–199	9
200–209	6
210–219	3

a Draw a histogram of these results.

b What type of variation is shown by hand span?

Passing on information

Like mother, like daughter

'Doesn't she have her mother's eyes?' 'Isn't she like her father?' are typical of the comments that friends and relatives make when they first see a young girl. How are these features inherited?

The diagram below shows the main events that take place during **fertilisation.** What does this diagram tell you about how genetic information can be passed from parent to offspring?

When the nuclei of a sperm and egg join together, the first cell of a new individual is formed – the zygote.

Many of this baby's characteristics have already been determined.

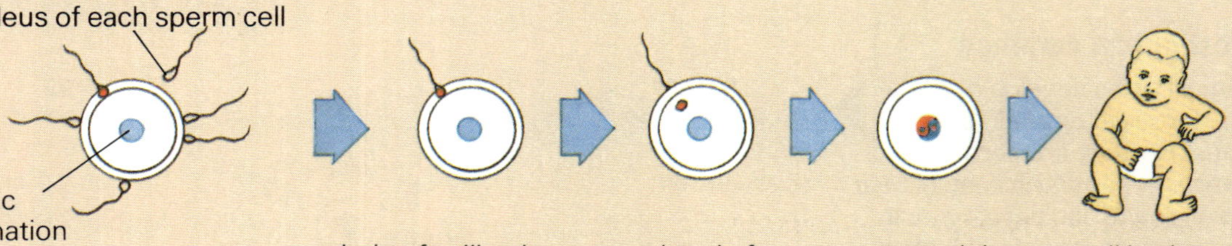

The material of inheritance

A new life starts when the nucleus from a sperm *fuses* with the nucleus of an egg at fertilisation to form a single-celled **zygote**. The material that is present in the nuclei of the sperm and egg is the *only* material that passes from parents to their offspring. The sperm and egg contain information which affects how we grow and what we look like. This is called **genetic information**.

When a cell is not dividing, the nucleus appears as a dark region inside the cell. During cell division, thread-like **chromosomes** can be seen in the nucleus. Each chromosome contains enough genetic information to control thousands of characteristics. The chromosomes in eggs and sperm carry genetic information from the mother and father to their offspring.

Through a microscope, you can see thread-like chromosomes when cells divide.

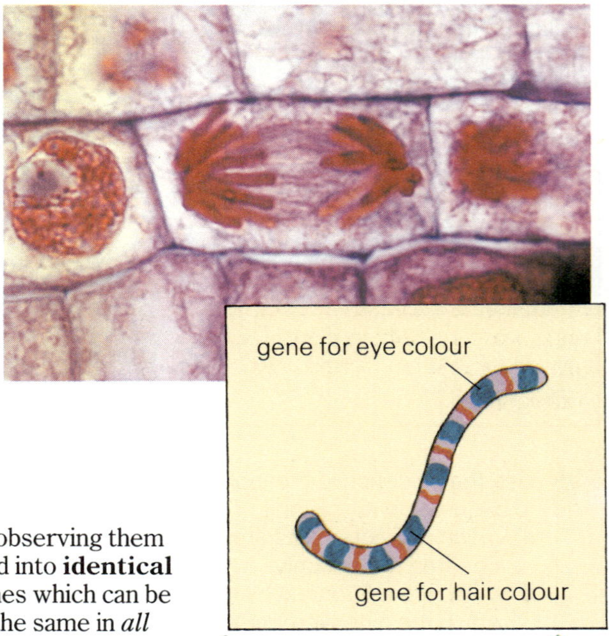

Each gene in a chromosome controls a particular characteristic.

Pairing up

Chromosomes appear in different shapes and sizes. By observing them very carefully, the chromosomes in a cell can be grouped into **identical pairs**. For example, human cells contain 46 chromosomes which can be grouped into 23 pairs. This number of chromosomes is the same in *all* body cells – you have 23 pairs of chromosomes in each of your skin cells, eye cells, bone cells and so on.

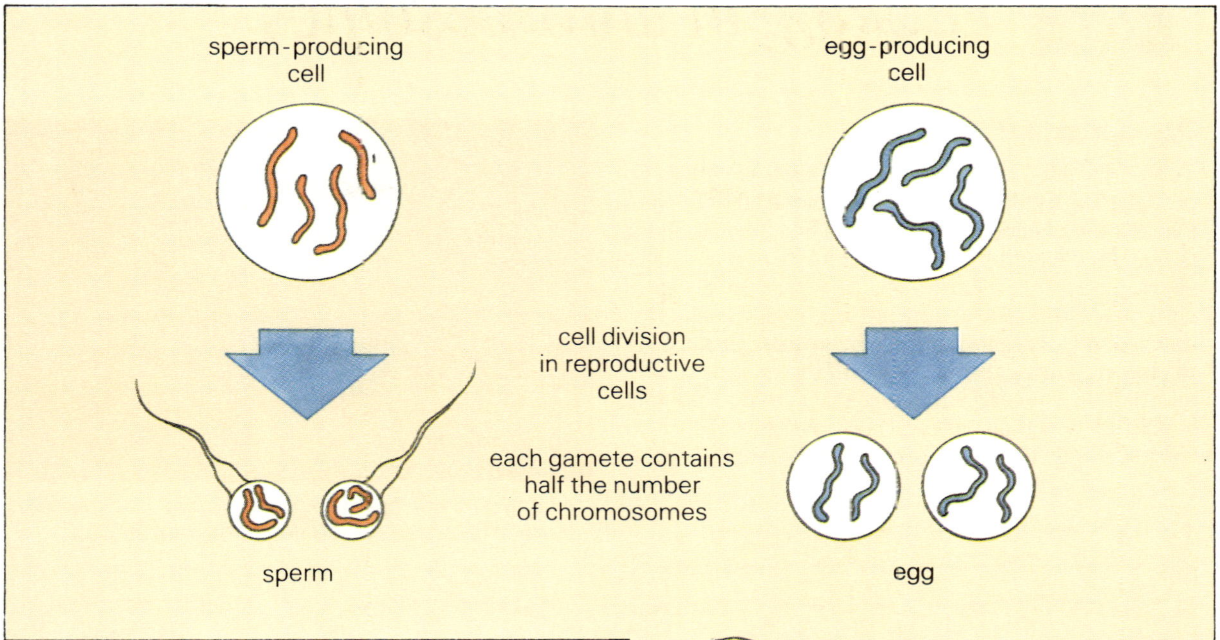

Halving the number of chromosomes . . .

Chromosomes are passed from parents to their offspring by reproductive cells called **gametes**. Gametes are produced by a special form of **cell division** that takes place in reproductive organs. During this process, the pairs of identical chromosomes separate from each other and move into different cells. The gametes formed by this cell division contain only *half* the number of chromosomes in normal body cells. For example, each sperm or egg cell contains 23 chromosomes.

. . . and restoring the number of chromosomes

The first cell of a new individual is formed when gametes fuse at fertilisation. Each gamete carries a single set of chromosomes, so the zygote that is formed by their fusion contains *both* sets. For example, when a human sperm carrying 23 chromosomes fuses with a human egg carrying 23 chromosomes, a zygote is formed with 46 chromosomes. The chromosomes in the zygote are again found as identical pairs. Each pair has one chromosome from the male gamate and one from the female gamete.

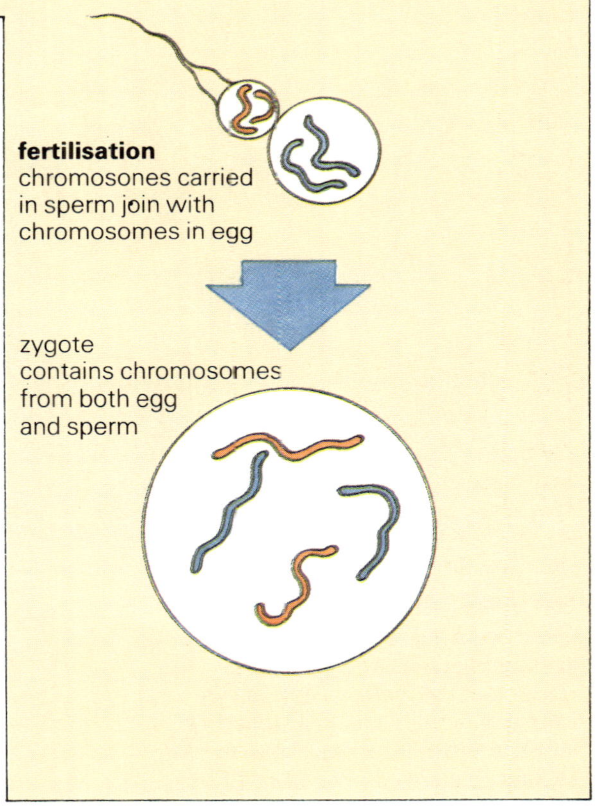

1 The number of chromosomes found in the cells of a particular species is always the same. Human cells contain 46 chromosomes while the cells of cats have 38. How many chromosomes will be found in

a a cat skin cell?
b a cat sperm cell?
c a cat muscle cell?
d a cat zygote cell?

2 The diagram below shows the chromosomes in the root cell of a plant.

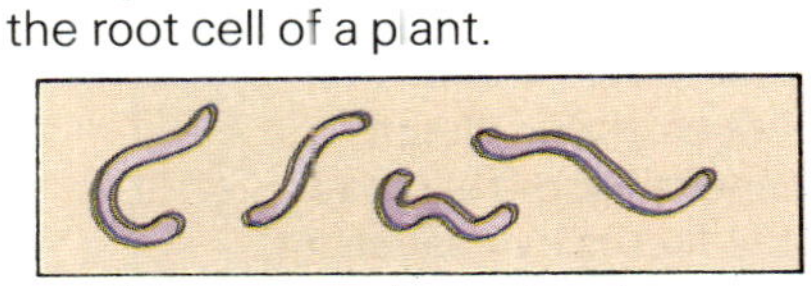

Draw diagrams to show the chromosomes in
a a leaf cell,
b a pollen grain, of the same plant.

YOU CAN READ MORE ABOUT REPRODUCTION ON SPREADS 5.13 AND 5.14.

Looking at chromosomes

The start of life

Your life started from a single cell called a zygote, produced at fertilisation. This contained all the genetic information needed to make you. The information that determined whether you became a boy or a girl, tall or short, blue-eyed or dark-eyed, was present in the chromosomes in the zygote. All your body cells developed from this single cell by **simple cell division**. During this process, *all* the genetic information is copied into new cells so that all the cells in your body contain an *exact* copy of the chromosomes that were present in the zygote.

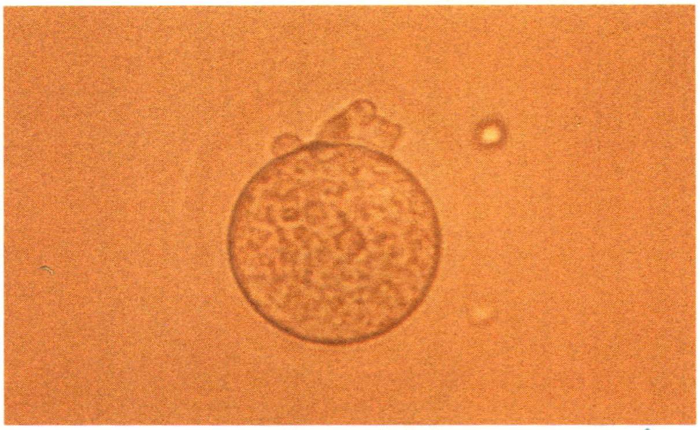

When you were 'one' you had just begun . . . you started life as a single zygote like the one above.

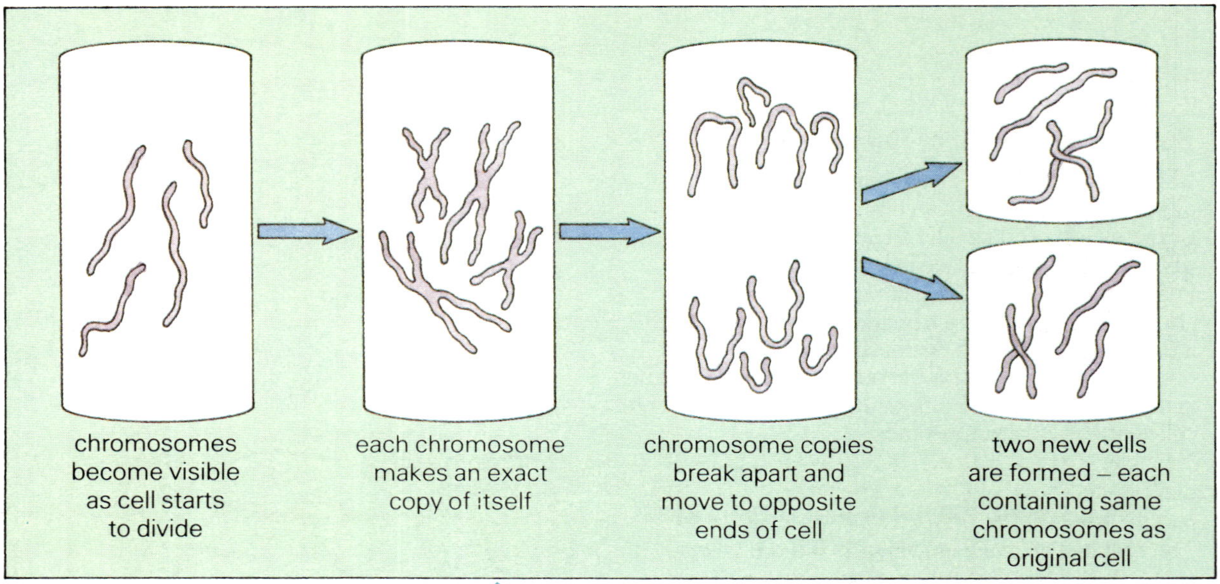

Simple cell division – making copies of cells.

Checking development

Some women are given a special test during their pregnancy to check that the foetus is developing normally. During this test, called **amniocentesis**, a small amount of fluid is removed from around the foetus. The fluid contains chemicals and cells from the foetus which doctors can examine to check foetal development. For example, doctors can identify several abnormalities that may occur in the foetus by examining the chromosomes in the cells. They can also see whether the foetus is going to be a boy or a girl.

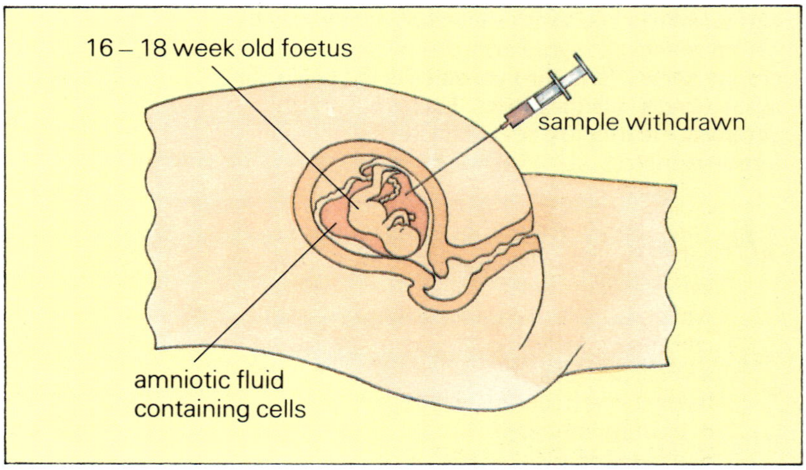

Boy or girl?

These diagrams show the appearance of some chromosomes from two healthy foetuses. Only 6 out of the 23 pairs of chromosomes are shown in each case. By looking at these chromosomes, doctors identified one foetus as male and the other as female. Can you identify any difference between the two sets of chromosomes?

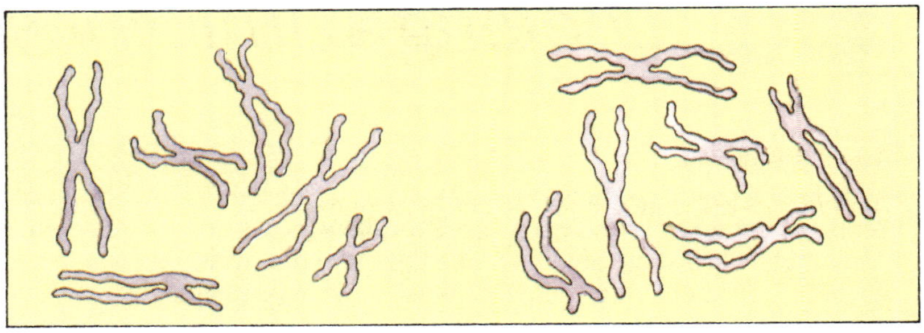

How do the chromosomes in the male differ from those in the female?

Sex chromosomes

Whether you became a boy or a girl was determined by one pair of chromosomes in the cells of your body – the **sex chromosomes**. In females, the sex chromosomes are identical to each other and are called **X chromosomes**. In males there are two types of sex chromosome: one is the same as the female sex chromosomes, an X chromosome, while the other is shorter and is known as the **Y chromosome**. So in females the sex chromosomes are XX and in males they are XY. As you can see from this diagram, sex is determined by the sex chromosome of the sperm that fertilises the egg.

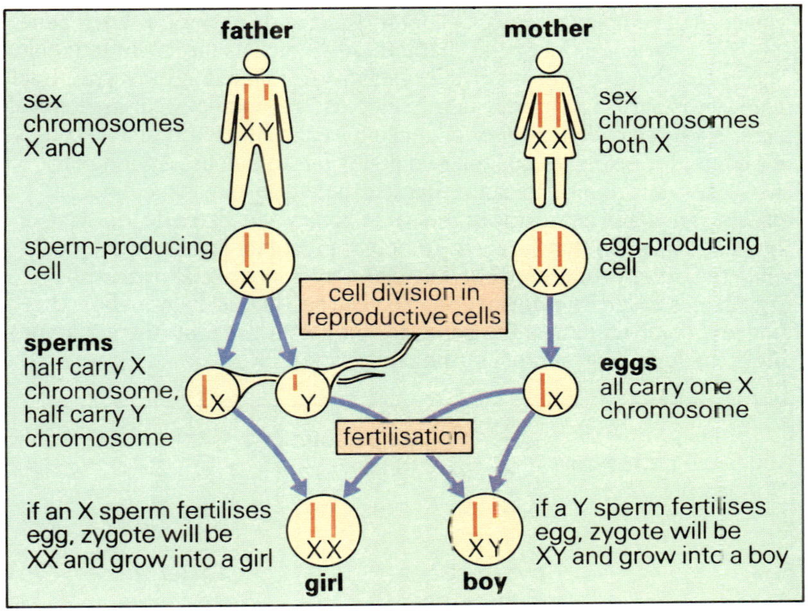

Checking for abnormalities

Examining the cells obtained by amniocentesis enables doctors to check for a disorder called **Down's syndrome**. Children with this disorder will have some mental retardation and may also have heart and respiratory (breathing) problems. The disorder is caused by a **mutation** – a change in the genetic material of an organism. Children with Down's syndrome have an extra chromosome in their cells, giving them 47 instead of the usual 46 chromosomes.

Many children with Down's syndrome lead happy lives, despite the disorder.

1 Draw a large, clear copy of the diagram of the chromosomes of the male foetus shown at the top of this page.
- **a** Draw a box around any two identical chromosomes,
- **b** draw a circle around the X chromosome, and
- **c** underline the Y chromosome.

2 The male foetus will eventually grow into an adult. Draw diagrams to show the appearance of chromosomes in this foetus's
- **a** cheek cells,
- **b** possible types of sperm cells.

3
- **a** What are the chances that the first baby in a family will be a boy? Explain why.
- **b** What are the chances of the next baby being a boy?

10.5 Genes and inheritance

The odd one out

Sandy kept a pair of pet brown rabbits and was pleased to find they were breeding. But when he looked at the litter, he was puzzled – three of the young rabbits had shiny brown fur like their parents, while one was completely different with white fur. What could have caused this unexpected variation?

Gene control

The cells of complex organisms contain thousands of **genes**. Each gene controls a *particular* inherited characteristic, such as fur colour in rabbits. The genes that are present in an organism are called its **genotype**. Each gene forms part of a chromosome. Since chromosomes occur in identical pairs, each cell contains a *pair* of genes for each characteristic. The cells of rabbits, for example, contain two genes for fur colour. Although the two genes determine the same characteristic they may have different effects. The different forms of the same gene are called **alleles**. One of the genes (alleles) that controls fur colour in rabbits produces brown fur while the other produces white fur. The way genes are shown in an organism is called its **phenotype**. You can see in this diagram how the different combinations of the genes for fur colour present (the genotype) affect the fur colour of rabbits (the phenotype).

Notice that a rabbit only has white fur when both *genes for white fur are present.*

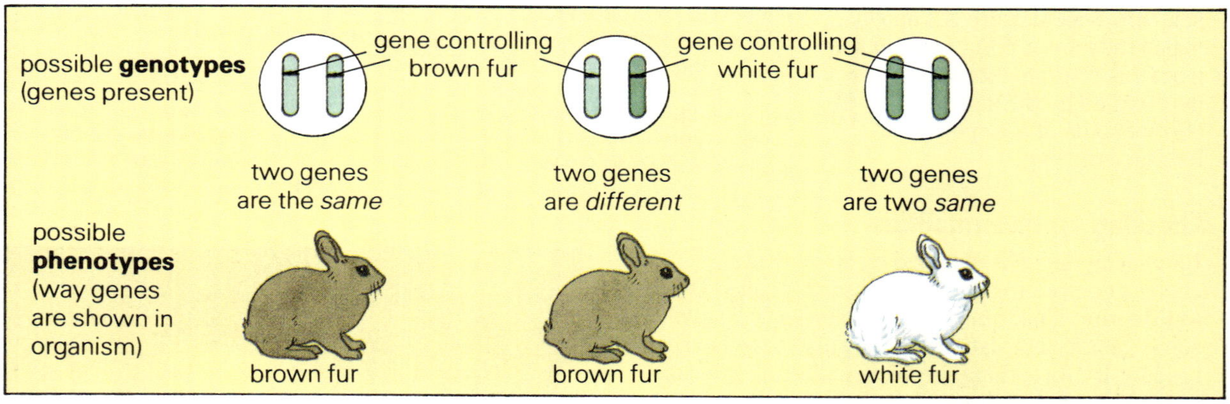

Dominant and recessive

When the gene for brown fur and the gene for white fur are both present, the rabbit is brown. This is because the gene for brown fur *masks* the other gene. The gene for brown fur is a **dominant** gene and the gene for white fur is **recessive**. A dominant gene is usually indicated by a capital letter and a recessive gene by a lower-case letter.

Explaining inheritance

The idea that some genes are dominant while others are recessive was put forward by **geneticists** – scientists who study genes and inheritance. Geneticists *observe* **patterns of inheritance** and try to *explain* them. They do this using a knowledge of what happens to chromosomes and genes during reproduction.

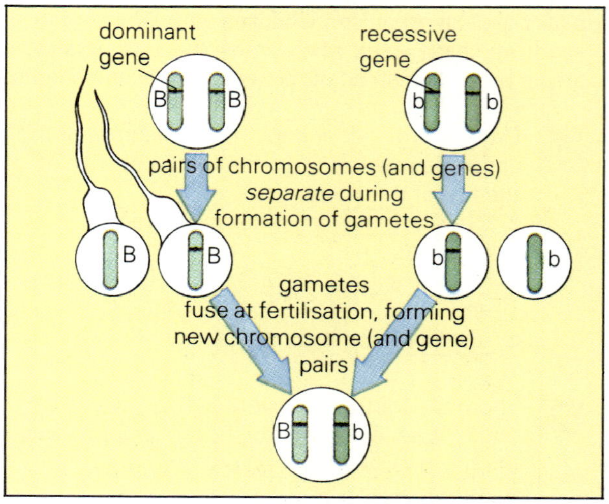

The two main events that occur during reproduction.

Tracing the path of chromosomes

How would geneticists explain the white rabbit? As a first step, they would make a **hypothesis** about the genotypes of the parent rabbits. Then they would trace the movement of chromosomes in reproduction to find out what genotypes the offspring are likely to have.

Follow the movement of chromosomes shown below, based on this hypothesis:

Hypothesis: both parent rabbits contain a dominant *and* recessive gene for fur colour, so both can pass on a recessive gene to their offspring.

Do you think the hypothesis is correct?

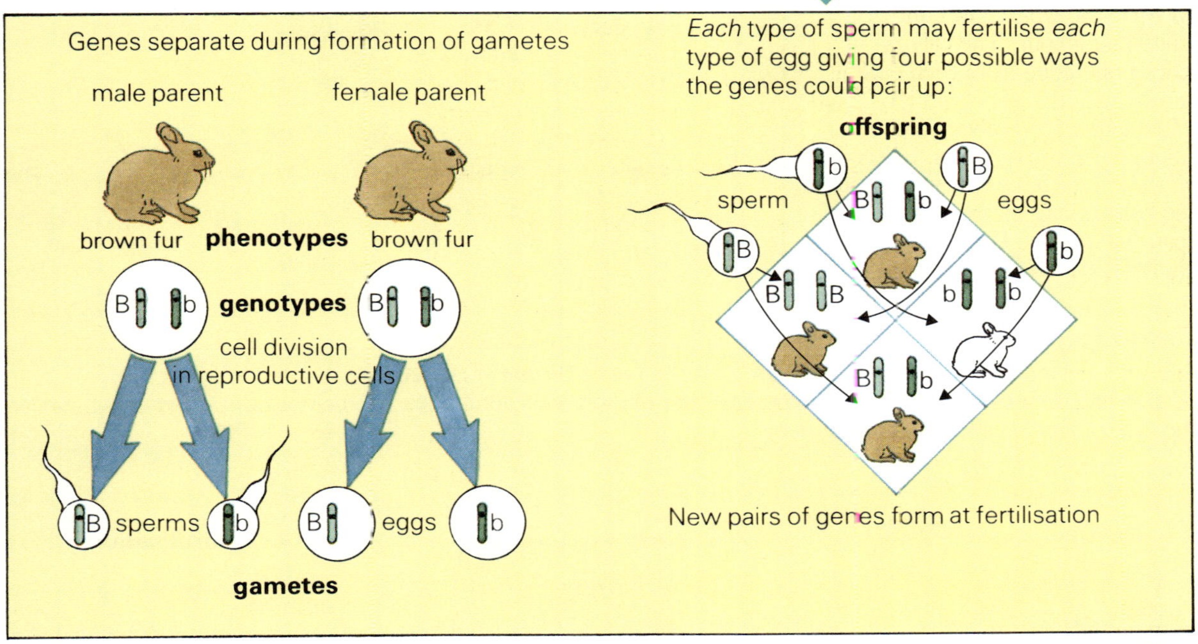

Predicting patterns of inheritance

You can use the knowledge of what happens to genes and chromosomes to *predict* the genotypes and phenotypes of offspring. This diagram shows a cross between a brown rabbit and a white rabbit. Study it carefully and then answer the question below.

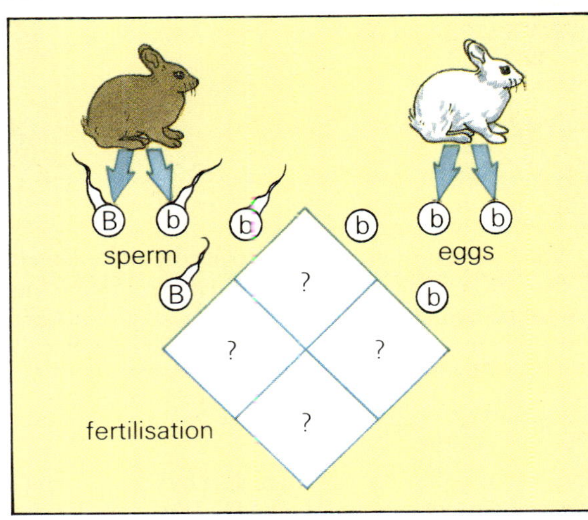

1 **a** Make a copy of and complete the table of gamete fusion.
b Predict the ratio of brown : white rabbits in the next generation.

2 Suppose Sandy's rabbits had two white young and two brown young. Would this mean that the hypothesis at the top of this page is correct? Explain your answer.

3 Flower colour in pea plants is controlled by a pair of genes. The gene for white flower colour is recessive (r) and the gene for red colour is dominant (R). When a heterozygous plant with red flowers was pollinated by a plant with white flowers, 40 new plants were produced.

a What hypothesis would you make about the genotypes of the parent plants?
b How many of the new plants would you expect to be white?
c The number of white flowered plants obtained was actually 13. Does this mean that your hypothesis in **a** is incorrect?

Interpreting patterns of inheritance

Unusual phenotypes

This diagram shows inheritance of coat colour in a breed of cattle called Shorthorns. There are two genes, R and W, that can control coat colour in Shorthorns. Both Genes (RR) in the red bull control red hair colour and both genes (WW) in the white cow control white hair colour. The calves inherit one gene from each parent and so have the genotype RW. You might expect the calves' coat colour to be red *or* white. Instead, *all* the calves have *both* white and red hairs giving them a pale red or roan coat colour. How does this phenotype come about?

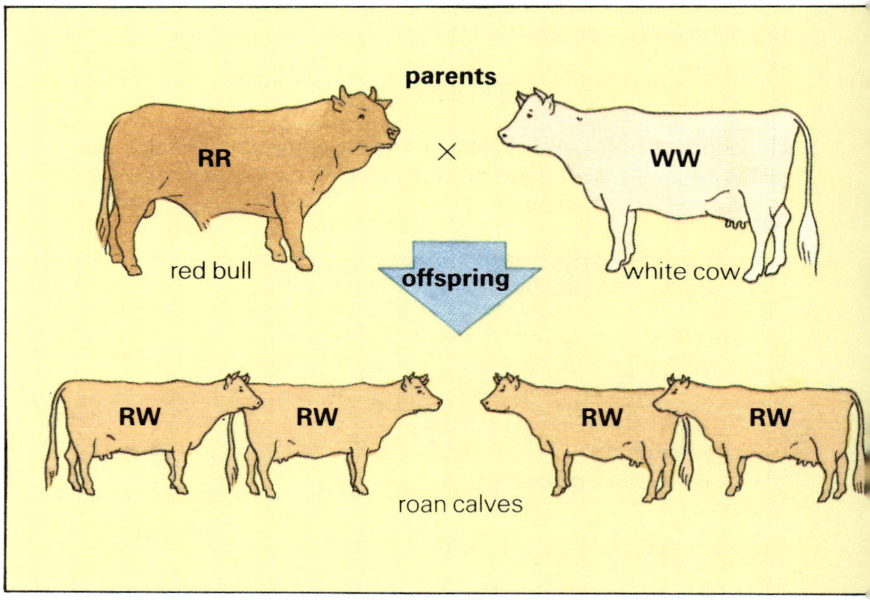

Co-dominant genes

Since the calves have red *and* white hairs, *both* the genes (R *and* W) must be showing their effect in the phenotype – neither of the genes dominates the other. This is called **co-dominance**.

Expected ratio of red : roan: white calves = ?

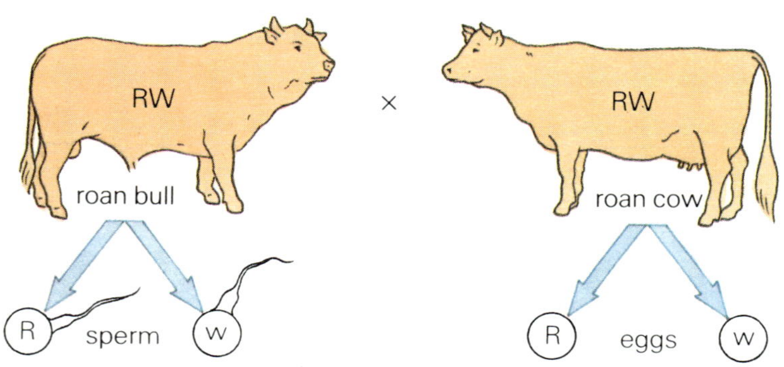

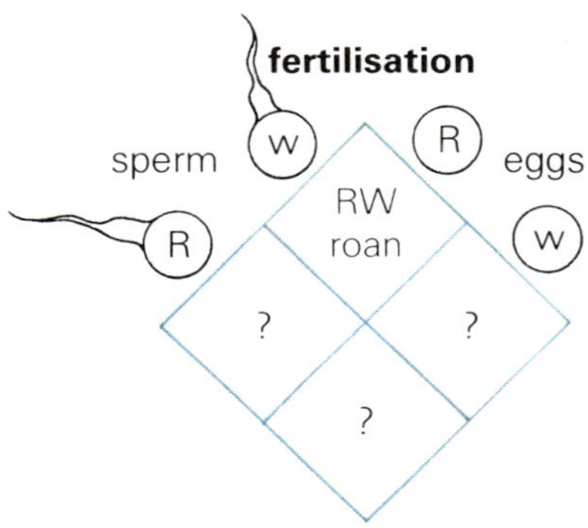

What happens if you cross a roan cow and a roan bull? Study this diagram carefully, and then copy and complete the table to show the possible results of gamete fusion. Use your table to predict the ratio of the phenotypes of the calves that will be produced from the cross.

Predicting blood groups

Your blood group may be controlled by co-dominant genes. There are four blood groups A, B, AB and O. These groups are controlled by three genes A, B, and O. Gene O is recessive to genes A and B. When both genes A and B are present, they show co-dominance. Since genes occur in pairs, only two of the genes are present in any one person.

Copy and complete this table.
Sam's father is blood group AB and his mother is blood group O. Which blood groups could Sam be? How did you arrive at your answer?

		possible genotypes
blood group	A	AA or AO
	?	BB or ?
	?	AB
	O	?

Your blood group is controlled by genes.

Colour blindness

Some people cannot distinguish between the colours red, brown and green. This is a type of colour blindness which can be tested for using charts like the one shown here. People who are colour blind can experience difficulties in many situations – for example, noting colour changes in chemicals during science lessons, or cheering the 'right' team!

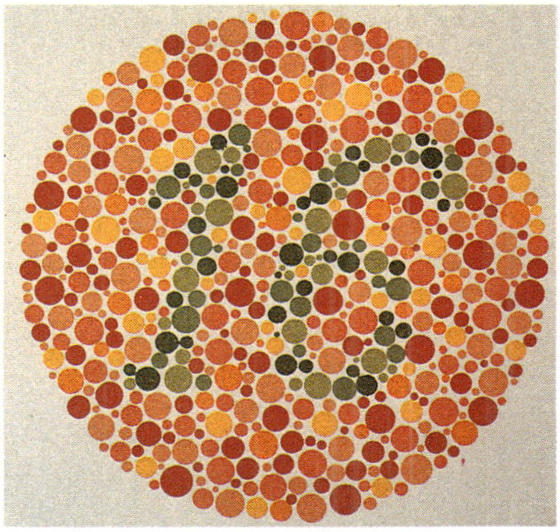

Not everyone can see the number in the dots.

This shows part of the family tree of Tim Walker, who is colour blind. Examine the pattern of inheritance carefully. Do you think that the gene that causes colour blindness is dominant or recessive?

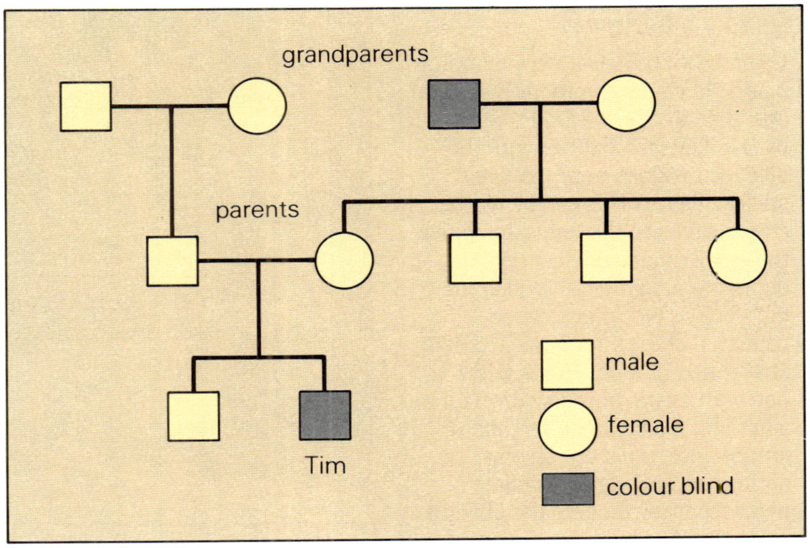

Sex-linked inheritance

One of Tim's grandfathers is colour blind, then the condition misses a generation and re-appears in Tim. This suggests that colour blindness is caused by a *recessive* gene. You can also see that both colour blind members of the Walker family are *male*. In fact, far more males than females are colour blind. This is because the gene for colour vision is carried on the X chromosome and is *absent* from the Y chromosome.

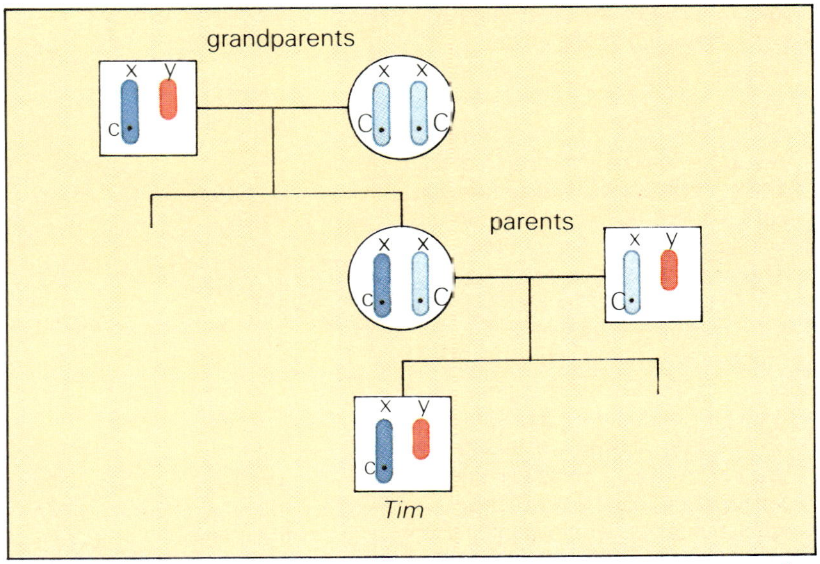

*Colour blindness is called a **sex-linked condition** because the gene is carried on a sex chromosome.*

1
- **a** Give some examples from everyday life when Tim Walker may experience problems because of his colour blindness.
- **b** From which parent, his mother or father, do you think Tim inherited the gene for colour blindness?
- **c** If Tim marries a girl whose family have *no* history of colour blindness, what are the chances that any son they may have will be colour blind? Explain your answer.

2 Mr Khan is blood group O and Mrs Khan is blood group A. One of their daughters is blood group O like her father.
- **a** Use this information to work out the genotype of Mrs Khan.
- **b** What are the chances of Mr and Mrs Khan having a child with blood group A? Explain how you arrived at your answer.

Inherited disease

Faulty genes

The genes present in the cells of your body control all your inherited characteristics. Some people inherit 'faulty' genes and these can cause **inherited diseases**. A faulty gene may result in only a minor defect, such as poor vision, but some cause very serious illness. Faults are produced by mutations (changes in genetic material) which can alter single genes or whole chromosomes. Down's syndrome is the result of **chromosome mutation** (*see 10.4*). Cystic fibrosis and haemophilia (excessive bleeding) are examples of inherited diseases caused by **gene mutation**.

Children with cystic fibrosis need regular physiotherapy to keep their chests clear.

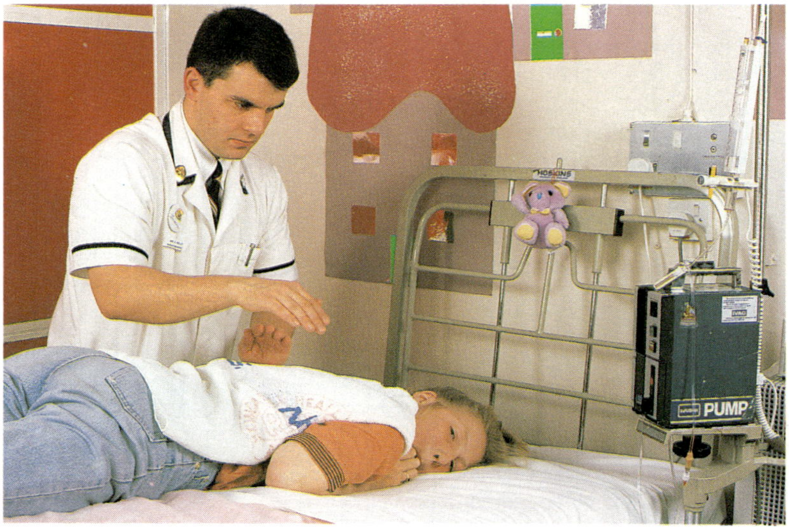

Deadly inheritance

Cystic fibrosis is a very common inherited disease in the UK – about one child in every 2 000 is affected by the illness. Children with the disease produce very thick and sticky mucus. This can block the air passages to the lungs and block the small ducts which carry digestive enzymes to food in the gut. These blockages cause repeated chest infections and poor absorption of food. In the past, no one with cystic fibrosis survived to adult life. Today doctors cannot *prevent* infections but strong antibiotics and vigorous chest physiotherapy do help the child to recover. However, each bout of infection leaves the lungs slightly more damaged so the child becomes gradually more and more ill.

Blood clotting

A serious loss of blood could make you very ill – or kill you. When you cut yourself, the wound in your skin is sealed by a **blood clot**. This stops blood loss and keeps the wound clean. The blood clot forms because **enzymes** (substances that enable chemical reactions to take place in your body) convert a *soluble* blood protein into a fibrous, *insoluble* protein. A blood clot usually only forms when blood vessels are damaged. What would happen if a blood clot formed in a healthy blood vessel?

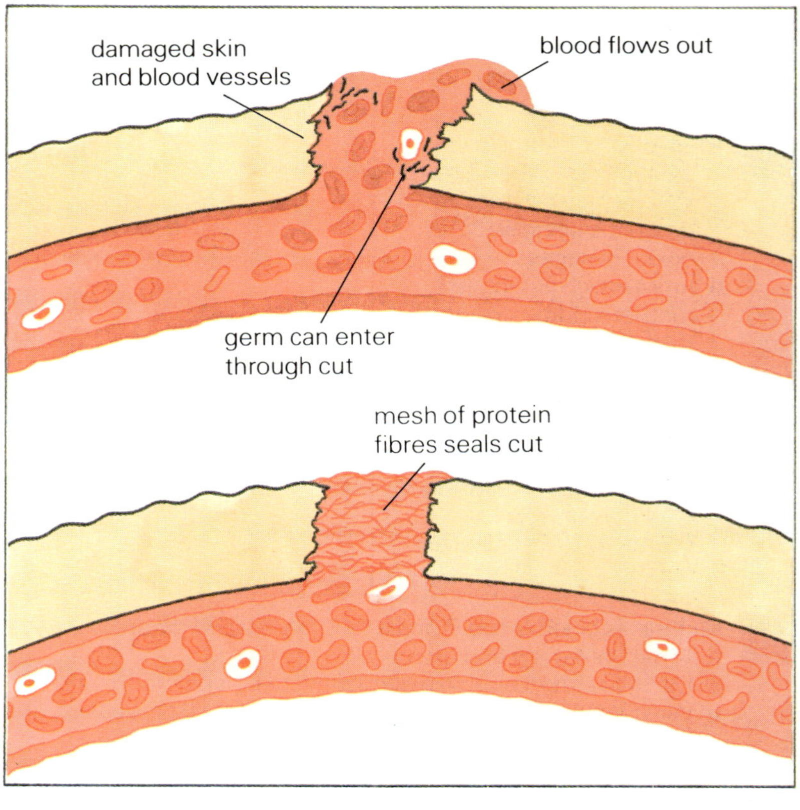

When your skin is cut, a clot forms. This stops you losing too much blood and prevents germs from entering your body.

Clotting factors

The enzymes that convert soluble blood protein into fibrous protein only work when certain **clotting factors** are present. This diagram shows how one important clotting factor – **factor 8** – works together with enzymes to clot the blood.

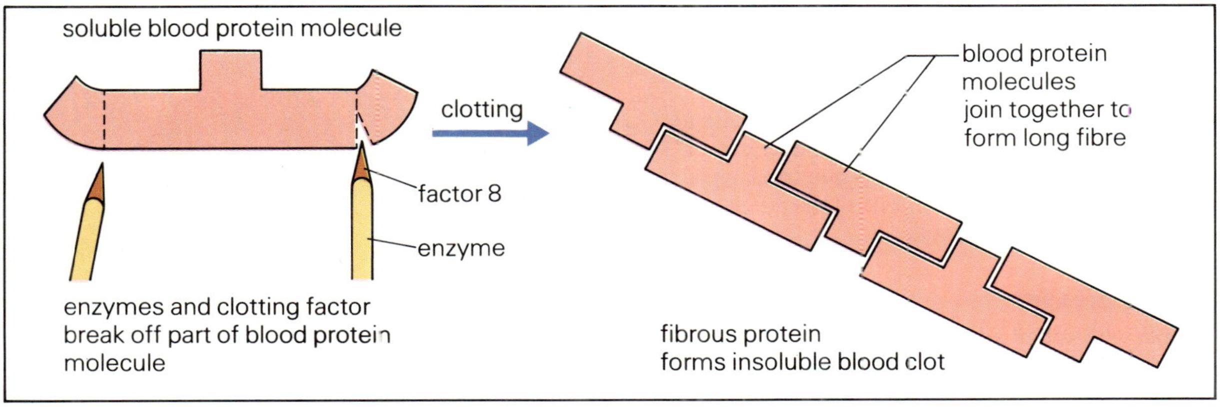

Lack of factor 8

Haemophilia is a disease in which the blood fails to clot or clots only very slowly. When a person with the disease is cut or bruised, they may bleed so much that they die. Haemophiliacs bleed excessively because their blood lacks the clotting factor 8. So the enzyme cannot work properly and no blood clot forms. The disease is due to a recessive gene which fails to produce factor 8.

Enzymes cannot work without the clotting factors.

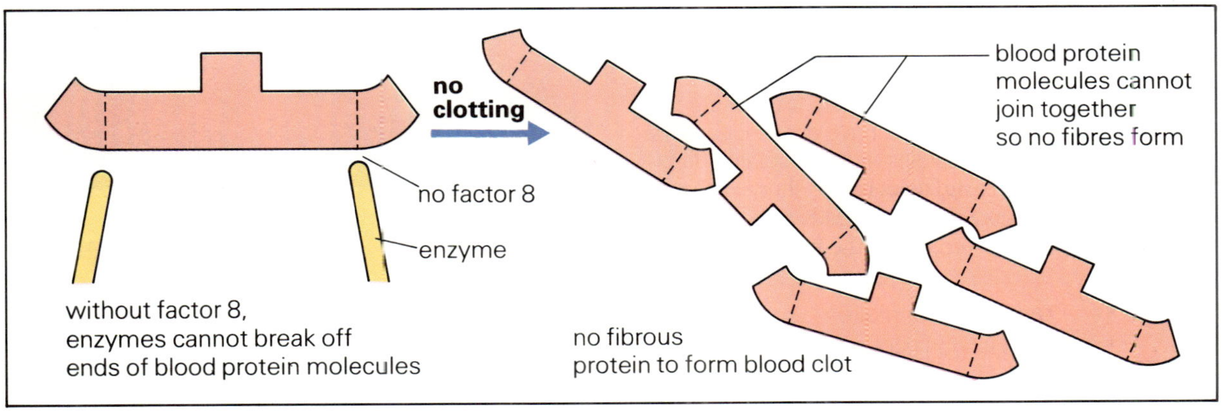

1 Cystic fibrosis is an inherited disease which involves a pair of genes.

Two healthy parents had three children. Two of the children were also healthy but the youngest child suffered from cystic fibrosis.

- **a** Is the gene that causes cystic fibrosis dominant or recessive? Explain your answer.
- **b** What are the genotypes of the parents?
- **c** What is the chance of a fourth child also having the disease? Draw a diagram to show your reasoning.
- **d** Inherited diseases, such as cystic fibrosis, are more common if the parents are cousins than if the parents are unrelated. Explain why.

2 Stephen is a haemophiliac. Neither of his two brothers have the disease. When Stephen asked his parents about his illness, they told him that two of his uncles also suffer from haemophilia.

- **a** Haemophilia is caused by a sex-linked recessive gene. Use this information to explain why only the male relatives are affected by the disease.
- **b** Stephen was told that his mother is a 'carrier' of the disease. What does this mean?
- **c** What are the genotypes of Stephen's brothers?

10.8 Bacterial factories

Lacking proteins

Many inherited diseases are caused by the body being unable to make an important substance – usually a **protein.** People with haemophilia lack the protein factor 8 which is needed to make the blood clot. **Pituitary dwarfism**, a disorder which results in severe underdevelopment, is caused by a lack of **growth hormone**. **Diabetes** is due to a lack of **insulin** which is needed to control the amount of glucose (sugar) in the blood.

Making proteins

People who suffer from these disorders need regular treatment with the protein that their body cannot make. Many people are diabetic so *large* amounts of the protein insulin are needed to treat them. In the past, the insulin had to be extracted from animals such as pigs and sheep. Some diabetics reacted badly to the animal insulin because animal proteins are *not identical* to human proteins. A technique developed over recent years has solved this problem by allowing *human* insulin to be made on a large scale.

The human cells that produce insulin cannot be grown easily outside the body. The cells of bacteria and other microbes can be grown on a large scale quickly and cheaply – but bacteria do not normally make insulin. By transferring human genes for making insulin into bacteria, scientists have created bacteria which do manufacture insulin – *human* insulin. This example of **genetic engineering** is shown below. Human insulin produced by bacteria is now widely available and is marketed under the name **Humulin**.

The insulin which many diabetics need to inject daily is now produced by bacteria.

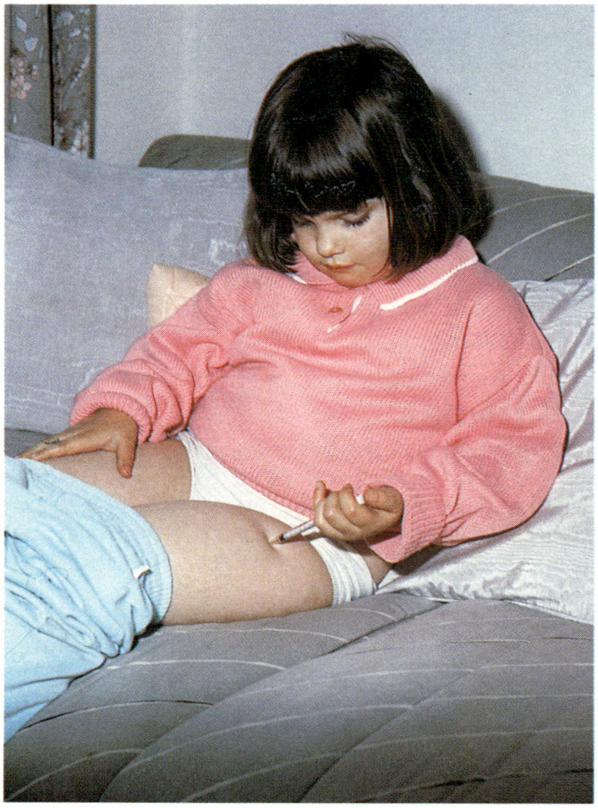

Making bacteria manufacture human insulin.

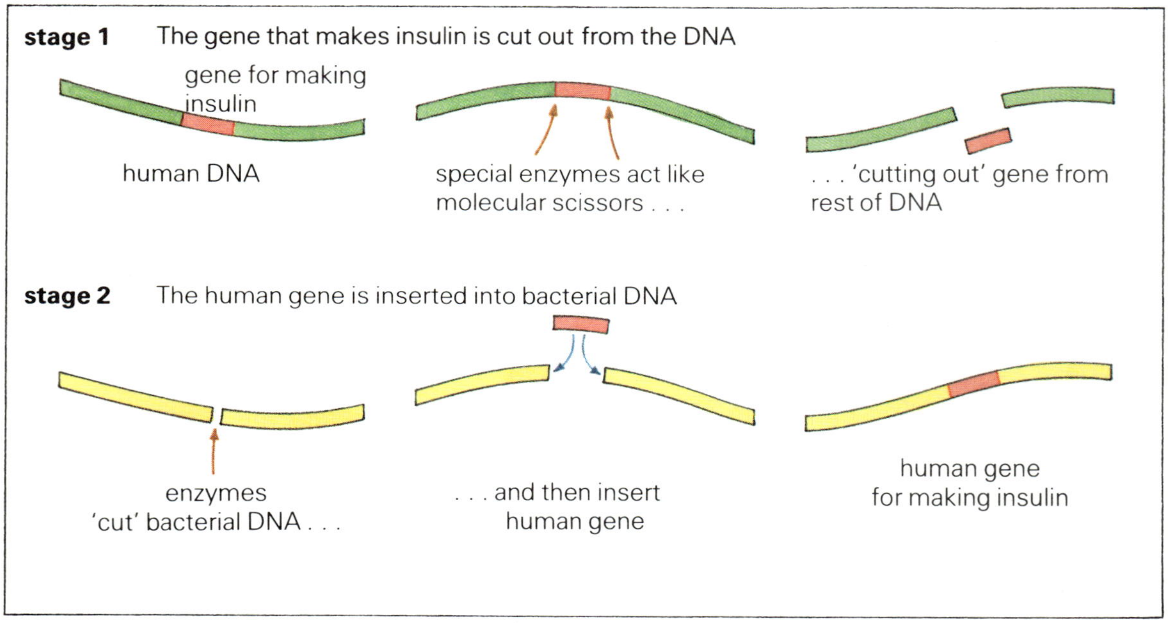

Large-scale production

Bacteria containing the human gene are grown inside huge industrial fermenters called **bioreactors**. These provide ideal conditions for the bacteria so that they grow and reproduce rapidly, forming millions of bacterial cells containing the human gene. Producing many copies of identical cells, each containing the same genes, is called **gene cloning**. Then the bacterial clones are collected, and the insulin they have made is extracted and purified.

Manufacturing human insulin (Humulin) on a large scale.

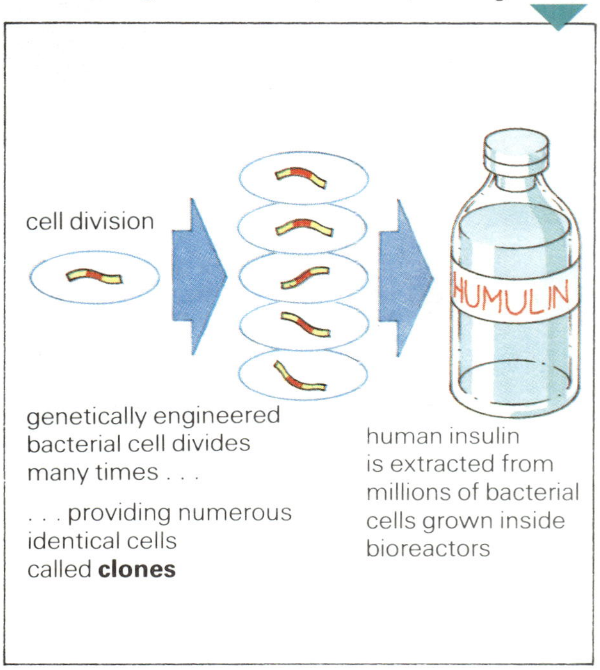

A bioreactor must maintain the perfect environment for bacteria to thrive and reproduce. What do you think bacteria need in order to thrive?

Cheaper and safer drugs

Through genetic engineering, bacteria can be made to produce many proteins vital to us. Human growth hormone used to be extracted from human tissue, which meant that it was extremely scarce and expensive. Nowadays human growth hormone produced by bacteria is widely available for the treatment of abnormally small children. Genetically engineered bacteria not only make drugs available in greater quantity – the drugs they produce are also *safer*. In 1985, three patients died from a virus that was present in the human tissue containing growth hormone they received. Genetic engineering has meant that more children can be given life-saving drugs which are uncontaminated with any virus.

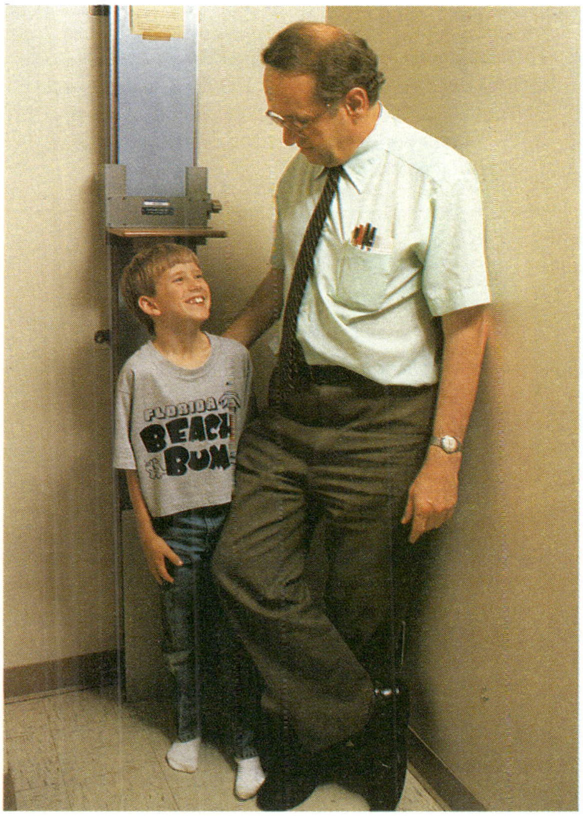

The growth hormone which this boy lacks can now be manufactured in 'bacterial factories'.

1 List *three* conditions that need to be controlled in bioreactors to produce the best growth of bacteria.

2 Why is factor 8 (the clotting factor lacking in haemophiliacs) made by bacteria safer to use than factor 8 extracted from human tissue?

3 Scientists can manipulate and change the genetic instructions in cells using genetic engineering.
- **a** What are the advantages of this process?
- **b** What possible disadvantages can you think of?

YOU CAN READ MORE ABOUT BLOOD GLUCOSE ON SPREAD 3.14.

10.9 Genetic fingerprinting

Unmistakable identity

Just as your fingerprints are unique to you, so is the pattern of genes in your DNA. Unless you are an identical twin, no one else will have a 'genetic fingerprint' exactly like yours. In 1984, scientists found a way of *identifying* sections of DNA – a technique called **genetic fingerprinting**. The technique produces a pattern that looks rather like the bar codes you see on groceries in the supermarket. Everyone has a different bar code – it is nature's own identity system.

A blood sample is often used to produce a genetic fingerprint.

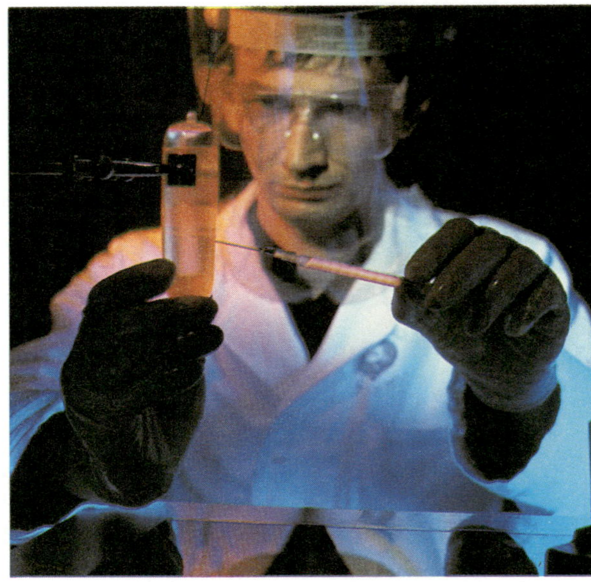

Inheriting DNA patterns

The patterns of DNA in a father's sperm and a mother's egg mix when the sperm and egg fuse at fertilisation. So each child's genetic 'bar code' contains half the father's and half the mother's patterns.

This diagram shows the genetic fingerprints of the members of two families. Can you see sections of DNA the children have inherited from each parent? Have *all* the children inherited sections of DNA from *both* parents?

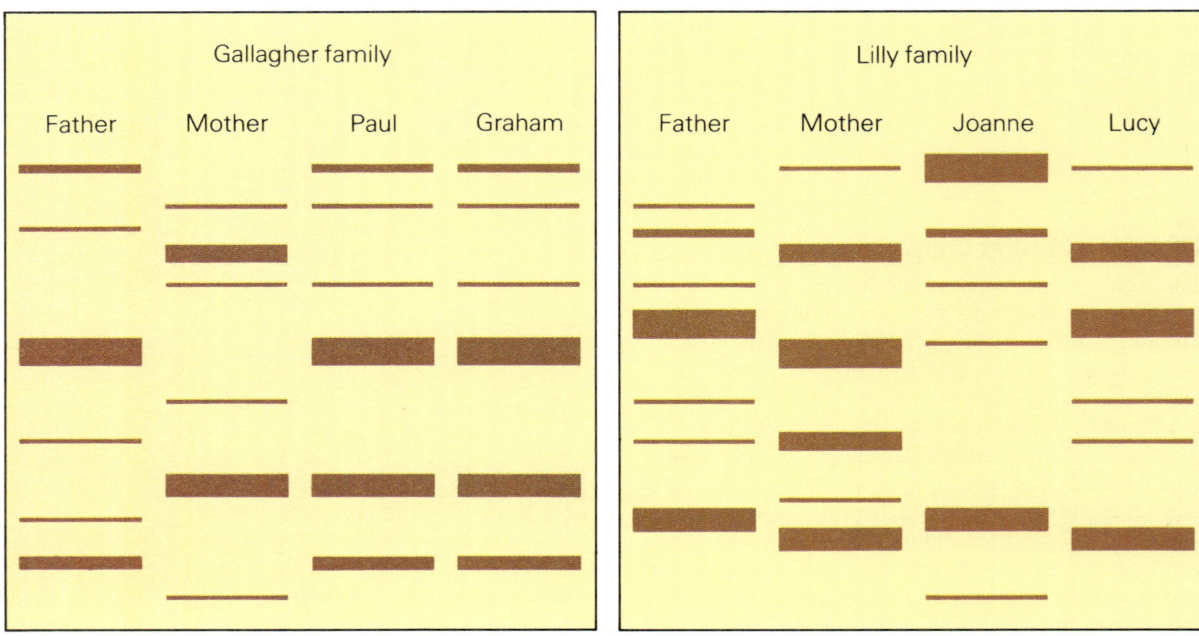

Identifying family ties

One of the first uses of genetic fingerprinting involved a boy who was born in Britain and emigrated to Ghana to live with his father. When he tried to return to this country to rejoin his mother, the immigration authorities refused to let him enter Britain. They claimed that he was not the mother's real son. The boy's genetic fingerprints showed that he shared half of the mother's DNA pattern. This evidence proved that he was her son and the authorities agreed to allow him to join his mother.

The fingerprinting process

Genetic fingerprinting was first developed by Professor Alec Jeffreys at Leicester University. The diagram shows the main stages in producing a DNA fingerprint.

The process of genetic fingerprinting.

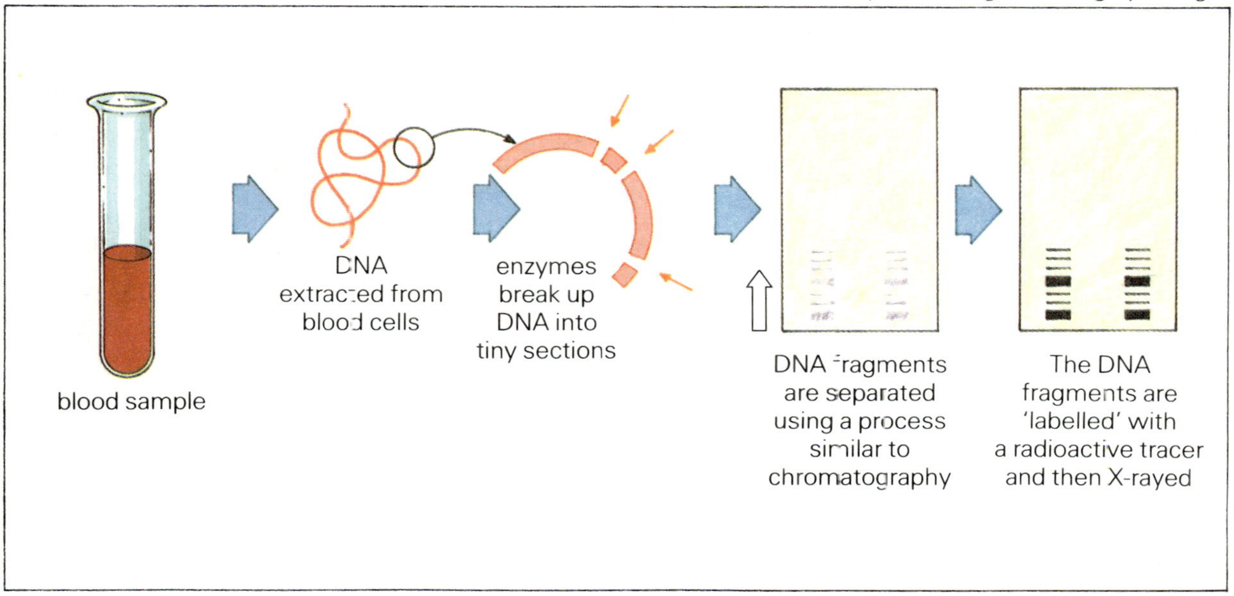

Criminal evidence

Forensic scientists examine any blood, hair, semen or other tissue found at the scene of a crime. In the past, the tissue could only give some clues about the criminal, such as his or her blood group. Now a genetic fingerprint taken from the tissue can pinpoint the offender. The 'bar code' produced from the tissue is compared with the genetic fingerprints of suspects – a match identifies the criminal, while a mismatch clears the innocent.

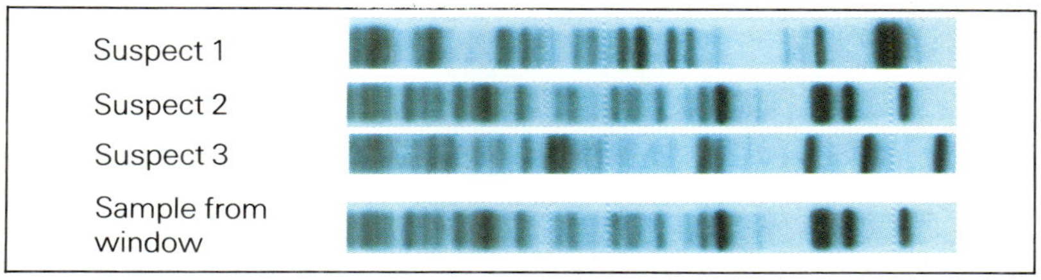

Three of these genetic fingerprints are from men suspected of burglary, while the other is from blood found next to a broken window used to gain entry.

Using genetic fingerprinting

The technique is now widely used in forensic science and in proving family relationships – including confirming the pedigrees of dogs and horses! Genetic fingerprinting is also a valuable tool in medicine. The success of transplant surgery depends partly on how well the organ being transplanted matches the recipient – and genetic fingerprinting can ensure the best match. The technique also helps to identify certain inherited diseases.

1 Use the genetic fingerprints of the two families shown on the opposite page to answer these questions:

- **a** What can you deduce about the relationship between Paul and Graham?
- **b** Joanne's mother died when she was very young. Since then her father has remarried. Explain the DNA patterns shown by Joanne and her younger sister.

2 What can you deduce about each of the burglary suspects from the evidence shown above?

3 In a recent murder hunt, the police obtained blood samples from more than 5 000 people for genetic fingerprinting. The Home Office is considering creating a data base which will contain everyone's genetic prints. Do you think that this would be a good idea? Give reasons for your answer.

10.10 Building proteins

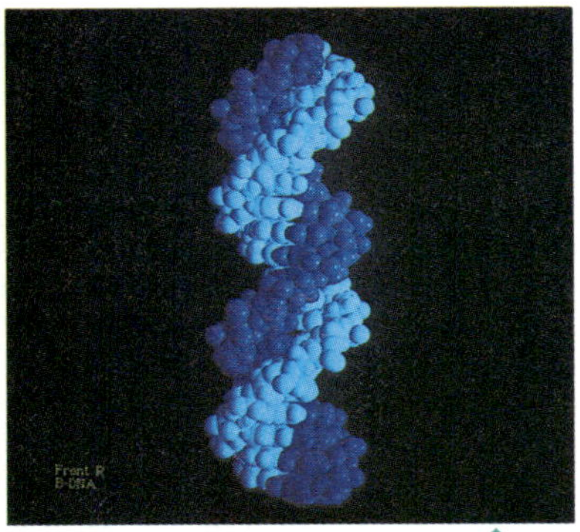

A model of a DNA molecule showing the two strands twisted round each other in a spiral or helix.

Revealing the structure of DNA

Genetic engineering, genetic fingerprinting and other recent developments in genetics were made possible by the discovery of the **structure of DNA**. In the early 1950s scientists knew that DNA carries coded instructions for making proteins, but no-one knew *how* the code worked. The discovery of DNA's structure by James Watson and Francis Crick in 1953 was one of the major advances in science. Watson and Crick pieced together the findings of other scientists researching DNA and arrived at the now-famous **double helix structure**. They suggested that each molecule of DNA has two long strands twisted around each other like a spiral staircase.

Four kinds of bases link the backbones – A (which stands for adenine), T (thymine), C (cytosine) and G (guanine). A always pairs with T, while C always pairs with G. This is called ***specific base pairing****.*

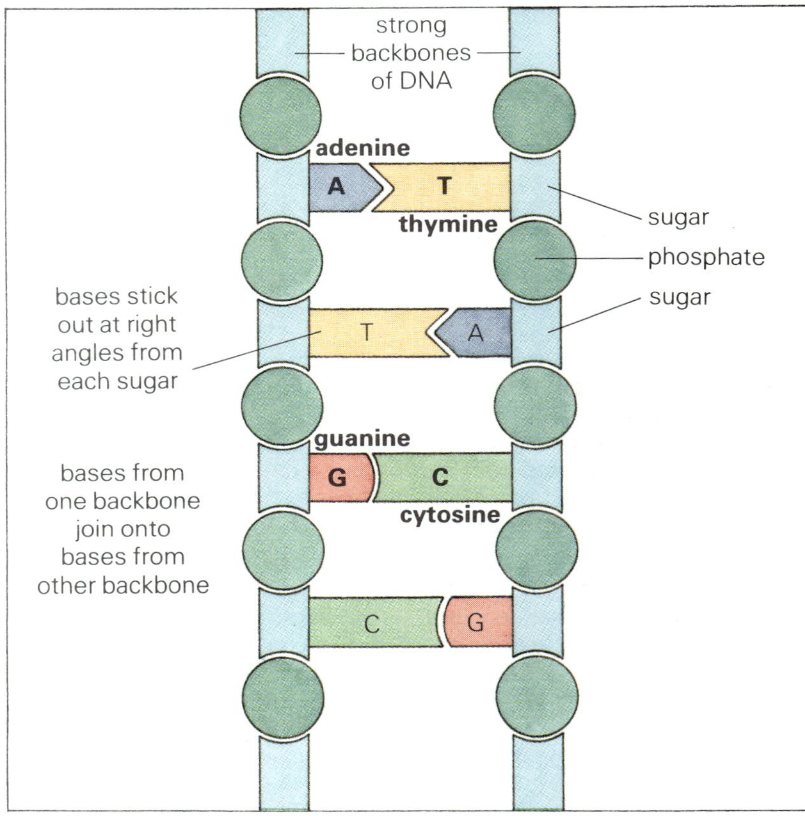

The backbone of each strand is joined to the other strand by bases.

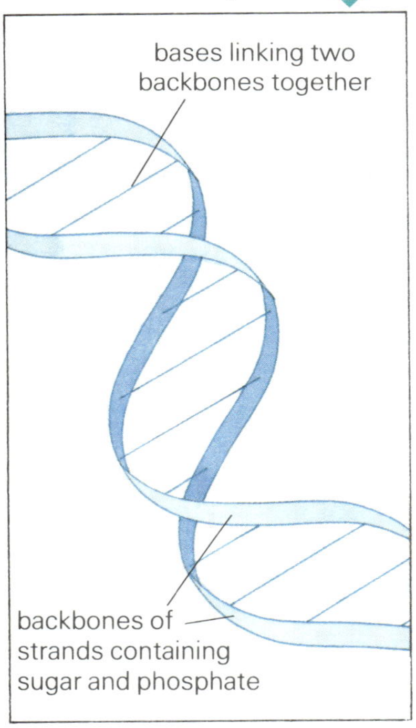

A scientist called Chargaff was working on the structure of DNA at the same time as Watson and Crick. He found out the amount of each of the four DNA bases that is present in different organisms. Some of his findings are shown in this table.

Watson and Crick used Chargaff's data when putting forward their model of DNA. How do Chargaff's findings support their model of DNA?

	Relative amount of each base			
	adenine	thymine	cytosine	guamine
Salmon DNA	30	30	20	20
Mouse DNA	29	27	22	21
Human DNA	30	29	19	19

Breaking the code

After Watson and Crick had worked out the structure of DNA, they went on to find out how the coded information in DNA is used by living organisms to make proteins. They discovered that the *order of the bases* in each strand of DNA forms the code. Proteins are made up of chemicals called **amino acids**. The order of the bases in DNA controls the order in which amino acids are joined together during the making of proteins. By controlling the synthesis of proteins, DNA determines the inherited characteristics of each individual.

The type and order of amino acids in a protein are determined by the DNA code.

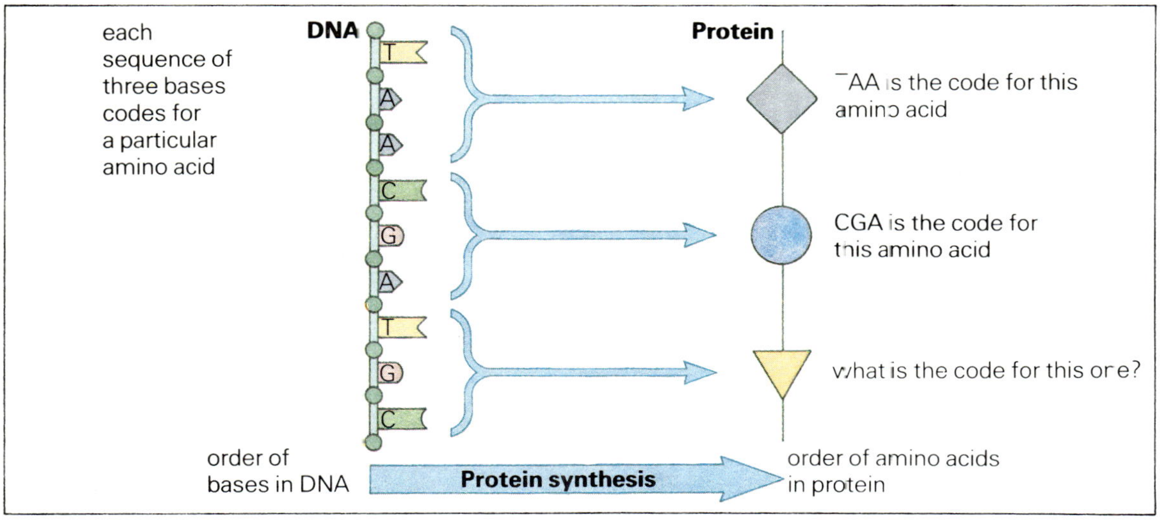

Amino acids – the buildings blocks

All proteins are polymers (long, chain molecules) made of chains of amino acids. There are just 20 amino acids found in proteins, but they can be arranged in billions of different ways. Every living organism contains a large number of proteins. You contain about 100 000 different proteins, each carrying out an essential job in keeping you alive and well. The properties of each protein depend on the order and types of amino acids that make up its structure. A protein may not do the same job if only *one* amino acid in its structure is changed. DNA controls *which* amino acids will be in the protein and the *order* in which they will be joined.

1 **a** Explain what 'specific base pairing' means.
b The bases in a strand of DNA are in the order:

A C T T G C C T A A

What will the order of bases be on the other strand of DNA?

2 A gene can be described as the sequence of bases in DNA that controls the synthesis of a protein.
a A protein was found to consist of 100 amino acids. How many bases would there be in the gene that makes this protein?
b Predict how the structure of the protein might change if just one of the bases in the gene was changed for another one.

Amino acids are like an alphabet for making proteins. If the amino acids are put together in a different order, a different protein is 'spelt out'.

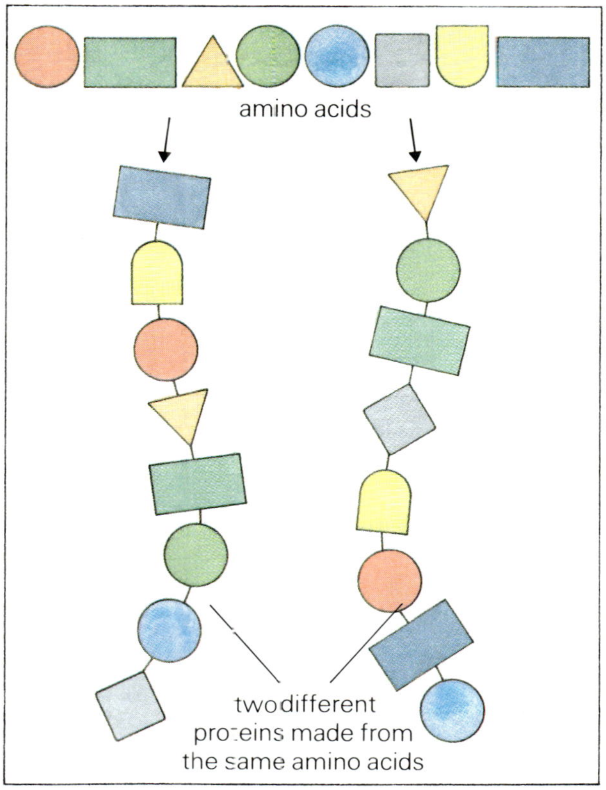

Replicating genes

Copying the code

All the characteristics that you inherited from your parents are controlled by the sequence of bases in the DNA in your cells. DNA can form exact copies of itself so that the coded instructions for making proteins can be passed on to new cells and new individuals. The coded instructions that make up each gene are copied each time a cell divides. Every cell in your body contains an exact copy of the genes that you inherited from your parents. This diagram shows how a DNA molecule copies itself during **replication**.

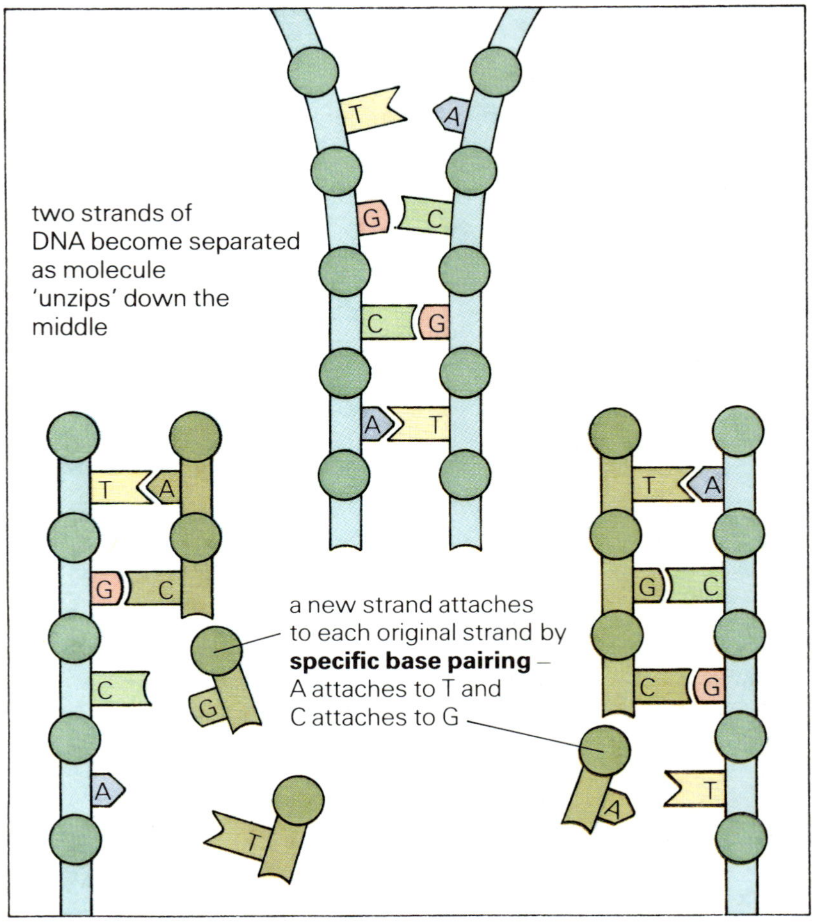

The order of bases in each original strand controls the order of bases in the new molecule. So the two new molecules of DNA formed are identical to *the original molecule.*

Making new cells

DNA is contained in chromosomes surrounded by a protein coat for protection. New DNA and new chromosomes are made during cell division. So the *amount* of DNA in cells *changes* during cell division.

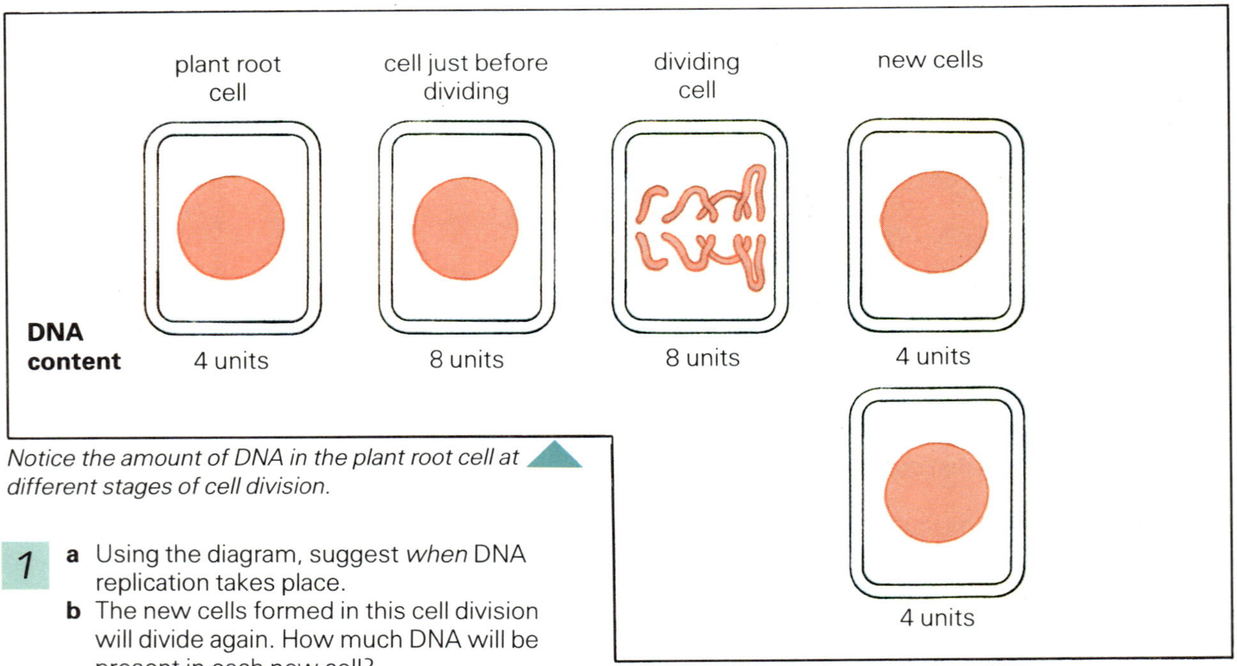

Notice the amount of DNA in the plant root cell at different stages of cell division.

1
- **a** Using the diagram, suggest *when* DNA replication takes place.
- **b** The new cells formed in this cell division will divide again. How much DNA will be present in each new cell?

Making incorrect copies

When animals and plants reproduce, genes are passed to the next generation through gametes (*see 10.3*). This means that it is *usually* possible to predict patterns of inheritance. But sometimes completely **new varieties** of offspring are produced. For example, budgies, which have been kept as pet birds for many years, always used to have green feathers. When they bred, their offspring had green feathers too. Suddenly, after many years of breeding, a blue-feathered variety appeared. A sudden change in phenotype such as this is the result of **gene mutation.** It occurs when the base sequence in DNA that makes a gene is not replicated *exactly* during cell division, creating a *new* form of the gene. Individuals with the new gene are called **mutants**.

The first blue budgies were a result of a mutation in the gene coding for feather colour.

Causing mutation

Certain factors known as **mutagenic factors** increase the chance of mutation. Exposure to ionising radiation or to ultraviolet rays in sunlight can increase the chance of mutation occurring. Some forms of **skin cancer** are mutations caused by prolonged exposure to strong sunlight. There are also mutagenic chemicals, including certain dyes, food additives and food preservatives.

Forming new varieties

A new variety may appear if the mutant gene is *inherited.* This can only happen when the mutation occurs in *gamete-producing* cells. The majority of new genes created by mutation are recessive. So a new phenotype will not appear unless *two* mutant genes occur together – that is, unless the mutant gene is inherited from *both* parents.

Which tomato would you choose? Apart from the normal red, there are many colour varieties produced by mutation.

2 If the DNA content of a human body cell is 20 units, what amount of DNA will be found in
- **a** a human sperm cell?
- **b** a zygote?

3 Suggest explanations for the following.
- **a** The incidence of skin cancer in people living in the UK has increased over recent years.
- **b** In South Africa, skin cancer is very rare among black African inhabitants and more common in people of European descent.

4 Why do most mutations only appear many generations after gene mutation?

YOU CAN READ MORE ABOUT THE EFFECTS OF IONISING RADIATION ON THE BODY ON SPREAD 12.6.

Forming new species

Sorting living things

There is a huge variety of living things in the world. The millions of organisms have some features in common but they also differ from each other in many ways. These similarities and differences can be used to arrange organisms into groups – a process called **classification.** For example, nearly all living things can be classified as either animals or plants. The animals shown here are placed into a smaller group using their *similar* features. Their *different* features can be used to divide this group into even smaller groups.

The smallest group that scientists use is called a **species** – you and all the other people in the world belong to the species *Homo sapiens*. Animals and plants that belong to the same species have so many features in common that they can *interbreed* to produce offspring.

These water animals are all classified as arthropods because of their similar *features, such as exoskeletons and jointed limbs. What* differences *do you think could be used to separate them into smaller groups?*

Evolving ideas

The Swede, Carolus Linnaeus, was one of the first scientists to classify organisms. Like many other people in the sixteenth century, he thought that animals and plants had remained the same since the world was created. As they learned more and more about plants and animals, some scientists began to question the theory that species had always been the same. Instead they suggested that species *change* and that *new* species are being formed all the time. This is the **theory of evolution** which proposes that all species evolved from a common ancestor by a process of *gradual change*. Many scientists accepted this theory but Charles Darwin was the first to collect evidence and put forward an explanation of how evolution takes place.

Scientists believe that all mammals – including you – evolved from a small shrew-like creature through gradual change over millions of years.

Gathering evidence

In 1831, the young Darwin was offered a place as a naturalist on the survey ship *HMS Beagle*. The five-year voyage took Darwin all round the world, and he was amazed by the tremendous variety of animals and plants he found. After returning to Britain, he spent the next 20 years studying and trying to explain the origins of his enormous collection of animals, plants and fossils. Eventually he put forward the theory that evolution might have occurred through **natural selection**.

Struggling to survive

Darwin's theory of natural selection is based on the four ideas shown here.

1. Organisms produce many offspring.

2. Organisms struggle to survive.

3. Members of a species vary.

4. Characteristics that give an organism an advantage are more likely to be passed on to the next generation.

The Galapagos finches

During the *Beagle's* voyage, Darwin became fascinated by the animals and plants found on the small Galapagos Islands in the Pacific Ocean off the coast of South America. He noticed that the species on these islands were similar to species found on the South American mainland – but many of the Galapagos species differed from their mainland relatives in small ways. For example, there are 13 species of Galapagos finches that are found nowhere else in the world. Some islands even possess particular species of finches that are not found on the other islands. To explain these observations, Darwin suggested that a few finches had strayed to the islands from the mainland. As they bred in their *different* and *isolated* environments, the finches gradually changed or evolved into new species.

There are no woodpeckers on the Galapagos Islands so these woodpecker finches have adapted *to feed on the insects in tree crevices.*

1 The main groups used in the classification of living things are:
phylum species class kingdom genus.

Place these groups in order of their size, starting with the largest. You may need to use reference books to do this.

2 In the struggle to survive, some organisms are killed by predators while others survive. What other factors affect the survival of organisms?

3 Darwin realised that variation is necessary for natural selection to occur. He searched for an explanation of variation but was unsuccessful. Using your knowledge of genetics, try to explain the causes of variation.

4 Why was *isolation* on separate islands an important factor in the evolution of the Galapagos finches?

10.13 Selection in action

Testing the theory

According to the theory of natural selection, the characteristics of a population slowly change as individuals become *better adapted* to their environment. Darwin gave examples of populations that he thought had changed through adaptation. Since then, many investigations have been carried out which show natural selection in action.

Changing with the times

A good example of natural selection is shown by a species called the peppered moth. There are two varieties of this moth – a pale and dark variety. The first dark moth was found near Manchester in 1848. At that time the dark variety was rare, but since then it has become very common in *industrial* areas. Scientists believe that this change in numbers of the dark variety is the result of natural selection.

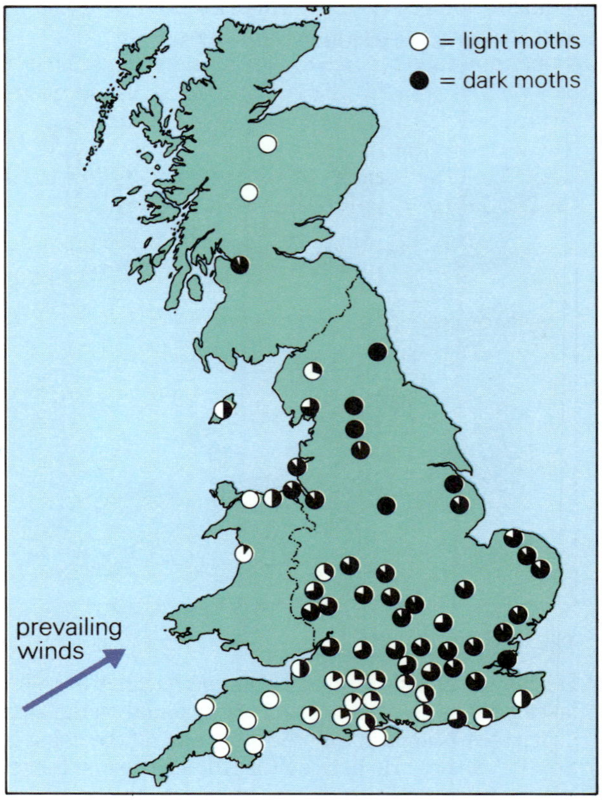

The proportion of dark and light varieties of peppered moth found in different areas of Britain today.

Peppered moths feed at night and rest on tree trunks and branches during the day. In areas with little or no industry, tree trunks are encrusted with lichens giving them a mottled grey appearance. In industrial areas, pollution in the air kills the lichens and blackens the trees. The dark variety of moth has an advantage in this environment because it is better camouflaged against the dark trees. So the dark variety is more likely to *survive* and *produce offspring* in industrial areas than the pale variety.

The pale and dark varieties of peppered moth . . .

*. . . in each picture, which of the **two** moths will survive?*

Super rats

If you had rats in your house, they would gnaw through any stores of food. As well as being pests, rats are also a serious health hazard – by contaminating food with harmful bacteria they can spread diseases to people. So wherever rats are found, poison is put down. Warfarin started to be used as a rat poison in the 1950s. By 1980, many areas in Britain had populations of warfarin-resistant rats. These 'super' rats failed to die even when they ate large doses of warfarin. Many pest species develop a **resistance** to the pesticides used on them.

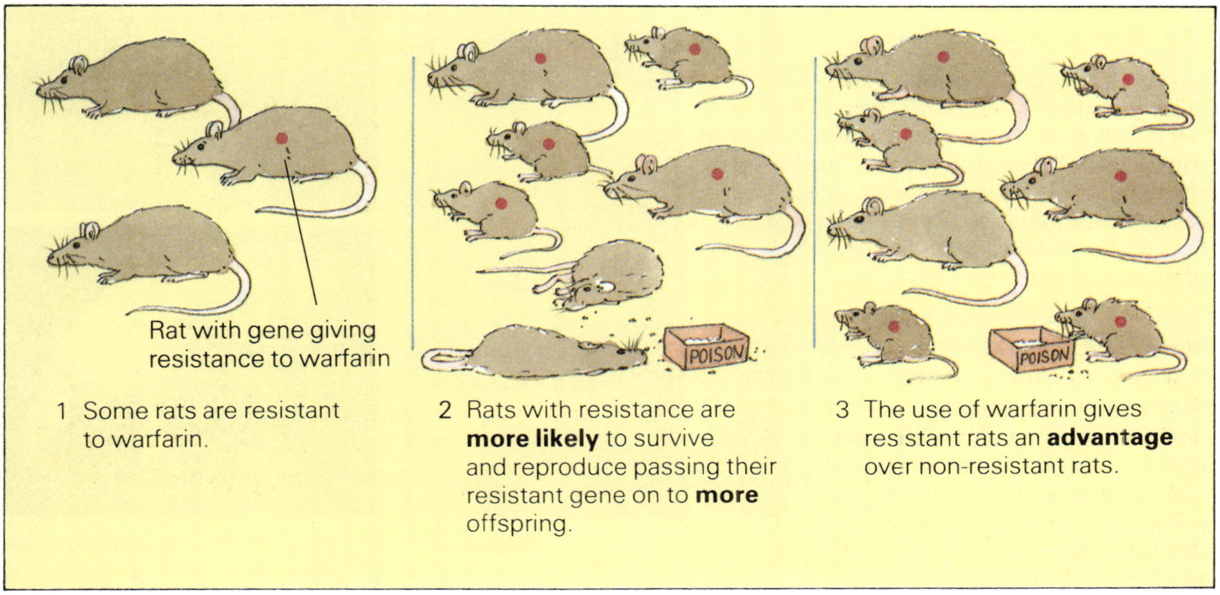

How resistance to warfarin spreads in a population of rats.

The three possible genotypes and phenotypes for resistance in rats.

Genotype	Phenotype
WW	warfarin resistant but needs large amounts of vitamin K
Ww	warfarin resistant and needs only small extra amounts of vitamin K
ww	killed easily by warfarin

Genes controlling resistance

Warfarin kills rats by stopping their blood from clotting. Resistance to warfarin is controlled by a *dominant* gene, W (*see 10.5*). Recent studies have shown that rats which have two dominant genes (WW) require very large amounts of vitamin K – a vitamin which is also needed for blood to clot. If these rats fail to get enough vitamin K they bleed to death.

1 Study the distribution map and photographs of the peppered moth on the opposite page and then answer these questions

- **a** In which areas are pale moths more common?
- **b** How does being well camouflaged aid survival?
- **c** Why is the *pale* variety more common in some areas than others?
- **d** What would happen to the peppered moth population if the industry in north-west England changed and the amount of pollution in the air decreased? Explain your answer.

2

- **a** Which genotype gives the best advantage to rats? Explain why.
- **b** If two rats with this genotype bred, what genotypes could the offspring have? Predict the ratio of these genotypes.
- **c** Will the recessive gene that causes rats to be killed by warfarin ever be totally wiped out? Explain your answer.

10.14 Tailor-made plants and animals

'Improving' nature

People have grown crops and kept domesticated animals for thousands of years. Until recently, no one knew how inheritance worked, but it was obvious that characteristics were passed from parents to offspring. So people *controlled* the breeding of plants and animals to develop the characteristics they wanted, such as faster growth, higher yields and more resistance to disease. They selected and bred from plants and animals with the desired characteristics. The process is called **artificial selection** and has resulted in many new varieties of animals and plants.

More milk from cows

Farmers have increased milk production through careful breeding programmes, using only the bulls and cows with the most suitable characteristics. These programmes have gradually developed **breeds** of cattle with much higher milk yields than their ancestors. The breeding programmes have been helped enormously by **artificial insemination** – taking semen (fluid containing sperm) directly from the male and inserting it into the female. Using artificial insemination, a single bull can pass on desirable characteristics to many offspring without actually mating. By freezing semen, it is even possible for a bull to continue to sire offspring after its death. However, as this table shows, not all animals are suitable for use in artificial insemination programmes.

Why is artificial insemination particularly useful for cattle?

Farm animal	Volume of semen obtainable from a single sample (cm^3)	Easily frozen	Number of inseminations from a single sample
horse	50–100	no	90
cattle	5	yes	500
sheep	1	no	25
pig	200–250	no	35

Modern varieties of crops, such as this high-yielding wheat with lots of 'ears', have helped to increase our food supplies.

Many years of careful breeding have increased the meat yield of domestic pigs – and made them very different from their ancestor, the wild boar. What differences can you see?

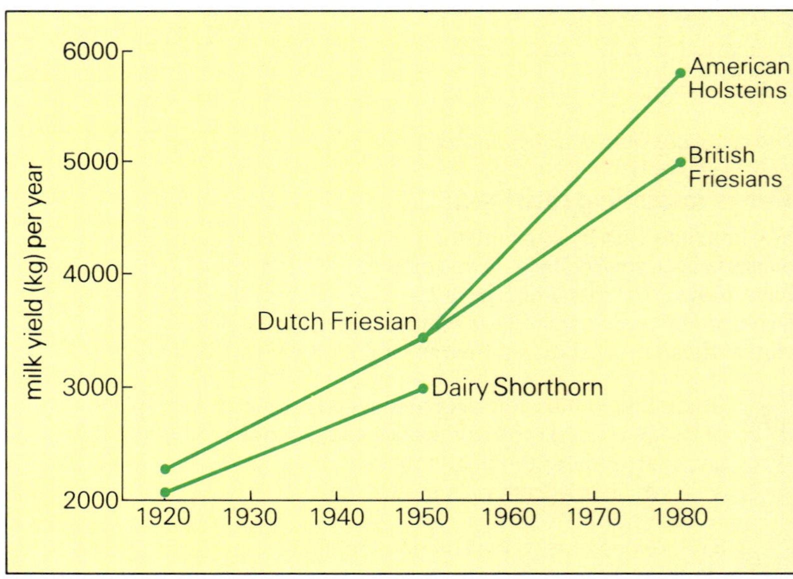

This graph shows the increase in milk yields of some breeds of cattle, produced by artificial selection.

Speeding up breeding

Only the 'best' cows (those with the required characteristics) are selected for breeding. The number of offspring that could be produced from selected cows used to be limited by the long **gestation period** – the time it takes for the embryo calf to develop. This problem can now be overcome by extracting eggs from the best cows and fertilising them outside the body (**invitro fertilisation**). Alternatively, the eggs can be fertilised inside the mother and the fertilised eggs or **zygotes** extracted.

Multiplying and checking offspring

A short time after fertilisation, the zygote has divided many times, forming a ball of *identical* cells. Each cell of this developing young or **embryo** can be separated and grown into a new embryo, using a technique called **tissue culture**. This enables a large number of embryos *with identical genes* to be produced from a single embryo. The individuals that develop from these embryos will be identical – they will be **clones**. Each embryo is then transplanted into an 'inferior' cow. Before transplantation, each embryo's DNA may be tested for inherited diseases. In 1990, scientists identified the gene that determines the sex of an individual. So in the future, breeders may be able to control the sex of calves. This is very important if you are a dairy farmer and want only cows.

Modern technology has given animal breeders far more control.

Semen is taken from bulls with the most suitable characteristics.	Sperm may be: – sexed (X or Y) – checked for genetic defects – frozen.	Selected cows are treated with hormones to increase egg production, then artificially inseminated.	Embryos extracted may be – check for faulty genes – sexed – cultured & cloned – frozen.	Embryos may be transplanted into 'ordinary' cows, so that selected cows can continue to produce 'superior' eggs.

1 List five types of animal or plant that have been changed or 'improved' for our benefit. In each case, state their use to us.

2 Look at the graph opposite
- **a** Why did milk production increase rapidly in 1950?
- **b** Explain why milk production continued to increase after this year.

3
- **a** List the advantages to breeders of using
  - (i) artificial insemination.
  - (ii) embryo transplants.
- **b** Do you think such techniques should be used on farm animals? Discuss this question in a group.

YOU CAN READ MORE ABOUT INVITRO FERTILISATION ON SPREAD 5.13.

10.15 Sickle-cell disease

Blood disease . . .

Your blood transports vital materials, such as food and oxygen, around your body. The oxygen is carried by a substance called **haemoglobin**, contained in red blood cells. These cells are usually disc-shaped. In 1910 doctors found that a large number of children in west Africa were suffering from a very severe form of **anaemia** – a disease in which the blood fails to carry sufficient oxygen. The red blood cells of these children were sickle-shaped and so the disease was named **sickle-cell anaemia**. People with the disease died early in childhood.

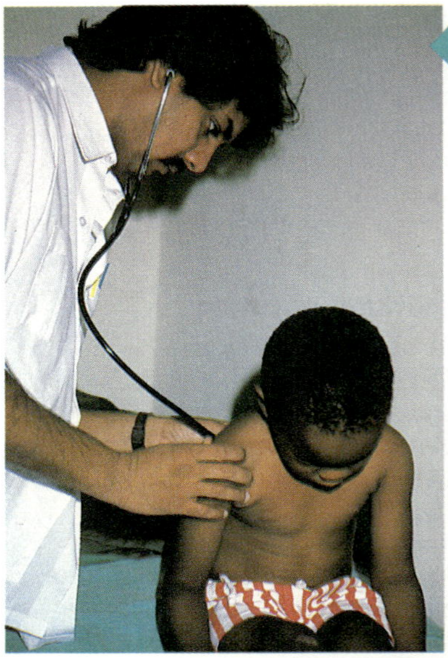

This child has sickle-cell anaemia – a painful deadly disease caused by a faulty gene.

. . . caused by genes

Shortly after discovering the disease, doctors found that the parents of children with sickle-cell anaemia had a very *mild* form of anaemia known as **sickle-cell trait**. This caused little, if any, ill effect. Children with sickle-cell anaemia were *only* born into families in which *both* parents had sickle-cell trait. From this evidence, doctors concluded that sickle-cell anaemia is an *inherited* disease and that it is caused by a **co-dominant gene** (*see 10.6*). It is now known to be caused by one of the co-dominant genes controlling the production of haemoglobin. The gene N controls the production of normal haemoglobin, while the gene S leads to the production of *abnormal* haemoglobin which distorts red blood cells into a sickle shape.

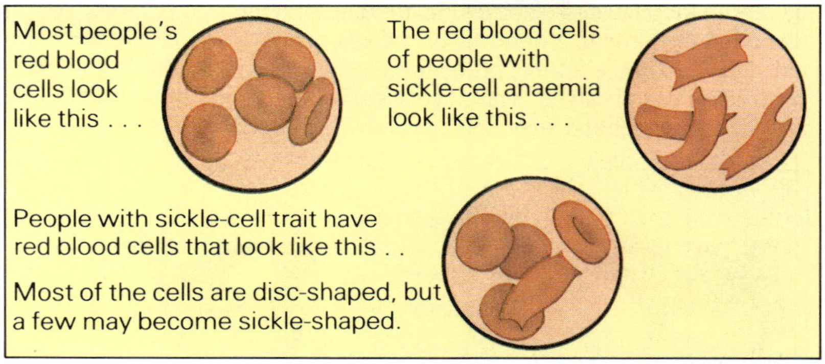

A puzzling distribution

Since most people with sickle-cell anaemia died before they had children, doctors expected that few people would inherit the abnormal S gene and that the disease would become less and less common. Yet the number of children born with sickle-cell anaemia remained at the high level *in certain areas*. Then people noticed that the disease was most common in areas of the world where another deadly disease, **malaria**, also occurred. Malaria is caused by a parasite that spends part of its life in red blood cells. But how could malaria affect the distribution of sickle-cell anaemia?

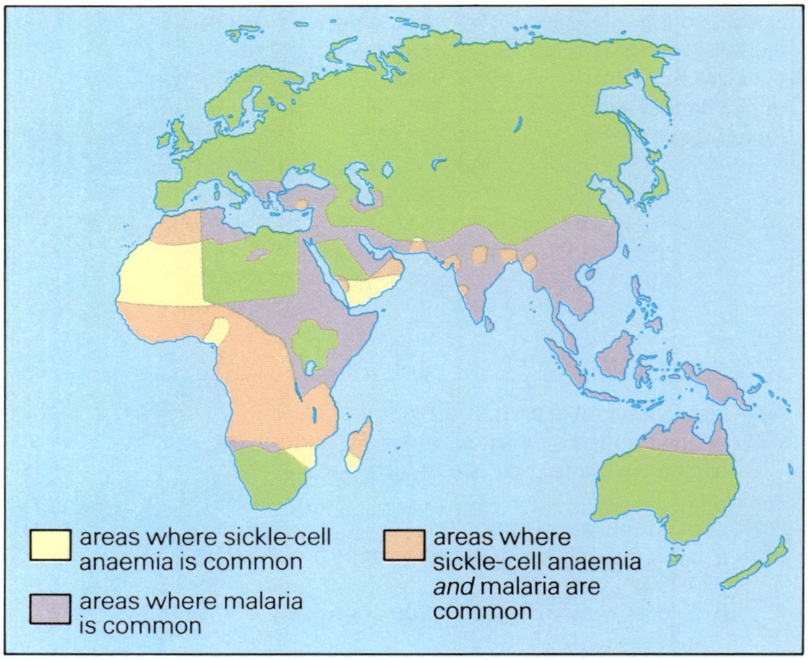

YOU CAN READ MORE ABOUT BLOOD AND HAEMOGLOBIN ON SPREAD 3.9.

The link with malaria

Malaria affects the distribution of sickle-cell anaemia because the abnormal S gene provides **resistance** to malaria – people with the S gene are unlikely to die from malaria. This diagram shows the possible combinations of N and S genes (the genotypes) and their effects.

Which genotype do you think would be of most advantage in
- malaria areas?
- non-malaria areas?

Explaining the distribution

The distribution of sickle-cell anaemia can be explained by **natural selection** (*see 10.12*). Many people die of sickle-cell anaemia or malaria before they are old enough to have children. So in areas where *both* diseases occur, N and S genes are *removed* from the population. But N and S genes are also *passed on* in the population because people of genotype NS are most likely to survive. These two effects of natural selection maintain both the N and S genes in populations in malaria areas – and maintain the number of children with sickle-cell anaemia.

Preventing genetic disease

Doctors help couples with sickle-cell trait to consider the risk of having a child with sickle-cell anaemia. After such **genetic counselling** couples may decide not to have children. Doctors can also diagnose many genetic disorders, including sickle-cell anaemia, in the very early stages of pregnancy. This provides couples with the choice of whether to continue the pregnancy. Medical scientists are now developing a technique called **gene replacement therapy**, which will enable them to replace one gene with another – for example, replace S genes with N genes. In the future, this technique may cure sickle-cell anaemia and many other inherited diseases.

1 **a** What evidence is there to show that sickle-cell anaemia is an *inherited* disease?
b Explain why doctors concluded that the disease is caused by a *co-dominant* gene.

2 Why is sickle-cell disease much more common in west Africa than in Britain?

3 Gene replacement therapy may provide a cure for inherited diseases – and allow *other* inherited features to be changed. Many people are worried about this technique.
a Why do you think people are concerned about replacing genes?
b State, with reasons, whether you think research into gene replacement therapy should continue.

Genotype | **Effect**

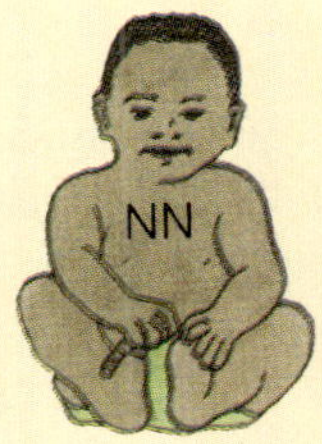

People of genotype NN produce *normal* haemoglobin – and have *little* resistance to malaria.

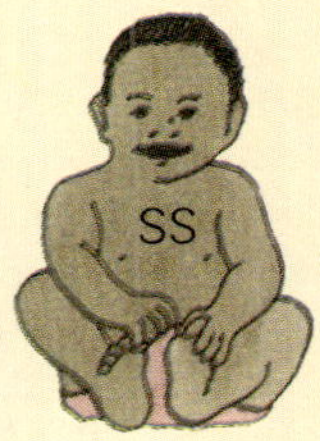

People of genotype SS have *abnormal* haemoglobin and suffer from sickle-cell anaemia. They are resistant to malaria.

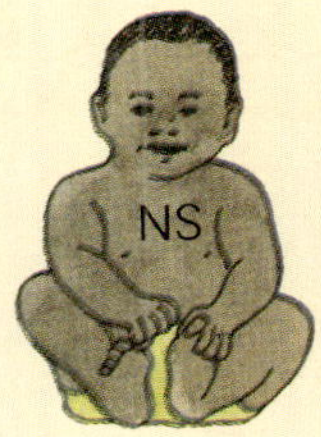

People of genotype NS have the very mild sickle-cell trait. They are resistant to malaria.

In areas where malaria is common, people with NS genotype are most likely to survive and have children . . .

. . . and 1 in 4 of their children is likely to suffer from sickle-cell anaemia.

Index *(refers to spread numbers)*

For additional information, see the following modules:
3 Humans as Organisms
4 Environments
5 Maintenance of Life

Photo acknowledgements

These refer to the spread number (in italics), and where appropriate, the position on the page (lh = left-hand page, rh = right-hand page).

Allsport Photographic Ltd. (Tony Duffy) *10.1 lh bottom*; Frank Lane Picture Agency *10.11 rh top*; *10.14 1h*; Sally & Richard Greenhill *10.1 lh top*; *10.2 1h*; *10.3 lh top*; Holt Studios Ltd. *10.14 rh*; NHPA (M. Savonius) *10.11 rh bottom*; (Roger Perry) *10.12 rh*; Science Photo Library *10.1 rh*; *10.2 rh*; *10.3 lh bottom*; *10.4*; *10.6*; *10.7*; *10.8*; *10.9*; *10.10*; *10.15*.

Picture Research: Jennifer Johnson, Norman Franks

11 NUCLEAR POWER AND ELECTRICITY

In different ways, both electricity and radioactivity arise from the structure of the atoms of certain materials. This module shows you what causes **radioactivity**, how it can be harmful and helpful, and how **nuclear power** (like many energy sources) can be used to **generate electricity**. You will see that a lot of energy is wasted in generating, distributing and using electricity – and how the increasing demand for electricity can pose a threat to our world.

Relevant National Curriculum Attainment Targets: Old ATs (8), (11), (13), New ATs (4), (5)

Our energy needs

Energy to survive

To survive, you need energy – the energy in food, light energy, heat for warmth and cooking. Until a few hundred years ago, people used energy mainly to meet these **basic energy needs**. Most people lived in small, scattered communities, and hunted and grew their own food. Many used firewood for warmth and cooking, while wind and flowing water powered machines. All these were **renewable energy sources** – the wind still blew, water continued to flow and new trees grew to provide firewood. People took the energy they needed *without* reducing the planet's energy resources.

Producing food can be hard but simple . . .

Energy on demand

Today, our demands on the environment are vastly greater. In industrialised **developed countries**, such as Britain, many of us live in densely populated cities. Our basic energy needs must be *provided* for us *where we live*. We expect energy to be available immediately – without having to wait for the wind to blow or build a fire. Thousands of power stations convert energy from sources – such as the **fossil fuels**, coal, oil and gas – into electrical energy. This is supplied to homes and factories so that we have energy when we want, where we want.

. . . or easier but far from simple.

We no longer use energy simply to survive. Energy is consumed in producing a huge range of materials that we have become used to and in powering machines that make our lives easier and more enjoyable. To meet these demands, the planet's energy resources are being used up at an ever-increasing rate.

A developing demand

In **developing countries** the demand for energy per head of population is much lower. Many people live in rural communities, produce their own food and use firewood to meet their other basic energy needs. But as the populations in developing countries rise, the consumption of wood increases. In some parts of the world firewood is being used up faster than it can be replaced – so the wood is no longer a renewable resource.

The lifestyles of people in many developing countries are changing. The countries are trying to industrialise and people are moving from the rural areas into the towns and cities. As lifestyles change, the demand for energy to survive – and to do many other things – will increase.

This graph shows the rise in the amount of electrical energy we use. At one time, the USA used nearly as much energy as the rest of the world put together.

What do you think happened in the USA in the 1930s?

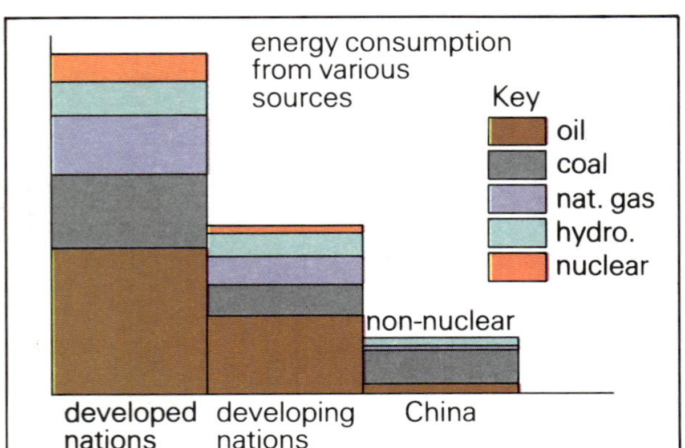

As countries develop, their energy needs will increase.

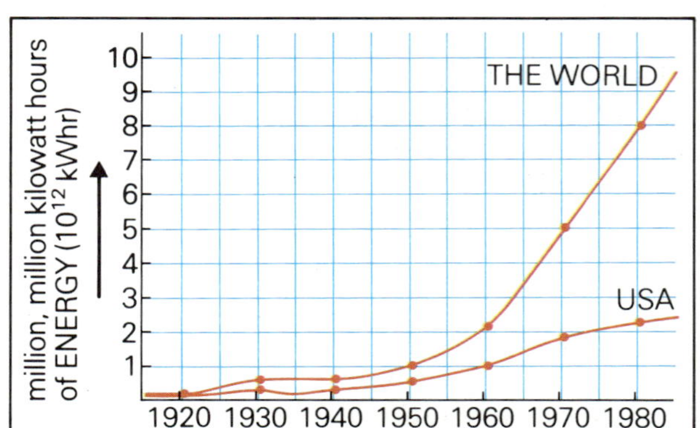

What reasons can you think of for the increase in our energy demands?

Vanishing resources

Urban areas demand huge amounts of energy in the form of electricity. We exploit a range of energy sources to meet present demands. Most of the electricity used in developed countries is obtained by burning fossil fuels. These take millions of years to form and so are **non-renewable energy sources** – and fossil fuels are running out fast.

In some parts of the world, fast-moving water is used to generate hydroelectricity. Other renewable energy sources have proved difficult to use *on a large scale*.

Our consumption of fossil fuels has risen dramatically – and will fall just as dramatically as they run out.

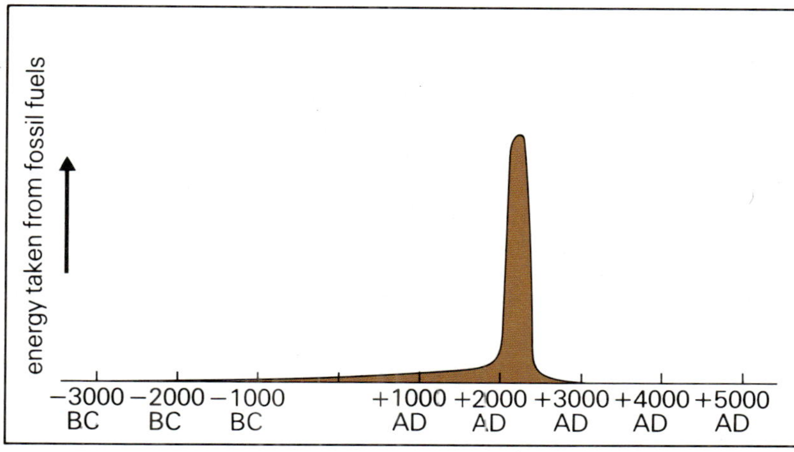

Nuclear energy to the rescue?

Another form of energy – nuclear energy – can provide a large amount of the electricity we use. A number of countries have built nuclear power plants and so reduced their need for fossil fuels. Although nuclear energy is non-renewable, there seems to be sufficient resources to provide us with electricity for many thousands of years.

Unfortunately, there are problems with using nuclear energy – for example, dangerous radiation and waste materials are also produced. If these escape into the environment, they can cause serious damage to all life, including us.

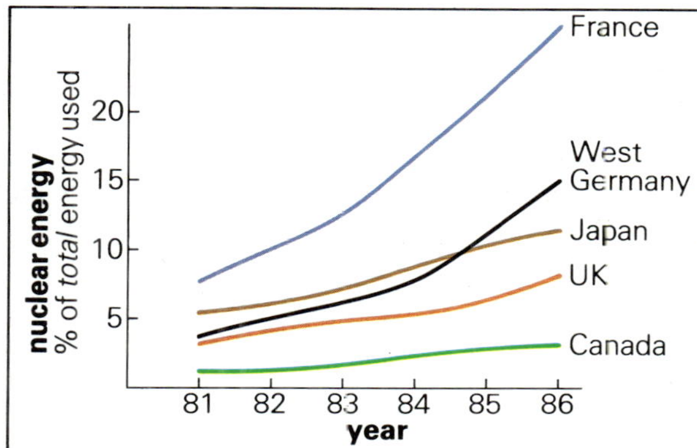

Nuclear energy is seen, in some countries, as the only way to produce enough electrical energy. Do you think this may be so?

Planning for the future

It is estimated that by the middle of the next century, the world's population will have doubled, and 50 per cent of people will live in urban areas. How can we provide enough electrical energy to meet the huge increases in demand this will cause? Could nuclear energy be the answer?

This module explores the promises and risks of nuclear energy so that you will be in a better position to consider this question.

Every country is likely to want more and more energy in the future.

1 List as many energy sources as you can. Divide the list into:
- **a** renewable sources
- **b** non-renewable sources.

2 What percentage of the UK's energy is provided by nuclear energy?

3 Find out:
- **a** When nuclear energy was *first* used in the UK to generate electricity;
- **b** How many nuclear power stations there are in the UK today.

Discovering a new energy source

The mystery rays

In 1896, the French scientist, Henri Becquerel, was investigating **phosphorescent chemicals** – chemicals that emit light after being exposed to sunlight. The previous year, the German scientist, Röntgen, had discovered new rays, called **X-rays**, while experimenting with a gas discharge tube. At the same time as X-rays were emitted, phosphorescent chemicals at one end of the tube started to glow.

Becquerel thought that the phosphorescent chemicals might be producing the X-rays (as well as light rays). He decided to find out whether phosphorescent materials placed in the sun would give off X-rays.

X-rays are very penetrating – even passing through skin and flesh – and will darken a photographic plate.

Becquerel's investigation

Becquerel investigated various crystals of phosphorescent materials, particularly compounds of **uranium**. He knew that both light and X-rays would darken a photographic plate. But X-rays could pass through black paper, while light rays could not. So he used photographic plates wrapped in black paper to detect any X-rays emitted.

The phosphorescent compounds of uranium caused blackening of photographic plates, forming an image of the crystals. Becquerel concluded that the uranium compounds had *gained* energy from the Sun and had then given out that energy in the form of rays.

Becquerel's investigations gave him a clear idea about what was happening – or so he thought.

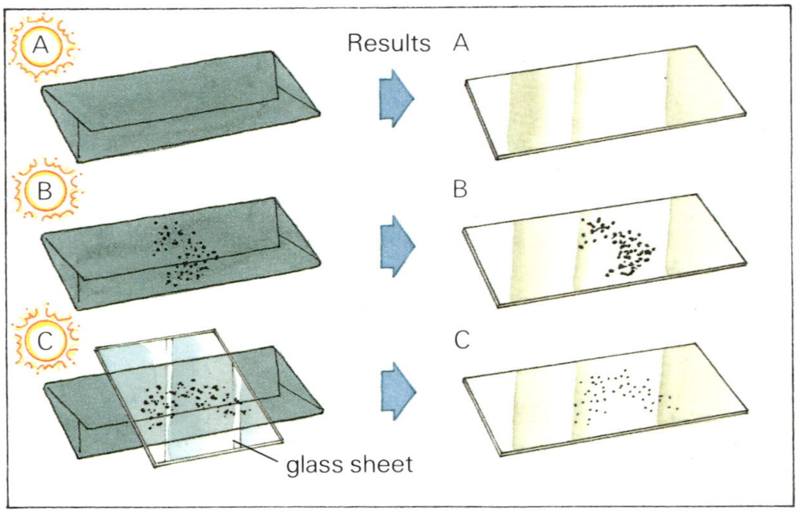

Do you agree with Becquerel's conclusion?

What else could Becquerel have done to test whether his ideas were correct?

In the dark

A short while later, Becquerel found a plate that he had accidentally left in a drawer with some uranium salts – and he noticed that the plate had become blackened. He assumed that the uranium compounds could *store* energy from the Sun and emit it much later.

The radiations emitted were found to be *different* from X-rays. For example, they took longer to blacken a photographic plate and produced fuzzier images than X-rays. Becquerel continued to investigate these new **Becquerel rays**.

This shows one of Becquerel's later investigations. Compare the results with those from Becquerel's earlier experiments. How do these results help explain where the rays come from?

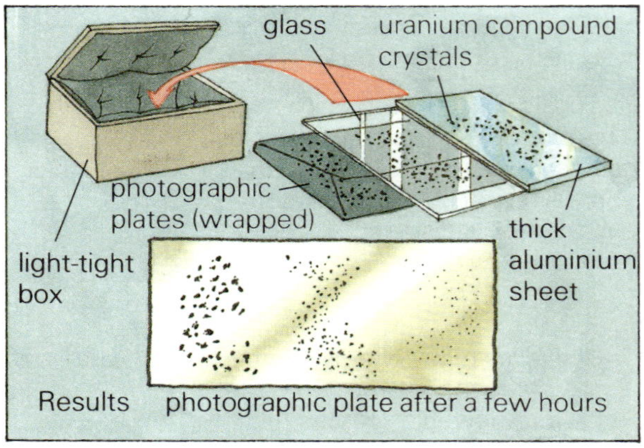

The glass and aluminium sheets were the same thickness. What does this tell you about the properties of the rays emitted?

YOU CAN READ MORE ABOUT X-RAYS ON SPREAD 7.12.

Radioactivity

The scientist Marie Curie found that the greater the *mass* of uranium salts used, the more the photographic plates were blackened. What do you think that told her?

Other investigations showed that Becquerel rays were *not* caused by the Sun's energy (as in phosphorescence) but came from the uranium salts. The ability of materials, such as uranium, to emit radiation because known as **radioactivity**. Soon scientists discovered that **thorium** compounds were also radioactive.

Marie Curie carried out many investigations on radioactive materials. To her surprise, pitchblende (a mineral containing uranium and thorium) produced far more blackening of plates than expected. Did pitchblende, she wondered, contain other substances apart from uranium and thorium that also produced 'Becquerel rays'? If so, they must be present in very tiny amounts (or they would have been discovered earlier) and so must be *very* radioactive.

She and her colleagues managed to separate a new material from the pitchblende. Many thousands of times more radioactive than uranium, the small pellet of the new element **radium** that she obtained proved immensely valuable in developing uses for radioactivity.

Life and death

Marie Curie became very interested in the use of radium, particularly in medicine. Its penetrating radiation could help in diagnosis. Soon after its discovery, radium was known to cause burns when held close to the skin. Later, radium was used to 'burn out' cancers in the human body.

'If we take a practical point of view', she said on her tour of America in 1922, 'then the most important property of the rays is the production of physiological effects on the cells of the human organism.'

It is now known that lower amounts of radiation can damage cells and *cause* cancer. Marie Curie died of cancer in 1934.

Marie Curie at work in lab.

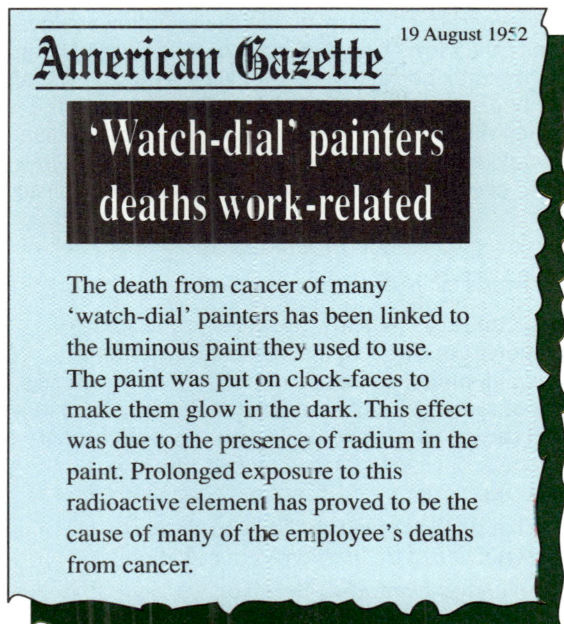

American Gazette 19 August 1952

'Watch-dial' painters deaths work-related

The death from cancer of many 'watch-dial' painters has been linked to the luminous paint they used to use. The paint was put on clock-faces to make them glow in the dark. This effect was due to the presence of radium in the paint. Prolonged exposure to this radioactive element has proved to be the cause of many of the employee's deaths from cancer.

The use of radium proved fatal for some workers.

1 Becquerel had an idea about how X-rays and other rays were produced. What was his idea?

2 **a** How did Becquerel make sure that his early tests were fair?
b What else do you think he should have done?

3 Using Becquerel's results, list some properties of 'Becquerel rays'.

4 Why did Marie Curie suspect that pitchbende contained previously unknown substances?

5 Today, the death of any 'watch-dial painters' would result in payment of compensation to the families concerned. Do you think this is right? Why do you think this did not happen at the time?

Investigating radioactivity

Bursts of energy

Radioactive materials give out radiation all the time. Becquerel detected the energy carried by this radiation using phosphorescent crystals. These gave out light when they absorbed energy from the radiation. At this time, light was thought to be a steady *stream* of energy – and Becquerel wondered if the new radiation was continuous.

One of the **detectors** which revealed the answer is the **spinthariscope**. This contains a screen covered with phosphorescent material. When a radioactive substance is placed near it, the screen glows. Through a magnifying glass, you can see that the glow is made up of many tiny *flashes* of light. From this and other observations, scientists realised that radiation was given out in bursts or *packets* of energy.

The energy from radium causes dark tracks to form on photographic film.

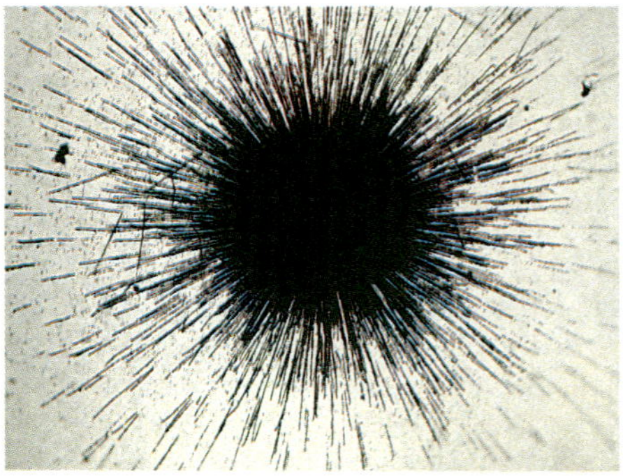

Vapour trails

Early experiments showed that the radiation could *ionise* (form charged atoms called **ions**) substances it passed through. Ionisation helps us to 'see' the radiation in a detector called a **cloud chamber**. The cloud chamber is a very cold container full of air saturated with vapour. The vapour will *condense* or form droplets around any ion. When a radioactive substance is placed nearby, radiation passes through the chamber. Each packet of energy forms ions along its path, which can be seen as a vapour trail.

Vapour trails in a cloud chamber. Here the path of non-colliding α-particles has been coloured green. One α-particle collided with an atom of the cloud, releasing a proton. Their paths have been coloured yellow and red.

Two kinds of radiation . . .

The pictures below show the trails produced by radiation from a radioactive material. Scientists quickly identified two kinds of trail, which meant two kinds of radiation. These were called α **(alpha) rays** and β **(beta) rays**. The trails were so straight that they were obviously formed by fast-moving **particles**.

What do these pictures tell you about the properties of the two types of radiation?

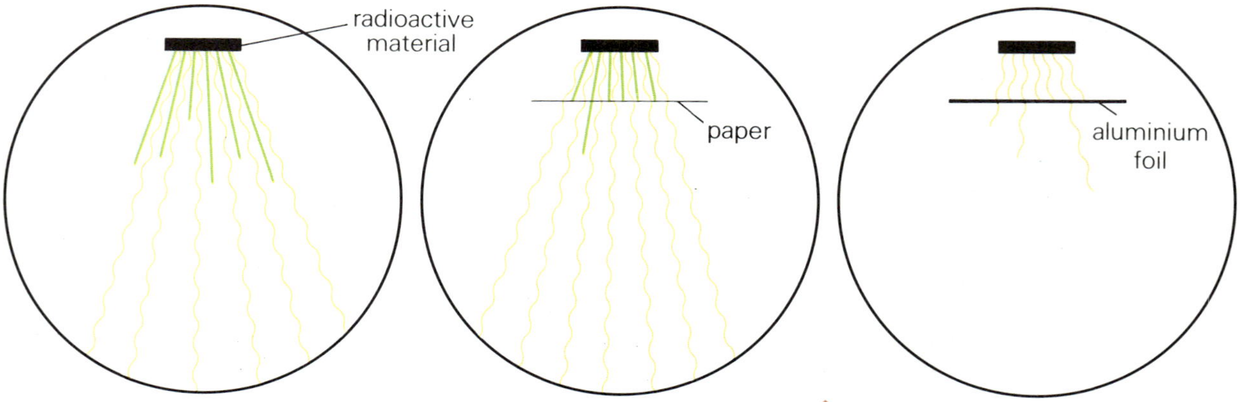

The particles which leave a thicker, brighter trail are called α particles, while the fainter trails are made by β particles.

YOU CAN READ MORE ABOUT IONS ON SPREADS 7.12 AND 8.11.

. . . and a third!

Further investigations revealed *another* kind of radiation. This was not a beam of particles but **electromagnetic radiation**, like light and X-rays. Called γ **(gamma) rays**, it was even more penetrating than X-rays and could pass through thick lead sheets.

Some radioactive materials, such as radium, emit all three kinds of radiation – and light and X-rays. Others may emit only one or two kinds.

Gamma radiation can even pass through thick metal, especially faults or cracks in welded joints.

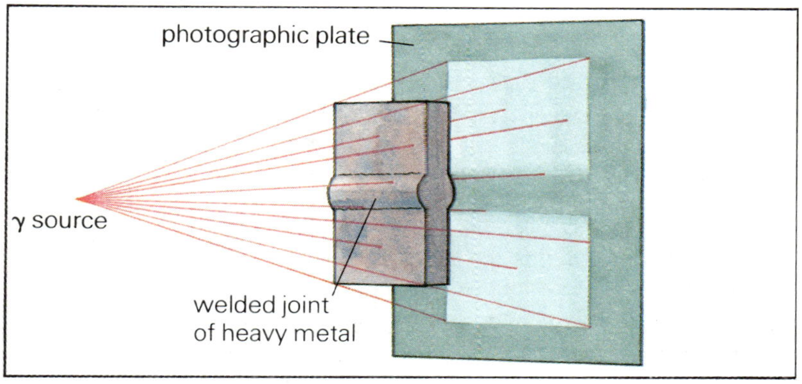

A charge on the rays?

Scientists also tried to find out whether any of the radiations carried electrical charges. To do this, they put a cloud chamber in between the poles of a magnet. They knew that if a wire carrying a current (a flowing electrical charge) was put between a magnet, the wire moved. So a beam of charged particles should also be deflected by a magnet – and the *lighter* the particles, the *bigger* the deflection.

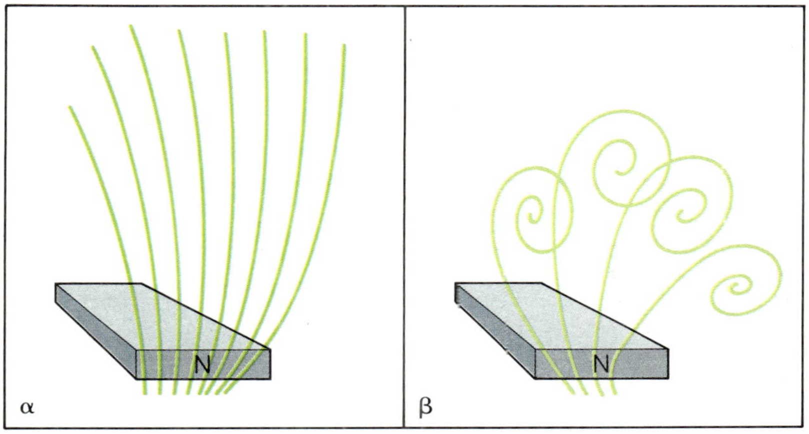

α and β rays responded differently to the same strong magnetic field. γ rays were not deflected. What does this tell you about each of the types of radiation?

Probing the atom

The α, β and γ rays seemed to come from the **atoms** of radioactive materials. At this time, an atom was thought to be a sphere containing positively and negatively charged particles *mixed up together*. Scientists wanted to find out more about the atom – and α-particles helped.

When α-particles were fired at metal foil, some of the α-particles bounced back. The α-particles were known to carry *positive* charges and so would be *repelled* by strong positive charges in the foil. But what were those strong positive charges? The scientist Ernest Rutherford suggested that *all* the positive charges in the atom were *concentrated at the centre* forming a positively charged **nucleus**. His ideas led to a new model of the atom – and the discovery of the **proton**.

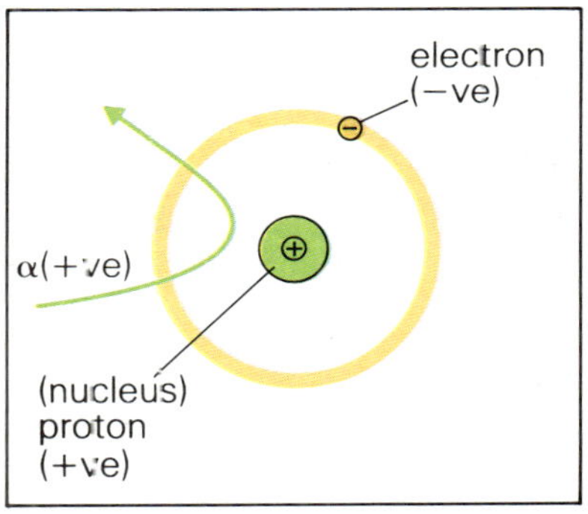

A model of the atom. It was later discovered that the nucleus of most atoms contains neutrons (which have no charge) as well as protons.

1. Why did scientists think that radiation was a continuous stream of energy?

2. What evidence showed that the radiation was made up of 'bursts' of energy?

3. **a** How did the cloud chamber help scientists to identify two kinds of radiation?
   b What were they?
   c How do the properties of the two kinds of radiation differ?

4. **a** Which kinds of radiation were deflected by a magnetic field? What does this tell you?
   b Which kind of radiation was deflected *most*? What does this tell you?

5. What safety precautions would you use when handling radioactive materials? (Think about the properties of α, β and γ rays.)

YOU CAN READ MORE ABOUT ATOMS AND ATOMIC STRUCTURES ON SPREADS 8.9 AND 8.10.

Patterns in radioactivity

Patterns among the elements

The new model of the atom helped in *classifying* the elements. Chemists had already arranged elements in order in the **Periodic Table**. They did this using the *properties* of the elements and the *relative masses* of atoms of the elements – but these did not always agree! The order of the elements was found to follow perfectly the *number of protons* in the atom.

Sections of the Periodic Table in which elements are arranged in order of their atomic number.

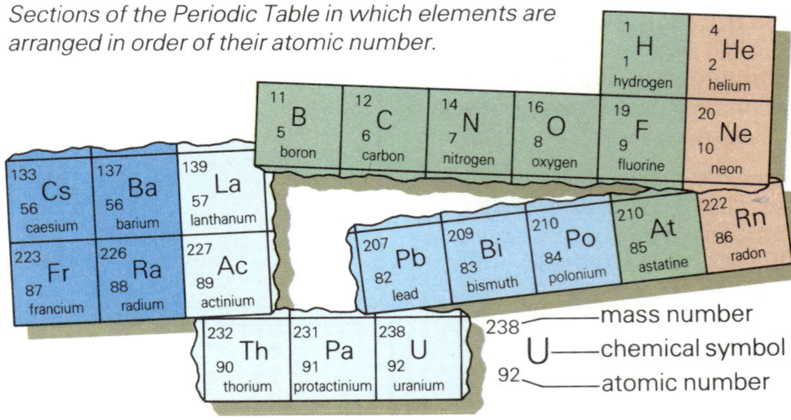

A modern Periodic Table shows the symbol of each element *and*:

- its **atomic number** – the number of protons in the nucleus
- its **mass number** – the number of protons and neutrons in the nucleus.

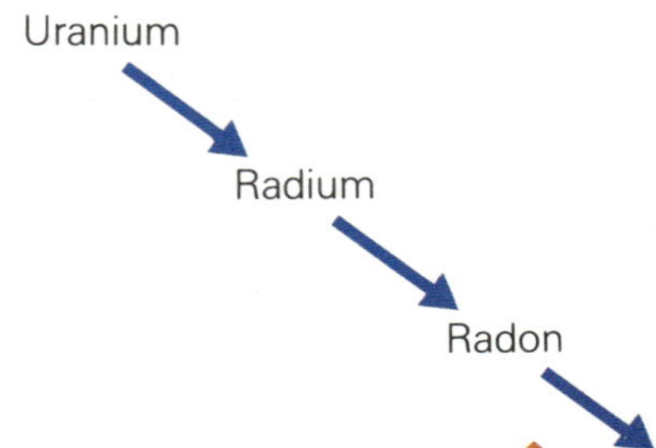

Part of the radioactive series of uranium decay, which eventually finishes with stable lead.

Modern alchemy

Ancient scientists called alchemists dreamed of changing or **transmuting** elements – particularly cheap metals – into gold. At the beginning of this century, scientists knew that atoms of an element could not change *during a chemical reaction*. Then Rutherford and other scientists studied the elements in radioactive materials carefully – and came to a startling conclusion: *radioactive elements transmute as they give out radiation!*

This is because radioactivity is *not* a chemical change. It involves the *nucleus* of an atom and is a **nuclear reaction**. When the nucleus of an atom emits α or β particles, the atom **decays** into the atom of a *different* element. The atom may decay again and again forming a series of elements known as a **radioactive series**.

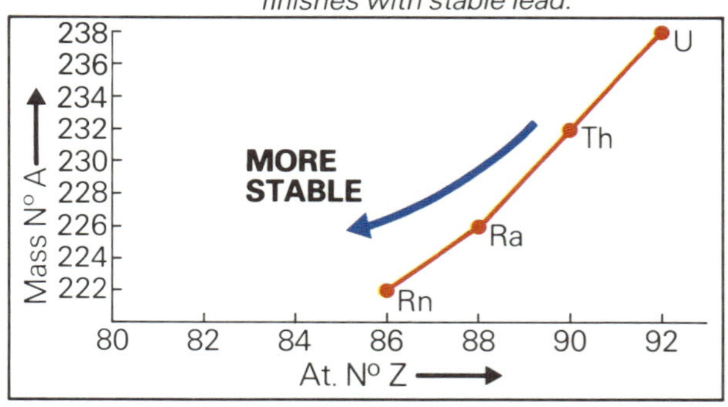

This graph shows how the mass number and atomic number change as uranium decays to radon. At each stage, an α particle is emitted. Can you work out what an α particle is?

Patterns of decay

By studying many radioactive series, and noting the positions in the Periodic Table of the elements formed, scientists found patterns of decay. For example, look at the positions in the Periodic Table of the elements formed in the section of the uranium series shown. What pattern can you see?

Nuclear reactions

The nucleus of an atom contains protons and neutrons held together by strong **nuclear forces**. Many nuclei are *stable* and don't undergo nuclear reactions easily. But some nuclei, particularly very large ones, are *unstable*. They can break down or decay, ejecting energy and particles.

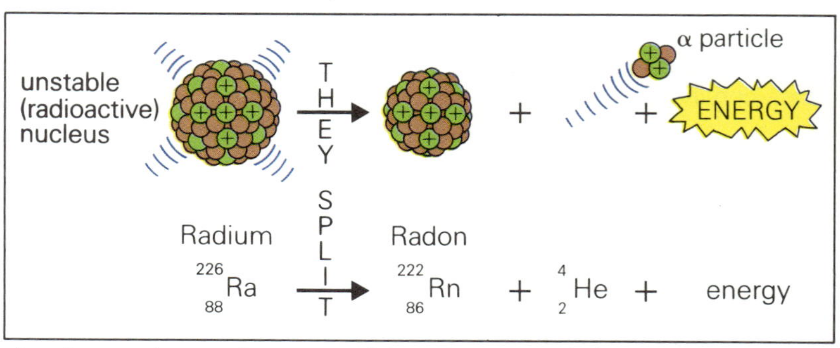

A radium nucleus emits an α particle and energy as it decays.

YOU CAN READ MORE ABOUT THE PERIODIC TABLE IN MODULE 9.

Isotopes

Close study of atoms and nuclei led to another revelation – all the atoms of an element are *not* necessarily the same. Atoms of the same element may take different forms, called **isotopes.** The isotopes of an element have the same number of protons but *different numbers of neutrons*. For example, the most common isotope of carbon ($^{12}_{6}C$) has six protons and *six* neutrons. Another isotope of carbon ($^{14}_{6}C$) has six protons and *eight* neutrons.

All the atoms of an isotope have the same mass number. So isotopes are often referred to by their mass number. The two isotopes of carbon may be written **carbon 12** (or C-12) and **carbon 14** (or C-14).

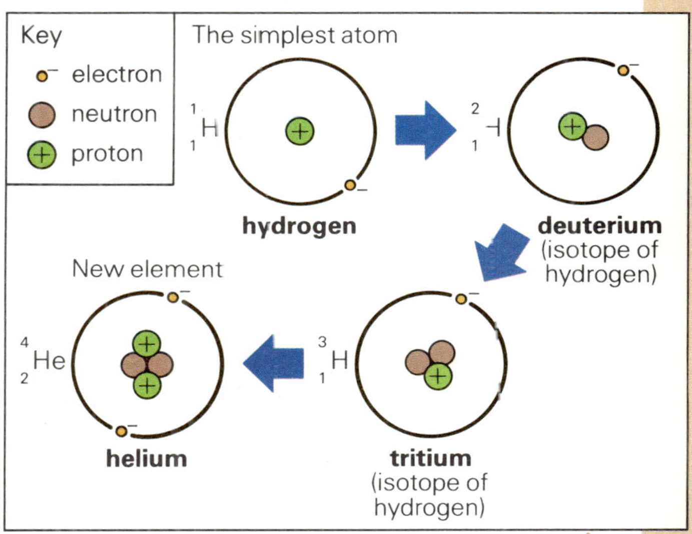

The simplest element, hydrogen, has three isotopes. Heavier elements may have far more

Radioisotopes

An isotope with unstable nuclei is radioactive and is called a **radioisotope**. An element may have some stable and some unstable isotopes. Most carbon (99 per cent) is made up of stable isotopes, mainly carbon 12. Carbon also has a number of radioisotopes, including carbon 14. The lighter elements tend to have mainly stable isotopes, while the isotopes of the heaviest elements are usually radioisotopes.

The rate of decay

A radioisotope decays all the time, and as each atom decays it emits a burst of radiation. You can find out about the decay by detecting and counting each burst. This reveals that the decay of atoms is *random* – any atom may decay *at any time*. Ten atoms may decay one second and none the next. So how can you find the *rate of* decay?

The answer is to count the bursts over a long enough period of time and to repeat the count at intervals. If you plot a graph of your findings, a pattern emerges – a **decay curve.** As atoms decay, there are fewer left to decay. So the rate of decay slows down, forming a curve.

Another pattern is that the length of time for a particular radioisotope to lose *half* of its radioactivity is *constant*. This time is called the **half life** of the radioisotope. Very unstable isotopes may have half lives of less than a second. The more stable radioisotopes can have half lives of thousands of years.

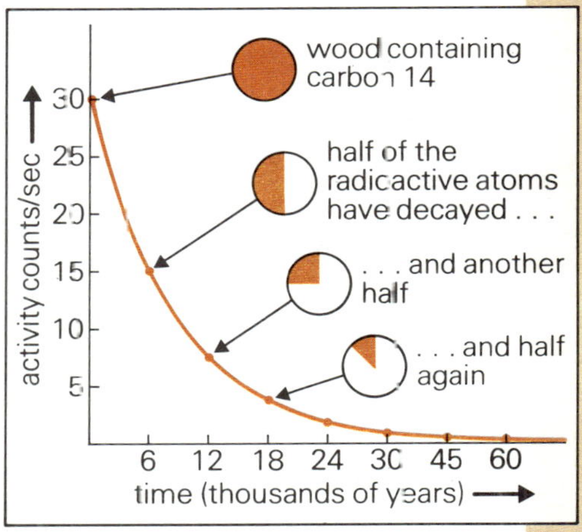

A decay curve of carbon 14.

1 How did the new model of the atom help chemists work out the order of the elements?

2
a What is an α-particle?
b Radon decays emitting an α-particle. What element does radon change into as it decays?
c This element also decays emitting an α-particle. What new element is formed?

3 An ore of uranium was found to contain impurities that did not come from the surrounding rocks and minerals.
a How do you think the impurities came to be there?
b What do you think the impurities might be?

4 An element used to be defined as 'a pure substance containing only one kind of atom'.
a Why is this definition wrong?
b Write a more accurate definition.

5 The carbon 14 in the wooden handle of an axe found in Egypt decayed at the rate of 13 counts per minute. When new, the handle would have given a count of about 20 a minute. Estimate how old the handle is. (Carbon 14 has a half life of 6000 years.)

11.5 Nuclear energy

Splitting apart

Radioisotopes (known as **parents**) usually decay to form a new element, called a **daughter**. Sometimes radioisotopes decay much more dramatically – literally splitting apart! This kind of decay is called **fission** and produces *two* daughters.

All radioactive decays release energy and fission can release *large* amounts of energy. Where does this energy come from?

Mass and energy

When scientists measured the mass of the parent atom and the mass of the daughter atoms and other particles produced in a fission reaction, they found there was a *difference* in mass. Mass had 'disappeared' during fission!

Albert Einstein had already shown in his famous equation that *mass and energy are related*:

$$E = mc^2 \text{ (where c is the velocity of light)}$$

Energy (J) = mass (kg) × $(3 \times 10^8)^2$ m/s.

So, a mass loss of 1 gramme would release:

$$\text{Energy} = 0.001 \times (3 \times 10^8)^2 \text{ J}$$
$$= 9 \times 10^{13} \text{ J}.$$

That is enough energy to lift the whole world population 18 metres into the air, at once!

A vast number of nuclei would have to be split apart to produce a mass loss of 1 gramme. Only a few of the heaviest radioisotopes split apart *naturally* – and they only do so occasionally. But if a fast-moving particle, such as a neutron, smashes into the nucleus of some heavy radioisotopes, the nucleus will split apart immediately. This is used to *make* fission reactions happen and is called **induced fission**. It produces energy in nuclear reactors – and in the atom bomb.

Uncontrolled energy

The atom bomb contains the radioisotope, uranium 235. When a neutron smashes into an atom of U-235, the nucleus splits apart ejecting fast-moving neutrons. In a *large* enough piece of *pure* U-235, some of these neutrons are likely to smash into *other* U-235 atoms – splitting the nuclei and releasing more neutrons. The **chain reaction** continues, releasing an enormous amount of energy in a fraction of a second – a nuclear explosion.

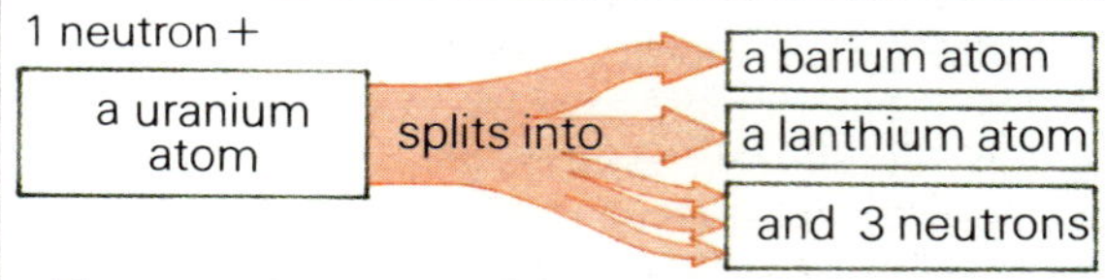

The actual masses of these atoms are

$^{235}_{92}$U = 235.091 $^{148}_{57}$La = 148.0 M $^{85}_{35}$Br = 84.9

$^{1}_{0}$n = 1.009

mass measured in atomic mass units

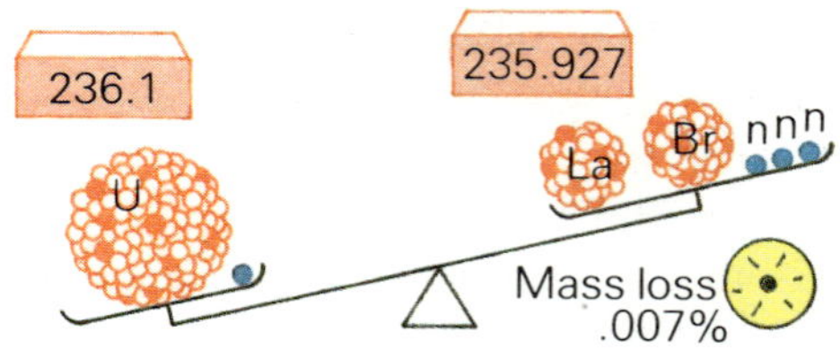

Mass has disappeared and energy has appeared

This energy can be used.
This kinetic energy is produced in the form of movement energy, electromagnetic rays and can be used to produce heat energy

The neutrons ejected from atoms can smash into other atoms

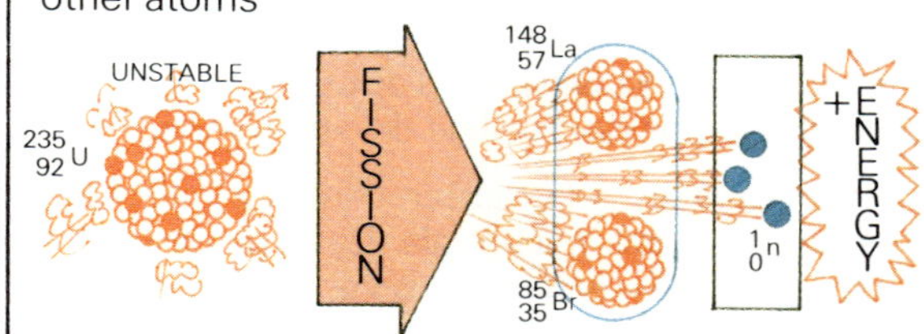

If *enough* uranium atoms are *close* together . . . .

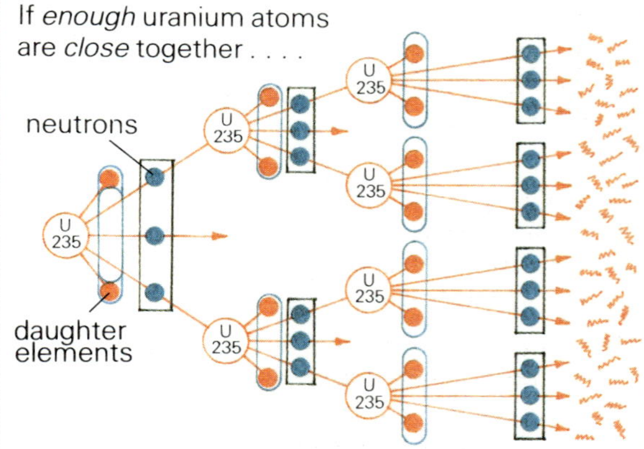

. . . the neutrons ejected as each uranium atom decays can smash into other atoms causing them to break apart in a *chain reaction*. This chain reaction can release all of the energy in a fraction of a second . . . a *nuclear explosion*!

The energy of stars

The matter and energy in radioactive materials originated deep inside stars. Indeed, all the matter around you – and all the matter you are made of! – was produced by nuclear reactions in stars. These reactions also produce all the energy we receive from the Sun. *Heavy* nuclei are needed for fission, yet young stars contain mainly *light* nuclei, such as hydrogen and helium nuclei. So what are *these* nuclear reactions?

At the very high temperatures and pressures inside stars, nuclei join together or *fuse* in a reaction called **nuclear fusion**. This produces the nuclei of heavier atoms – and, usually, other particles and energy.

In any nuclear reaction – fusion or fission – energy is only released if mass is lost.

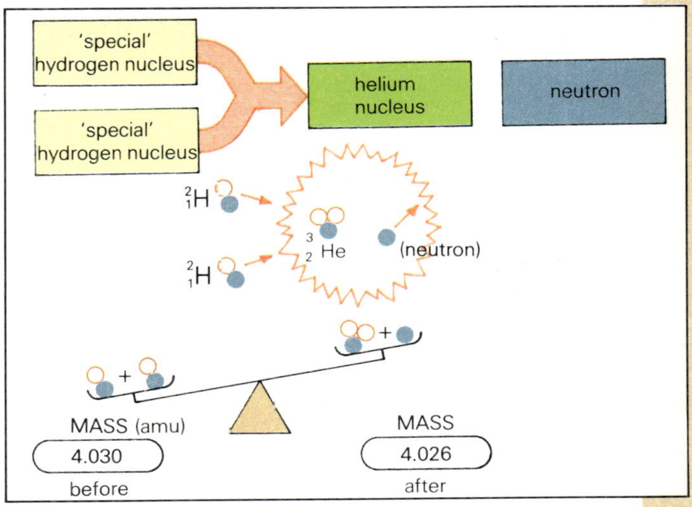

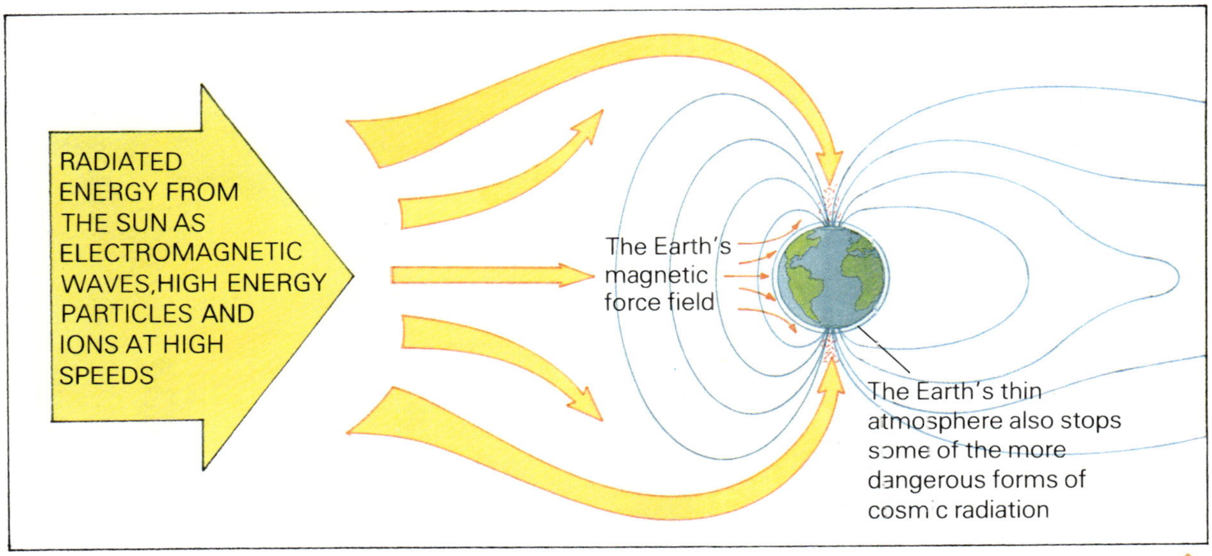

The Earth's cosmic protector

Nearly all the energy we use on Earth comes from the Sun's radiations. But the Sun and other stars also emit dangerous **cosmic radiation** – streams of charged particles or ions.

We are protected by the **Earth's magnetic field**, which deflects away much of the cosmic radiation. The protection is greatest at the equator, where the magnetic field is furthest from the Earth's surface. Near the poles, the radiation and magnetic field interact to produce light energy known as the **aurora**.

The ions that do enter the atmosphere smash into atoms forming radioisotopes – and some of these reach you. For example, cosmic radiation produces the radioisotope carbon 14. This mixes with the carbon in the air. Every living organism takes in carbon from the air, so every animal and plant contains some carbon 14.

Where the magnetic field dips towards the Earth's surface, charged particles enter our atmosphere – with devastating and brilliant effect.

1 What is a 'daughter' element?

2 In a nuclear reactor, 2 kg of radioactive material may be 'lost'. How much energy would this release?

3 What are the differences between nuclear fission and nuclear fusion? In what ways are they similar?

11.6

Radiation and health

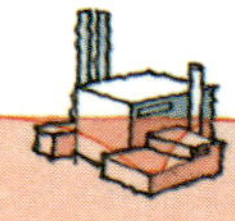

Long-lasting radioactivity

Nuclear fission, whether in a nuclear reactor or an atom bomb, produces radioactive daughters. Each of these will decay – and may decay to another radioisotope, forming a radioactive series. So fission results in a huge mixture of radioisotopes.

This table shows some of the radioisotopes produced by fission. Each emits one or more of the radiations α, β and γ – and these can damage living organisms. As you can see from their half lives, some will emit radiation for a very long time.

Isotope	Half life	Radiation emitted	Used by body
thorium $^{234}_{90}$Th	24 days	α	–
thorium $^{230}_{90}$Th	80 000 yrs	α	–
radon $^{220}_{86}$Rn	52 sec.	α	no but can be breathed in
plutonium $^{239}_{94}$Po	24 400 yrs	α	no but can be breathed in
iodine $^{131}_{53}$I	8.07 days	βγ	yes into thryroid gland
strontium $^{90}_{38}$Sr	28.1 yrs	βγ	yes into bones

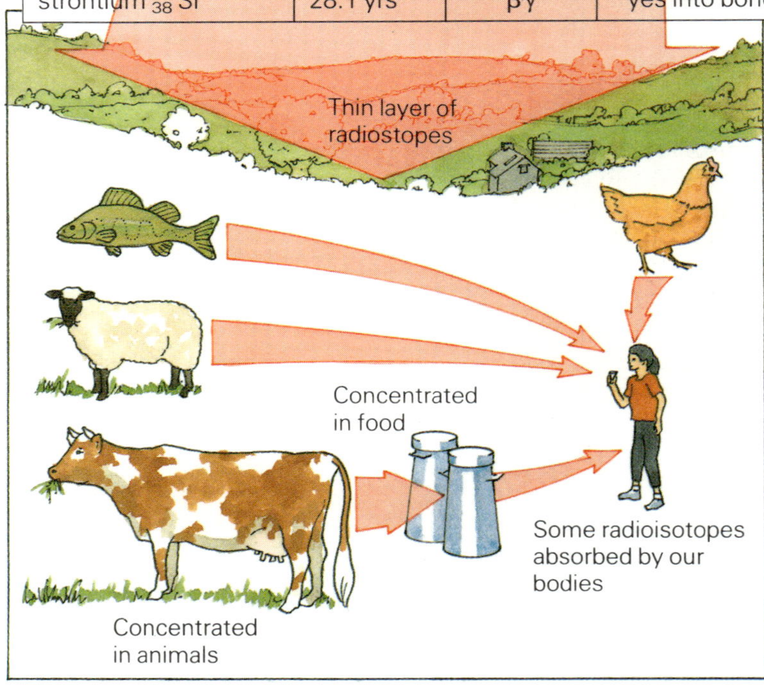

Radiation can become concentrated by passing through our food chain and then into our food.

Homing in on the body

Both α and β radiations seldom travel more than 1 metre and are stopped by paper or foil. Like light, γ radiation spreads out and loses its intensity the further away you are. So radioactive materials are safe if you stay away from them. The trouble is – you can't!

Many elements are absorbed by your body. Iodine is used in your thyroid gland. Strontium is used to make bones. Other elements are used in chemical processes in your cells. Just as carbon 14 is taken in along with stable carbon, your body may absorb radioisotopes of any element it needs.

Damaging cells

Radiation can damage the atoms used to make living cells. This damage can usually be repaired by your body, if it does not involve massive numbers of cells. But if the **genes** in cells are damaged, the cells can change or *mutate*, and some may become cancerous.

The different kinds of radiation vary in the extent or **quality (Q)** of the damage they cause. The α-radiation is thought to be the most damaging and has a Q value of 20. It is a stream of relatively large particles – helium nuclei – that collide with atoms and molecules, stripping electrons away to produce ions. The much smaller β particles and γ radiation are much less likely to collide with atoms and so are thought to be less dangerous. They both have a Q value of 1.

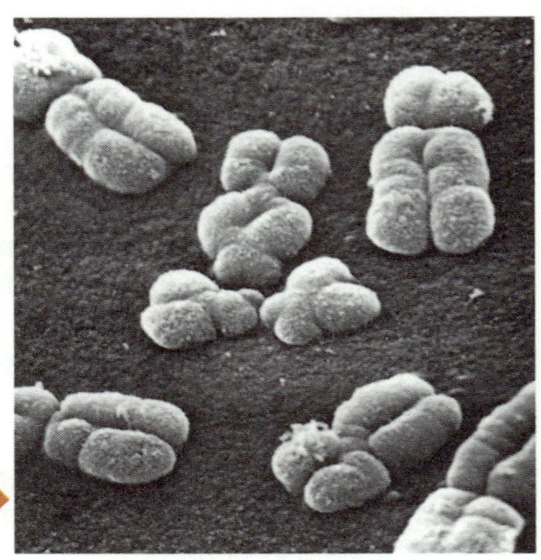

These irregular chromosome shapes show how the 'genetic message' of a cell can be altered by radiation. The cell may then develop into a different, possibly cancerous, cell.

YOU CAN READ MORE ABOUT GENES AND GENETIC DAMAGE ON SPREAD 10.11.

Measuring the damage

The more radiation we receive, the greater the risk of damage, so it is important that we keep a check on it. The amount of radiation – the number of radioactive decays per second – is measured in **becquerels (Bq)**. One Bq is equal to 1 radioactive decay per second.

But how much damage will the radiation cause? To find this out, we need to work out the amount of radiation *energy* absorbed by our bodies. This depends on the *quality*, Q, of the radiation and the amount of energy (J) received by a kilogram (kg) of flesh (measured in **greys, Gr**). This gives the **radiation dose** measured in **sieverts (Sv)**:

$$1\ \text{Sv} = 1\ \text{Gr} \times \text{Q}$$

In one year the average person should *not* receive more than about 0.005 Sv.

situation	dose (Sv)	effects
treatment of	100	cells *destroyed*
tumour/cancer	10	
accident/war	1	cells damaged
	.1	(short term)
maximum allowed	.01	possibility of
in industry		cancer
		(long term)
natural radiation	.001	
(1 yr)		
chest X-ray	.0001	
holiday in area of	.00001	possibility of
granite rock	.000001	genetic change
		(affecting future
		generations)

Even very low doses of radiation may cause genetic change, which can appear after many generations.

Are you getting your sieverts?

Radiation is all around you – and not just from nuclear reactors and atom bombs. Radioactive materials have been present in the Earth since its formation. Cosmic radiation continually bombards the atmosphere forming more radioisotopes.

All these radioactive sources produce **background radiation.** You are subjected to background radiation all the time. The amount of radiation you actually receive will depend on, for example, where you live, your occupation, your lifestyle and what you eat.

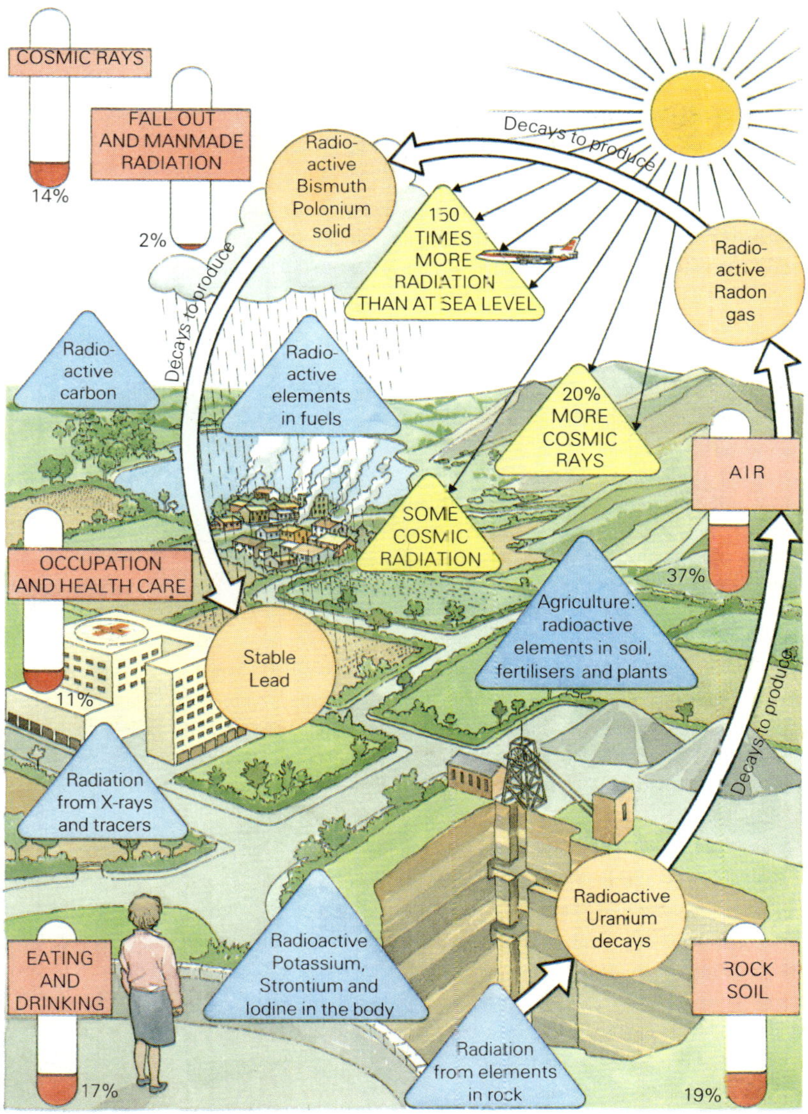

1 'The problem with the atom bomb isn't the blast'. Do you agree? Give reasons for your answer.

2 Draw a pie chart to show the amounts of background radiation we receive from different sources.

3 An accident at a distant nuclear power plant has released radioisotopes into the environment. Using the information on the opposite page, write an article for a local newspaper, explaining how the accident could affect people in *your* area.

Putting radioactivity to work

Using radiation

Radiation can also help us in many ways, and radioisotopes are widely used in medicine and in industry. Few naturally occurring radioisotopes are available in useful quantities. So artificial radioisotopes are usually used. These are made in a nuclear reactor, or with the help of a **particle accelerator**.

Often, a radioisotope emitting a particular type of radiation is needed. This is because the three types of radiation, α, β and γ, have different properties and so are used for different jobs.

Consider the properties of the different radiations and the three examples of uses shown below. Decide which of the types of radiation could be used in each example.

A particle accelerator, such as this proton synchrotron, provides a beam of high-energy particles. Firing these at a material causes nuclear reactions and produces radioisotopes.

Type of radiation	α	β	γ
penetration	Blocked by paper or human skin	Can pass through paper. Blocked by aluminium foil	Can pass through thick lead sheet
danger to health (ionisation)	Highly ionising – can cause a lot of damage	Moderately ionising – causes some damage	Poorly ionising – causes relatively little damage

Some of the properties of radiation.

Using radiation to check welded metal joints.

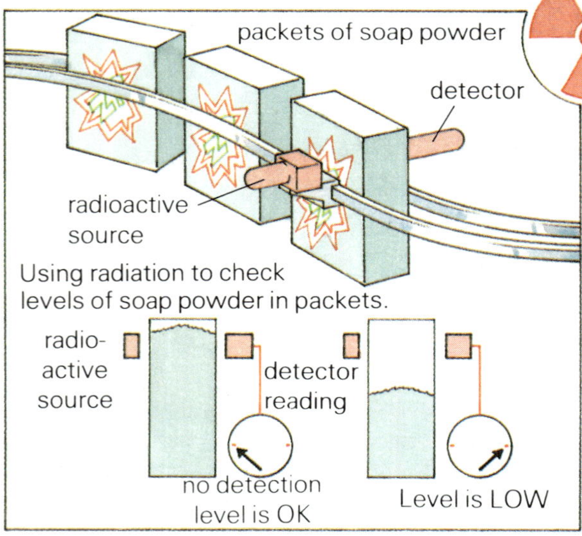

Using radiation to check levels of soap powder in packets.

Using tiny amounts of radioisotopes added to fluid in pipes to trace leaks underground.

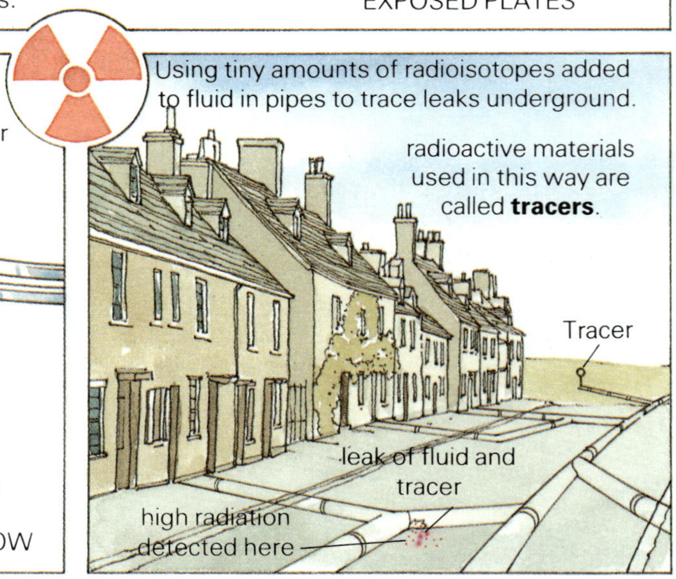

Tracing faults

Very tiny amounts of radioactive materials can be detected by the radiations they emit. So a tiny amount of a radioisotope of a substance *mixed with* the substance can act like a tag or label. It allows you to *trace* what is happening to the substance. Radioisotopes used in this way are called **tracers**.

Tracers are used in medicine to diagnose illnesses. Many substances need to move around the body and be absorbed properly for us to be healthy. A fault can cause illness and tracers help identify the fault. For example, this woman *may* have a blood clot forming in her leg – but has she? Injecting a tracer of a substance that will be taken up by any clot provides the answer. A radiation detector finds the location of the tracer – and the blood clot, which can then be treated.

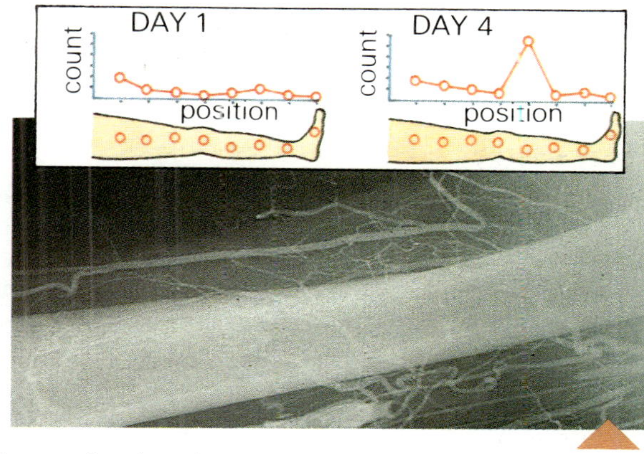

The graphs show how the radioactivity levels change as the tracer is taken up by the clot. The clot is shown as the white blob below the bone.

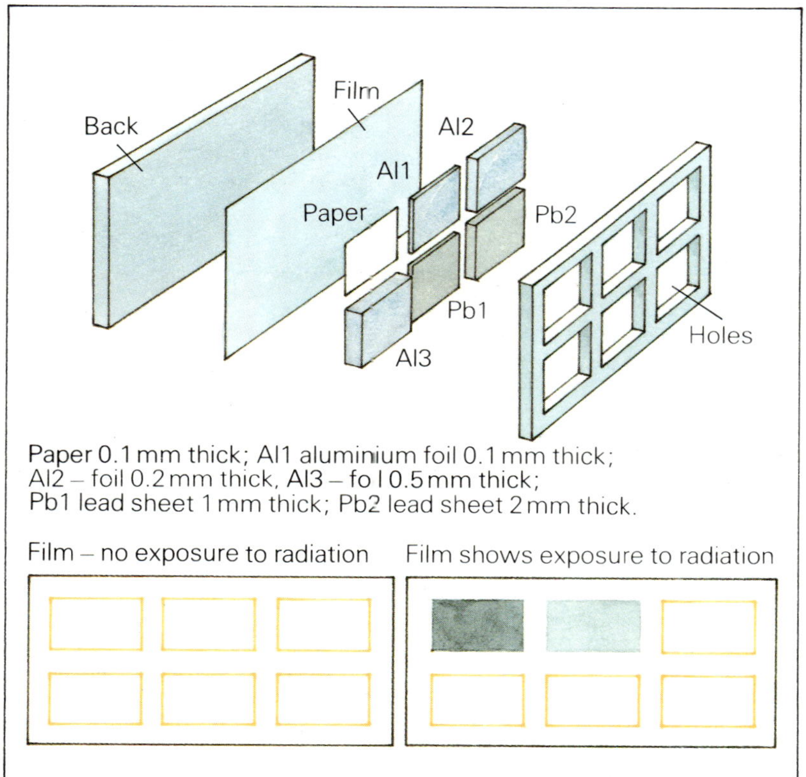

Radiation safety

People who work with radioactive materials – in nuclear power stations, in industry and in medicine – may receive too much radiation. Their exposure to radiation must be carefully and continuously checked. This is done using Becquerel's old idea of the photographic plate as a detector. Each person wears a **film badge** all the time they are at work. The film shows the *amount* and *type* of any radiation the person has received. The film in the badge is checked and replaced at regular intervals.

Look at the exposed film from a badge. What type of radiation has this person been exposed to?

1 The radioisotopes used in schools have to be stored in locked and sealed, lead-lined containers. These are low-level radiation sources – that is they emit fairly low amounts of radiation. Why do you think such precautions have to be taken?

2 What kind of radiation could you use to check the amount of powder being stored in metal tins in a factory? How would you use it?

3 The radioactive substances used as tracers in medical tests, usually:

are low-level radiation sources;
have a short half-life;
are β or γ emitters.

Why do you think this is so?

4 Stone pillars in Greek temples were pinned *inside* with iron rods. These rods eventually rusted and must now be located and replaced. How would it be possible to find the positions of the iron rods without destroying the pillars?

Changing energy

Easy energy

The amount of electrical energy that we consume has increased steadily since supplies were first introduced. At a touch of a switch, electrical energy provides light, heat, and energy for appliances, communication, transport and industry. If you want a hot bath you only need to flick a switch and then turn a tap. The ease and versatility of this form of energy has made electrical energy more and more popular.

. . . . all this just to have a hot bath.

All for one

We used to use energy in a variety of forms – the heat energy of coal drove steam engines, the kinetic energy of water turned millstones. Now we use few energy sources *directly*. Instead, coal, fast-moving water and other energy sources are used to make electricity in **power stations**. The generation of electrical energy has become a huge industry in itself.

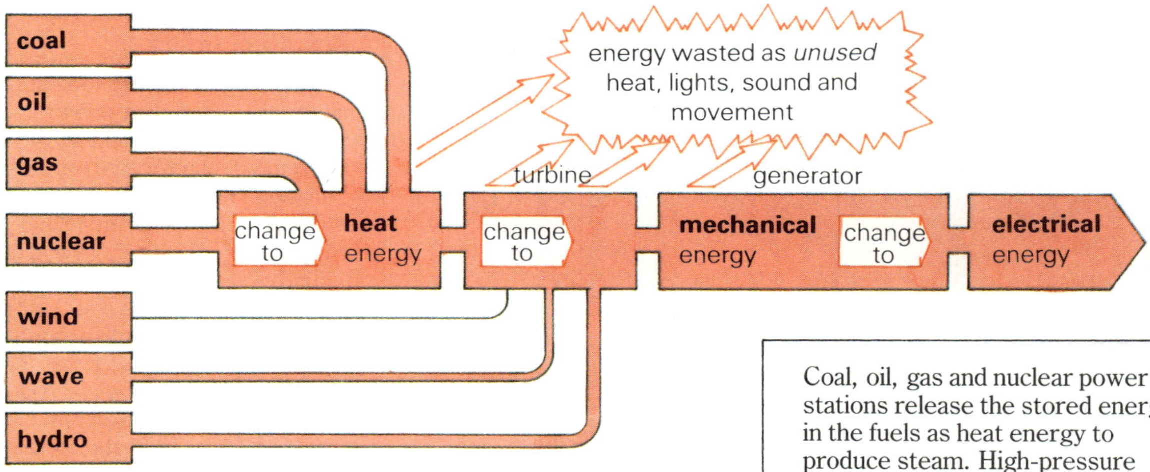

Coal, oil, gas and nuclear power stations release the stored energy in the fuels as heat energy to produce steam. High-pressure steam then turns a turbine, which drives a generator.

The energy in the wind, upland water and waves is used to turn turbines *directly*.

Changing the energy in different sources into electrical energy is very inefficient. Each time energy changes from one form to another, some energy is 'lost' to the environment. Which sources require more energy changes than the others?

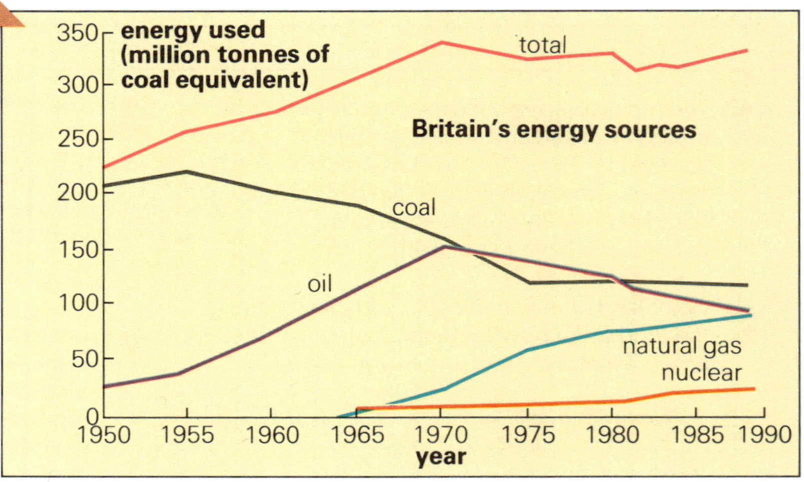

This graph shows the changes in the energy sources used in Britain for producing electricity.

Choices

Each method of producing energy has its advantages and disadvantages. Study the information on this page and then answer the questions below.

Fossil fuel power station

Oil is easier to transport and burns more efficiently than coal.

The new generating companies may import cheap coal to increase profits.

If we continue to use fossil fuels at the present rate, they will run out in a few hundred years.

More coal can be obtained but at a cost – using opencast mines.

Coal is a very rich source of chemicals we need.

Oil is needed to produce petrol, diesel and many other important chemicals.

Gas is more efficiently used directly for heating than to produce electrical energy.

Gas supplies are relatively small and difficult to find.

Burning coal produces acid gases that cause acid rain.

Acid rain kills animals and plants in forests, lakes and streams.

Burning fossil fuels produces carbon dioxide which is worsening global warming.

Nuclear power station

Nuclear energy produces heat energy more efficiently than fossil fuel burners.

Nuclear fuels could last for thousands of years.

Radioactive waste is difficult to store and must be kept safely contained for thousands of years.

Nuclear power stations can cause widespread pollution when accidents occur (e.g. Sellafield, Chernobyl).

Nuclear fusion could be the best way to produce all our energy.

To produce large-scale electricity from nuclear fusion energy much more research will be needed.

Wind/hydroelectric power station

Geothermal, wind, wave and water power do not cause chemical pollution.

Geothermal energy is easy to use – but is available in large quantities mainly in volcanic areas.

Geothermal energy will be produced as long as the Earth's core is active.

Solar energy can produce large-scale electrical energy in countries which are *sunny* for most of the year.

Hydroelectricity is important in countries with upland mountainous areas.

Building dams, tidal barrages and wind farms can damage the natural habitats of many rare animals and plants.

Developing the best ways of producing electrical energy from wind, wave or solar energy is likely to be very expensive.

Many of the world's power stations are like this one – they use fossil fuels. Will this still be so in the future?

1 Why do you think the use of electrical energy has increased?

2 How are the different energy sources used to produce electrical energy?

3 Using the information above, give reasons for the *changes* in Britain's energy sources shown in the graph opposite.

4 If you were in control, what choices would you make? Produce an article, explaining which is 'the best' policy for the government to follow on the production of electrical energy.

YOU CAN READ MORE ABOUT GEOTHERMAL, WAVE AND OTHER SOURCES OF ENERGY ON SPREADS 1.14 AND 7.2.

Nuclear power

Energy from uranium

The reactors in nuclear power stations produce large amounts of energy through the fission of uranium (or plutonium). Natural uranium contains a *small* amount of the *unstable* isotope **uranium 235 (U-235)** mixed with the *more stable* isotope **uranium 238 (U-238)**.

When a neutron collides with an atom of U-235, the nucleus may break apart. This fission releases energy in the form of γ radiation and the kinetic energy of three high-speed neutrons. These neutrons can give up their energy to – and even be absorbed by – other particles they collide with. If a neutron collides with another U-235 nucleus, fission may result – releasing *more* neutrons and energy. Repeated collisions *could* release large amounts of energy – but there is a catch. A neutron is *very unlikely* to hit and cause fission in another U-235 atom.

Uranium occurs naturally, locked up in uranium ore. Sometimes the colourful ore is even found on the surface.

Hit and miss

Uranium metal contains the isotopes U-235 and U-238 in the ratio of 1 to about 141. So a neutron is far more likely to hit a U-238 nucleus. This more stable nucleus will usually absorb the neutron *without* breaking apart. And most neutrons will not be absorbed by a nucleus at all! Such high-speed neutrons are most likely to bounce off the nuclei – or miss them altogether. So how can uranium produce large amounts of energy for us to use?

Isotope	% in natural uranium	stability	when hit by a neutron it is likely to:
$^{235}_{92}U$	0.7	unstable	?
$^{238}_{92}U$	99.3	relatively stable	?

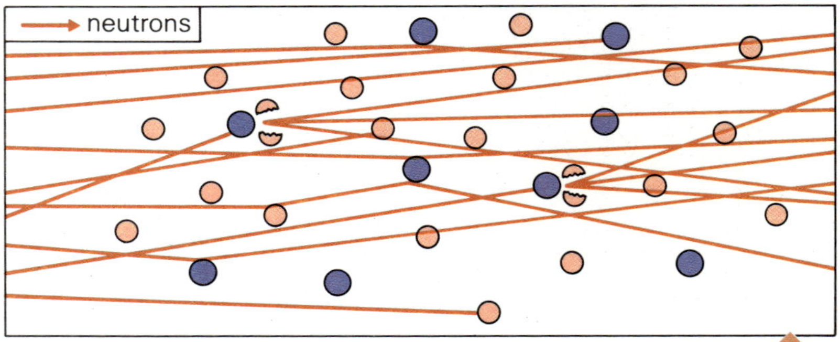

Enriching the uranium increases the energy released.

Increasing the odds

One way is to increase the *amount* of U-235. In **enriched uranium**, the ratio of U-235 to U-238 atoms is 1 to about 40. This enriched uranium is usually stored inside a nuclear reactor in rods called **fuel rods**.

Another way is to slow the neutrons down. Slower neutrons, often called **thermal neutrons**, are much more likely to be absorbed by U-235 nuclei and cause fission. When a high-speed neutron collides with some *small* atoms, such as carbon atoms, the neutron is slowed down slightly *but not absorbed.* Travelling across a 20 cm block of carbon, a neutron can have as many as 200 collisions – and each one slows down the neutron a bit more. Material such as carbon used to reduce or *moderate* the speed of neutrons in this way is called a **moderator**.

A nuclear reactor may use enriched uranium or moderator – or both – to increase the chances of collision between neutrons and U-235 nuclei. But if the odds are increased too much, the fission will get *out of control* – and result in a nuclear explosion.

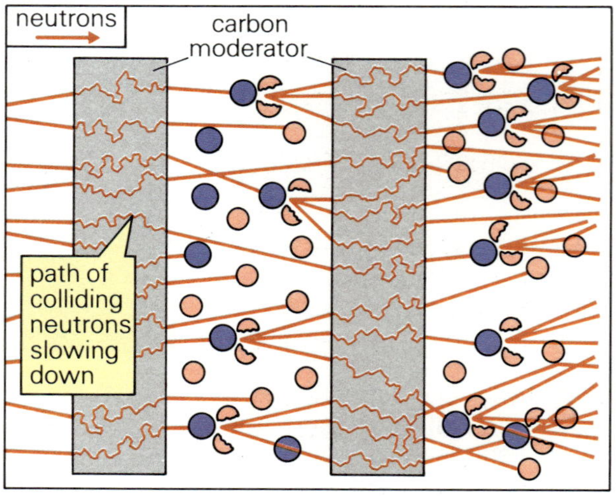

A moderator also increases the chances of fission. More energy and neutrons are released – which can build up into a dangerous chain reaction.

Fixing the odds

To avoid a dangerous chain reaction, *one* neutron from each fission should cause *one* other U-235 nucleus to split. The reaction can then continue steadily, releasing large amounts of energy in a *controlled* way. Steel rods coated with a material (such as boron) that *absorbs* neutrons allow us to control the rate of fission. The position of these **control rods** is adjusted to keep the rate steady. For example, if the chain reaction is going too fast, the control rods are lowered into the core to absorb the excess neutrons.

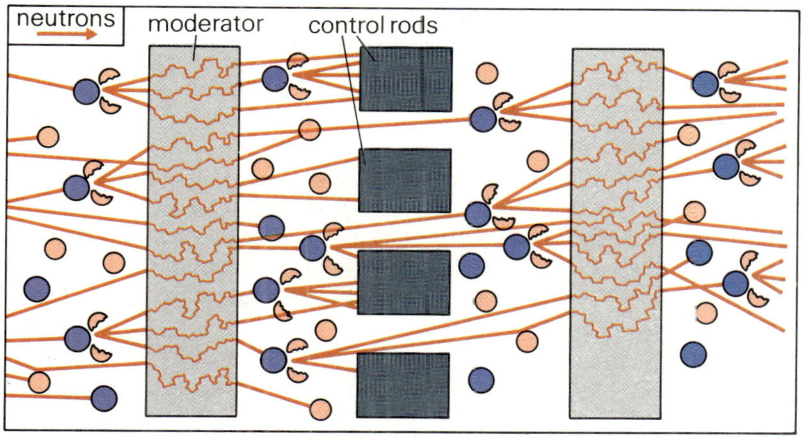

The control rods are raised and lowered so that they absorb as many neutrons as necessary to make the reaction safe.

A reactor core.

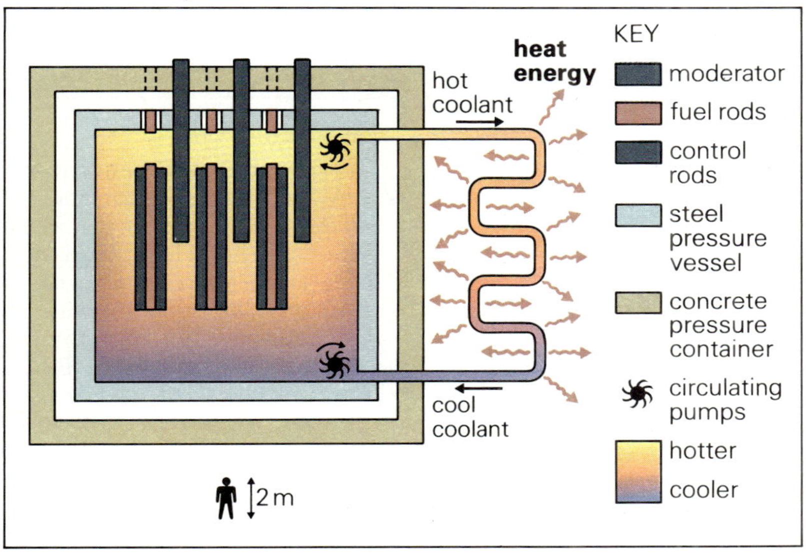

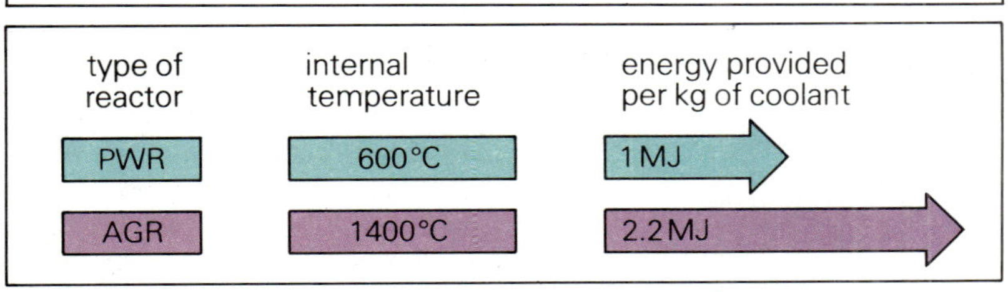

The hotter the core, the more effective the reactor.

The hotter the better?

Fission releases energy in the form of **heat** and the core of the reactor becomes hot. This heat energy is carried away by a gas or liquid known as a **coolant**, and used to generate electricity. But during the transfer much of the heat – up to two-thirds – is lost to the environment!

There are many different *designs* of nuclear reactor. How effective each one is depends on the temperature of its core. The hotter the core (and coolant), the more heat energy is transferred to produce electricity. For example, the **Advanced Gas Cooled Reactor (AGR)** is more effective than the **Pressurised Water Reactor (PWR)**. The gas coolant leaves the hotter AGR core at a temperature of about 650°C, while the PWR's coolant (water under pressure) leaves the core at about 400°C.

The greater effectiveness does have a cost. All the materials used in the AGR have to be able to withstand the much higher temperatures. And higher temperatures inside reactors can mean greater dangers. So is it the hotter, the better?

1 What is likely to happen to:
a a U-235 nucleus
b a U-238 nucleus
when hit by a high-speed neutron?

2 What is the purpose of a moderator in a nuclear reactor, and how does it work?

3 **a** How do control rods help to make a reactor safe?
b What properties must the control rods in an AGR reactor have?

4 The coolant circulates round the core, absorbing and transferring heat. What properties do you think a coolant must have?

5 At normal pressure, water boils at 100°C. Yet in the PWR, the water coolant reaches a temperature of 400°C.
a Explain how this is possible
b What safety problems might this cause?

11.10 Converting to electricity

Changing forms of energy

Nuclear power stations convert nuclear energy into the electrical energy we can use so easily. This conversion requires a number of stages. During the first stage, the energy stored in nuclear fuel is changed in the core of the reactor to heat energy. At each of the other stages, energy is also changed into a different form – and some energy is lost to the environment.

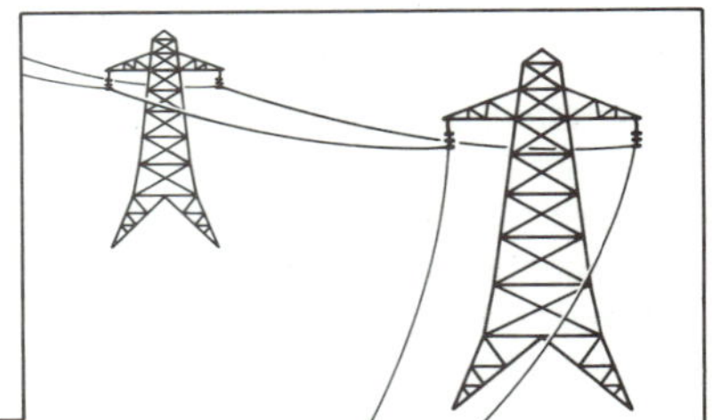

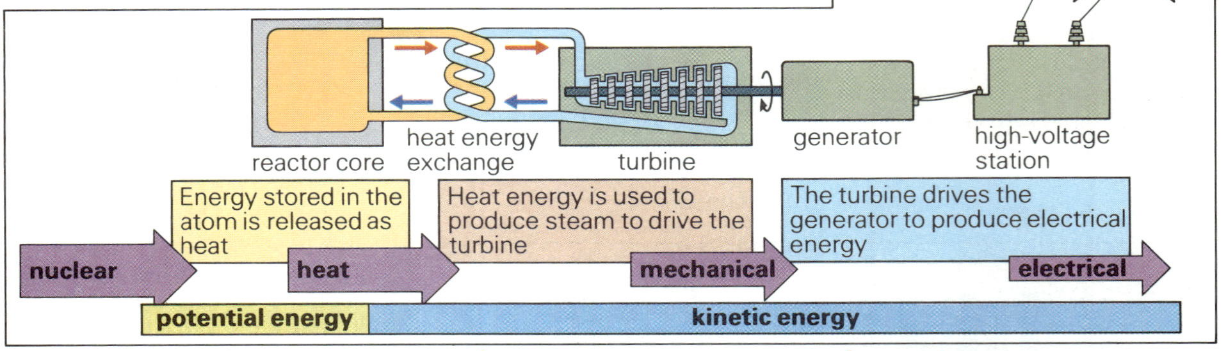

Energy changes in a nuclear power station.

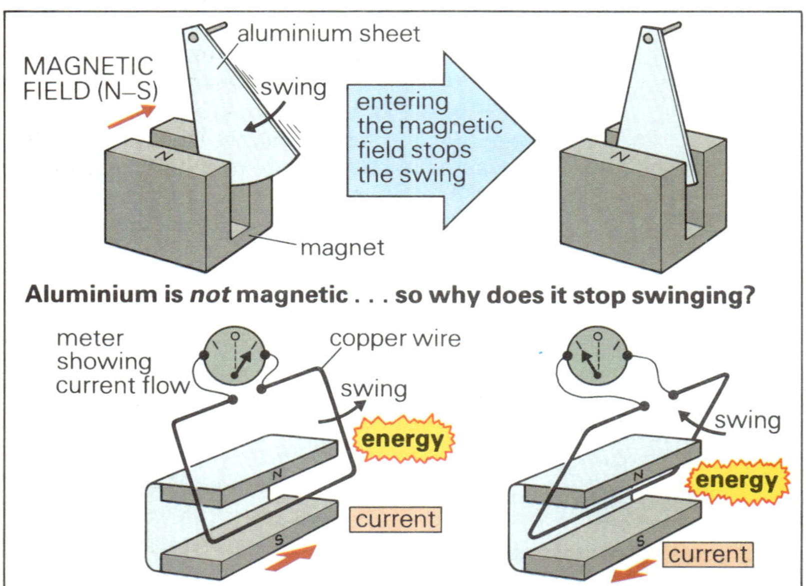
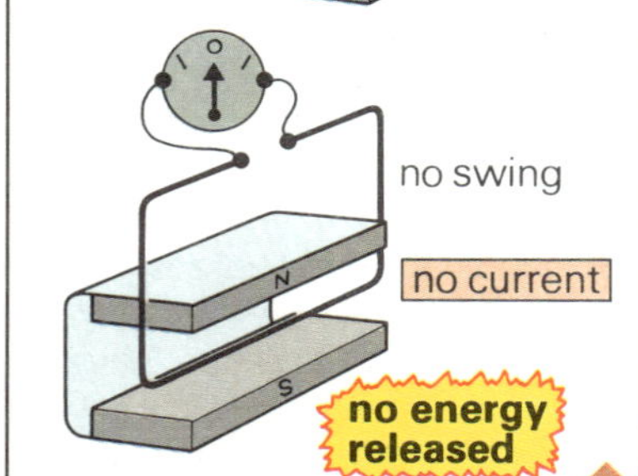

As the wire swings backwards and forwards or alternates, so does the current.

Generating current

In every **electrical generator**, a wire and a magnetic field move *relative to each other*. In the simple generator shown here, this is done by swinging a wire between the poles of a magnet. As the wire moves towards the magnet, it enters the magnet's **force field** – and an electrical current flows in the wire. Whenever a wire and a magnetic field move relative to each other, a current is *induced* in the wire. This is known as **electromagnetic induction**.

The induced current produces its *own* magnetic field. The magnetic force fields of the wire and magnet *oppose* the movement of the wire. Energy is needed to keep the wire moving against these magnetic forces. *Mechanical* energy can keep the wire moving, and so continue to produce *electrical* current in the wire. In this way, mechanical energy is *changed into* electrical energy.

Use Fleming's right-hand rule to check the direction of the current in these diagrams.

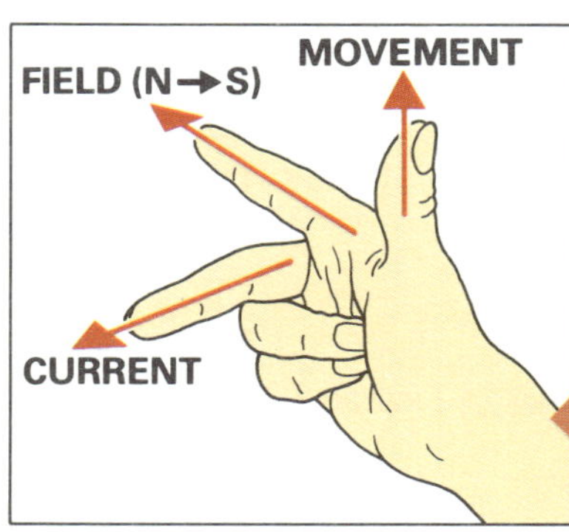

Fleming's right-hand rule. Using this simple rule, you can predict the direction of current flow in a generator.

Investigating induction

In the nineteenth century, a number of scientists investigated electromagnetic induction, including the German Heinrich Lenz and the British scientist Michael Faraday. They tried out different *strengths* of magnetic field and different *speeds* of motion. Each time, they measured the size and direction of the current induced. They explained what they had observed in their **laws of electromagnetic induction.**

Lenz suggested that the induced current always *opposes the motion producing it.* So, as the direction of the motion changes, the direction of the current changes. Faraday described how the size of the induced current changed. He found that the *stronger* the magnetic field or the *faster* the relative motion, the greater the induced current.

As the magnet's movement changes direction, so does the current

As the speed of the movement of the magnet doubles, the size of the current doubles.

It is easier to investigate induction if you use a coil of wire. This increases the size of the induced current – the more turns in the coil, the greater the current.

Faraday's generator.

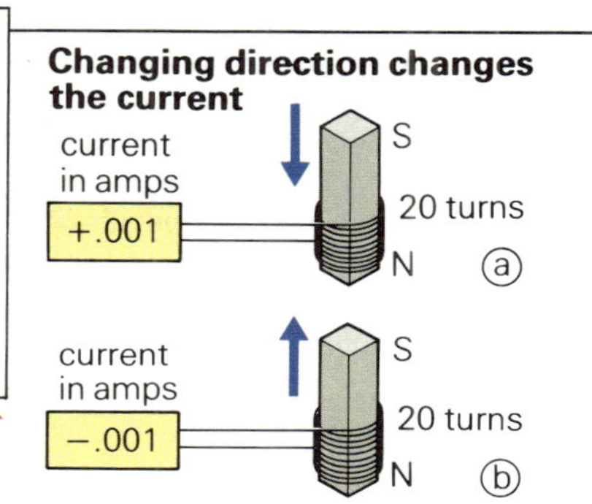

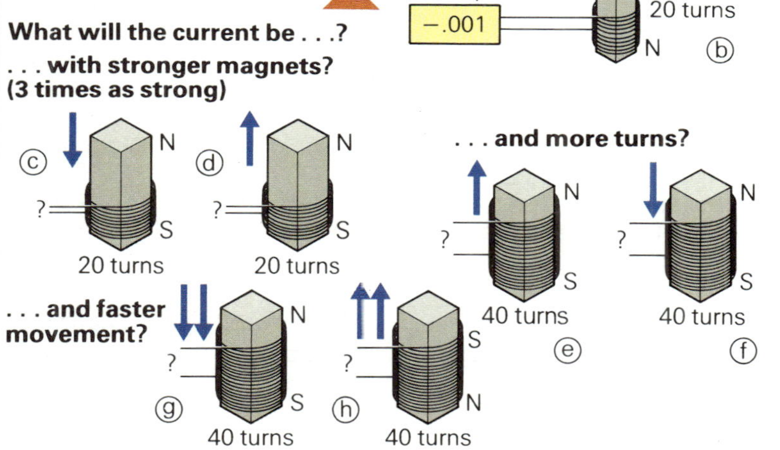

The first electrical generator

Michael Faraday used his ideas to produce the first electrical generator. It contained a coil of wire wound many times with a space in the centre for a magnet. He designed it so that both the magnet *and* the wire moved at the same time. Why do you think he did this?

These diagrams show some investigations into a generator similar to Faraday's. The value of the current recorded in the first two designs are given. Using these, and the ideas on this spread, predict what the values of the current for each of the other designs will be. (The actual values are at the bottom of the page).

1 How is the energy released from a reactor core changed into electrical energy for us to use?

2 What is produced in a wire that passes through a magnetic field? How does this help explain why a sheet of aluminium is stopped as it swings between the poles of a magnet?

3 What factors affect:
a the direction
b the size,
of an induced current.

Values of current (in amperes) for investigations shown above:
C – 0.003, D + 0.003, E + 0.006, F – 0.006, G – 0.012, H – 0.012.

4 Magnetic fields are sometimes produced in the metal of planes flying from Europe to America. But magnetic fields are *not* produced when planes fly south or north. Explain why.

5 Which would require more energy to push it through a magnetic field – a straight wire or a coil of wire? Give reasons for your answer.

6 Design a simple electrical generator that you think you could make at home or at school. It should generate an electrical current for at least one minute. Outline the problems that you think you might face in producing it.

Flowing energy

Losing the flow

Once generated, the electrical energy flows along wires to be distributed to homes and factories. *Enough* energy has to be distributed *safely* to everyone who needs it. For safety, the electricity used in homes should be at a low **voltage** (relative to the ground or **earth** at 0 volts).

The first electricity supplies were sent at a low voltage. Homes close to the supply received electricity at a similar voltage. But the more distant your home, the lower the voltage – and electrical energy –you would receive. This was because the wires connecting the homes had **resistance** to an electrical current – and changed some of the electrical energy into heat energy.

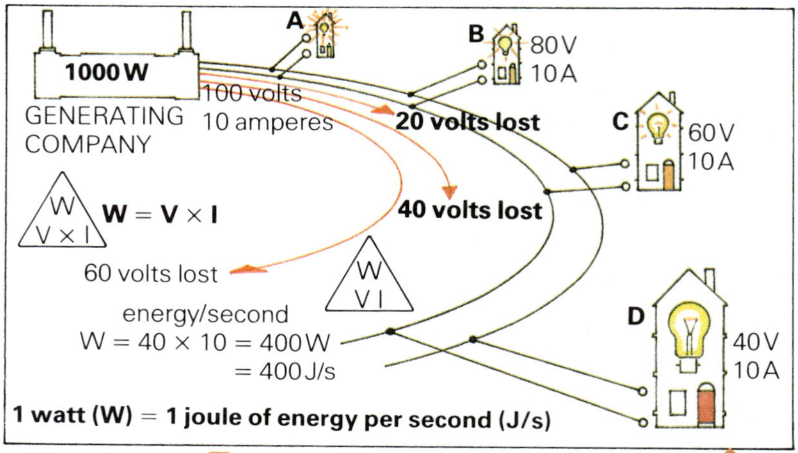

How much energy per second is wasted in delivering electrical energy to home D?
How much energy does each house actually receive?

Voltage drop

Getting *enough* energy to *distant* homes was a problem. Voltage was needed simply to drive current down the wires. The voltage used to drive current against the resistance of connecting wires is called the **voltage drop**.

The voltage drop along each *unit length* of wire depends on the *resistance* of the material the wire is made of and the size of the *current*. The voltage drop from the supply to homes depends also on the *length* of the connecting wire. Nowadays, vast lengths of wire connect your home to your nearest power station – how can you get the electrical energy you need?

V = I × R, where V is the voltage drop in volts (V), I is the current in amperes (A), and R is the resistance in ohms (Ω). Using this, fill in the missing values.
Why do you think the resistance of the wire increases?

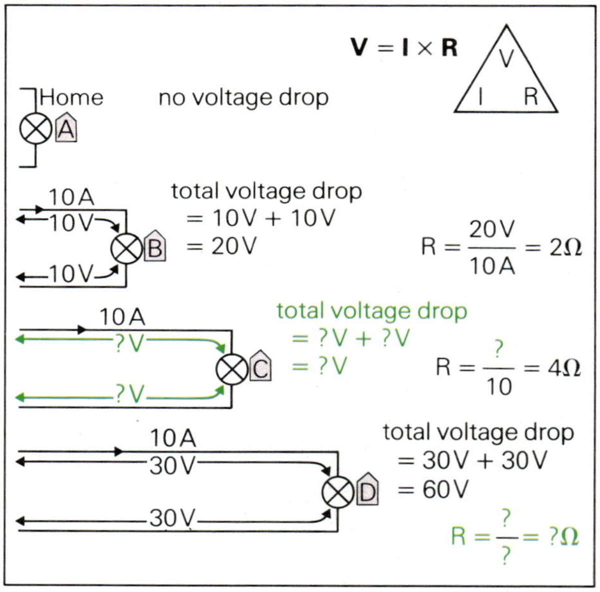

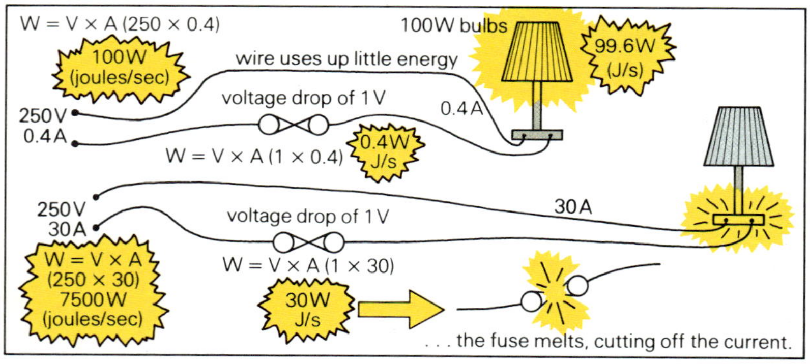

A voltage drop can be useful.

The current problem

To try to get enough energy to distant homes, the initial energy was increased. This meant that a *larger* current flowed, which increased the voltage drop. So more energy was wasted – and as more electrical energy was changed into heat energy, some of the wires started to melt! The early distributors had to find a way of raising the energy sent *and* keeping the current small. How could they do both?

YOU CAN READ MORE ABOUT CURRENT, VOLTAGE AND RESISTANCE ON SPREAD 1.8.

Transforming the problem

Lenz came upon a solution through his work on electromagnetic induction. He knew that when a voltage drives a current along a wire, there is a magnetic field around the wire. Lenz found that when the current (or voltage) *changes*, the magnetic field changes – and induces a voltage across a nearby wire. The **induced voltage** causes an induced current, which always flows in the *opposite* direction to the first or 'primary' current. That is, the induced or **secondary voltage** always *opposes* the **primary voltage** producing it.

Modern electrical distribution systems include **transformers**, which each contain two coils of wire. A voltage in the primary coil induces a voltage in the secondary coil *whenever the primary current (or voltage) changes*. The current can be changed by switching it on or off. It is even easier to use constantly changing **alternating current**. The electricity we receive alternates in current (and voltage) about 50 times per second or 50 **hertz (Hz)**.

Stepping up the voltage

The size of the secondary (induced) voltage depends on the number of turns in the transformers' coils. If both coils have the *same* number of turns, the secondary voltage is the *same* as the primary voltage. If the secondary coil has *double* the turns of the primary coil, the secondary voltage is double the primary voltage. This is used to increase or *step-up* the voltage in a **voltage step-up transformer**.

But how does this help the 'current problem'? The energy per second (**power**) in a wire is given by:

energy per second *in watts* (W) = voltage *in volts* (V) × current *in amps* (A)

Since the *total amount* of energy cannot change, doubling the voltage halves the current. By stepping up to high voltages, the current can be much reduced.

Work out the power (energy per second) in each coil of this transformer. Are they the same?

1 What problems do you think people who depended on the first electrical supplies might have had?

2 **a** What is meant by 'voltage drop'?
b What is the *percentage* drop in voltage if a wire of resistance 0.01 Ω per metre carries a current of 5 A at a voltage of 120 000 V over 2 km?

3 How does a transformer produce a high voltage when a low voltage is connected to it?

4 Why is it better to transmit electrical energy over long distances as high-voltage, low-current electricity?

Placing an iron rod in the coils helps transfer energy from the primary to the secondary coil.

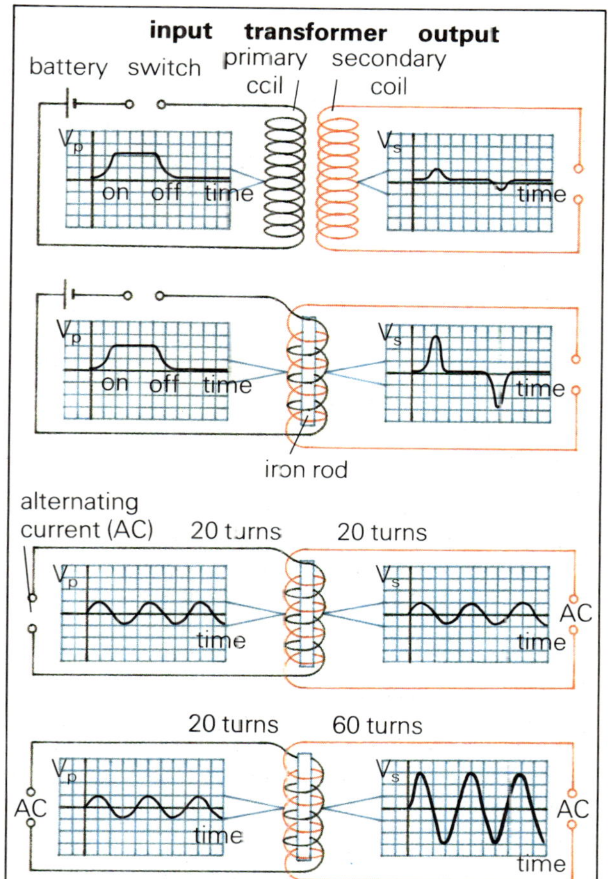

$$\left(\frac{20}{60}\right) \frac{\text{Number of turns (primary) } N_p}{\text{Number of turns (secondary) } N_2} = \frac{\text{voltage IN (primary) } V_p}{\text{voltage OUT (secondary) } V_s} = \left(\frac{2}{6}\right)$$

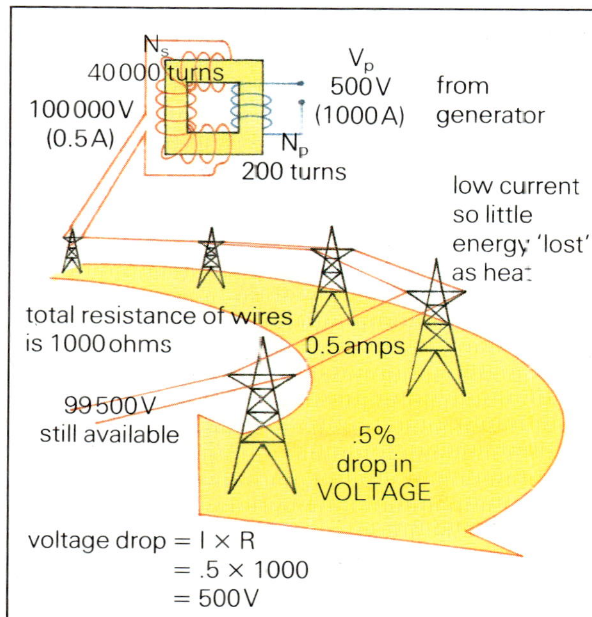

By producing high voltages and low current, transformers reduce voltage drop and energy loss.

11.12 Electricity in your home

Electricity supplies are stepped up in voltage for efficient transmission and then stepped down for use in industry and homes.

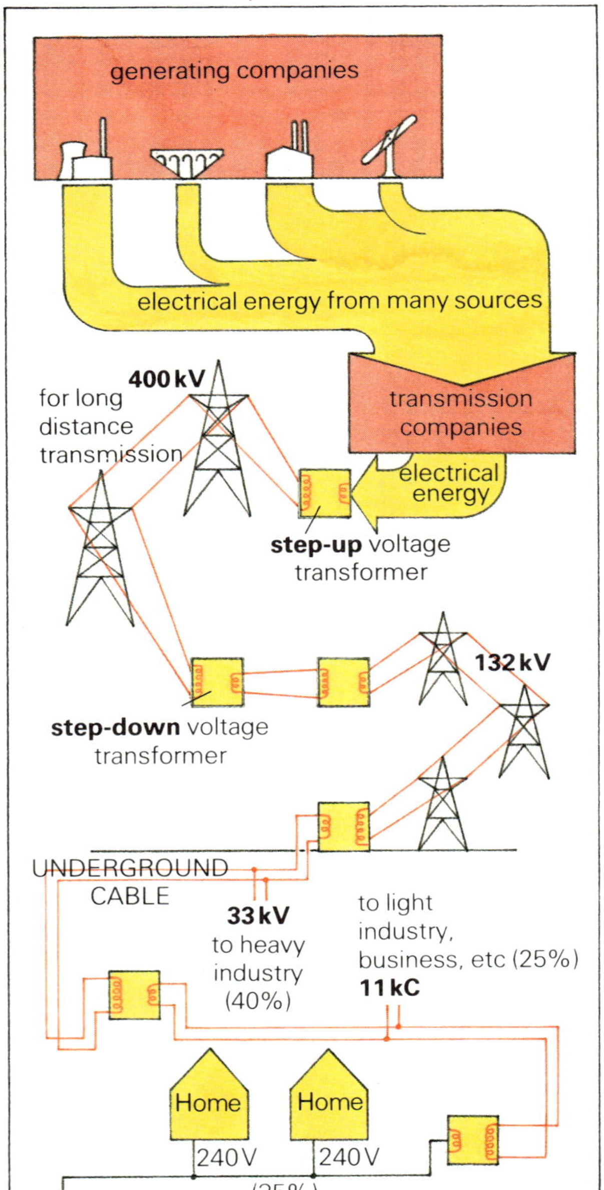

The super grid

Generating companies produce electricity in many different types of power station – hydroelectric, wind, fossil fuel and nuclear. The electricity is bought by other companies, which distribute the electrical energy and re-sell it to us. We use more electricity at home when it is cold, and more in the early mornings and evenings than at other times of day. We even use more energy at half time during the FA Cup final! So we require a supply system that can respond in seconds to large changes in demand.

All the supplies are *interconnected* in a **National Grid**, which allows electrical energy produced in one part of the country to be transferred to any other part. The electricity is transmitted along the grid at very high voltages, and can be switched to wherever it is needed. Step-up transformers *in reverse* act as **step-down transformers**, lowering the voltage to a safer 240 V before the electricity reaches your home.

Connected to your home

Each home is connected to the National Grid through a **consumer unit**. All the **electrical circuits** in your house are connected to this consumer unit. There are usually two kinds of circuit in homes – mains and lighting. The sockets that you plug appliances into are linked by mains circuits or **ring main**. A mains circuit can carry a large enough current to provide the **power** (energy per unit time) for heaters, cookers and other appliances. Lights need relatively little power and a lower current flows round the lighting circuits.

Even the low-voltage electricity used in homes can give you a serious shock or start a fire. An accident could happen if, for example, a fault in a circuit caused too much current to flow. The consumer unit contains **fuses** or **circuit breakers** which cut off electricity to a circuit if there is a surge in current.

The electricity in your home flows through the live and neutral wires. The earthwire is connected to the metal parts of appliances. Any electricity which 'escapes' into an appliance flows down the earth wire to the ground. This safety device has saved many lives.

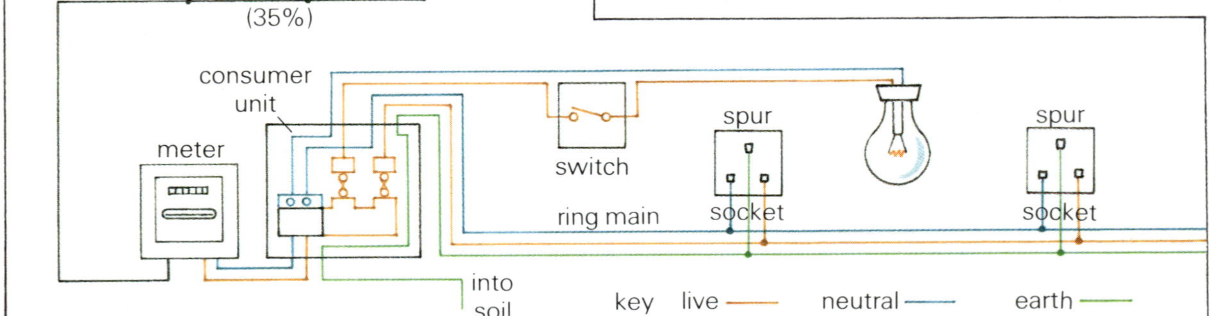

How much energy do you use?

Each electrical appliance in your home needs a certain amount of energy per second to function properly, and this **power rating** is usually shown on the appliance. The power actually delivered depends on the voltage of the electricity and the size of the current. Domestic appliances are *designed* to work at about 240 V. The resistance of an appliance allows *enough* current to flow (*at this voltage*) to provide the power the appliance needs. This table shows the power, current and resistance needed by a number of common appliances.

A fault in an appliance may change its resistance so that too much current flows. To prevent this, each appliance should be protected by a fuse.

You can buy fuses which will allow up to 1 A, 2 A, 3 A, 5 A, 7 A, 9 A, 13 A, 15 A or 30 A current to flow. Which fuse should you use for each of the appliances in the table?

APPLIANCE	Bulb	Refrigerator	T.V B/W	T.V colour	Drill	Iron	Toaster	Cooker	Immersion heater
voltage (volts) V	250	250	250	250	250	250	250	250	250
power (watts) W = **energy per second** (joules/sec)	60	150	200	350	400	800	1000 (1 kW)	?	7000 (7 kW)
current I (amperes) A (W / V I)	.24	.6	.8	?	1.6	3.2	4	20	28
resistance R (ohms) (approximate) (V / I R)	1041	416	312	178	?	78	62	12	9

W, V, I and R are interconnected. If you know two of these values, you can work the others out. What are missing values in this table?

What do you pay?

The electricity to your home passes through a meter which records the energy used. The number of joules of energy per second (watts, W) consumed in homes is inconveniently large. So the energy is measured in a unit called the **kilowatt hour (kWhr)**. This is the same as 1000 joules of energy per second being used for one hour – a total of 3,600,000 joules! The meter is read four times a year and each kWhr used is charged for on your electricity bill.

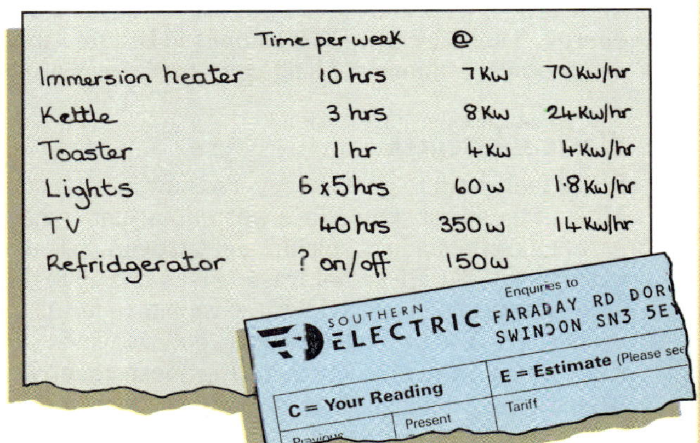

What power do you use . . . and have to pay for?

1 When you switch on a bulb it lights up immediately. How does the energy get to the bulb?

2 What is the difference between a step-up voltage transformer and step-down voltage transformer?

3 A current of 1000 A can flow at a voltage of 240 V. How much energy per second would this provide? What current would have to flow in the 400 kV long-distance transmission lines to provide this amount of energy?

4 The electrical circuits in your home have a number of safety features to protect you. What are they and how do they work?

5 Work out where the energy goes in your home.
- **a** Make a list of the appliances you have at home.
- **b** Find the power rating of each one (unplug the appliance first!)
- **c** Estimate how long each appliance is in use over one week.
- **d** Calculate the cost of this use if 1 kWhr costs 6p.
- **e** Which appliances cost the most?

6 How could you reduce the amount of energy used in your home? List as many ways as you can.

YOU CAN READ MORE ABOUT FUSES AND PAYING FOR ELECTRICITY ON SPREAD 1.10.

The cost of electricity

Resources to burn?

The more electricity you use, the higher the cost to you – and to the planet. Generating electricity makes our lives much easier, but it is very wasteful of the planet's resources. Although power stations are designed to produce electrical energy, fossil fuels and nuclear power stations actually produce *more* energy *in other forms*. At each stage of the conversion to electricity, some energy is changed into unwanted forms – light, vibration and, mainly, heat energy. In most power stations, only about 35% of the original energy is converted into electrical energy. So, each time *you* use electrical energy to power an appliance, *about twice as much energy is being wasted!*

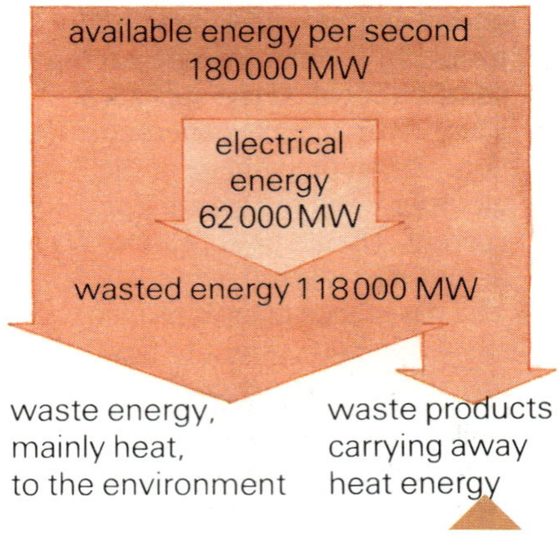

Over 65% of the energy used in a power station may be wasted. In a fossil fuel power station, some of the waste energy will be carried away by waste gases.

Waste heat

Most of the unused or **waste heat** energy is lost to the environment directly. For example, power stations often pump hot water directly into streams and rivers. This increases the temperature of the water, which can have dramatic effects on living organisms. Some rivers near power stations even contain large numbers of freshwater, tropical fish!

Instead of being wasted, this heat energy *can* be used. Many countries have built **combined heat and power (CHP)** stations. These provide heat energy for nearby homes and industry *as well as* electrical energy. There are few CHP stations in Britain – most of our power stations are built *away from* urban areas.

The heat in this geothermal power station is used twice – first to drive turbines, then hot water is pumped 27 km along the big pipe to the nearest town. Any power station could re-use its heat this way.

Waste substances

Fossil fuels burn to give energy *and* new substances. Most of these substances are wasted, including the gaseous compounds of sulphur and nitrogen (released mainly by coal). These hot waste gases rise up in the atmosphere and dissolve in water vapour to form weak acids. The prevailing north-westerly winds carry this **acid rain** to northern European countries, where it falls, damaging the land, vegetation and water systems.

This lake is so polluted by acid rain that alkaline lime must be added to neutralise the acid.

The infra-red trap

Burning fossil fuels also produce **carbon dioxide**. The huge quantities of this gas released by fossil fuel power stations are contributing to a very different problem.

The Earth receives energy from the Sun and produces its own heat energy. **Infra-red rays** carry the heat energy from the warm surface of the Earth up into the atmosphere. Some of the heat passes through to outer space, while some infra-red rays are reflected back down by carbon dioxide (and some other gases) in the atmosphere. By trapping some infra-red rays in this way, carbon dioxide and other gases have kept the Earth warm for millions of years. But now the amount of carbon dioxide is increasing, so *more* infra-red rays are being trapped – and the Earth is hotting up.

The trapping of heat energy by gases in the atmosphere is often called 'the greenhouse effect' because glass keeps a greenhouse warm in a similar way.

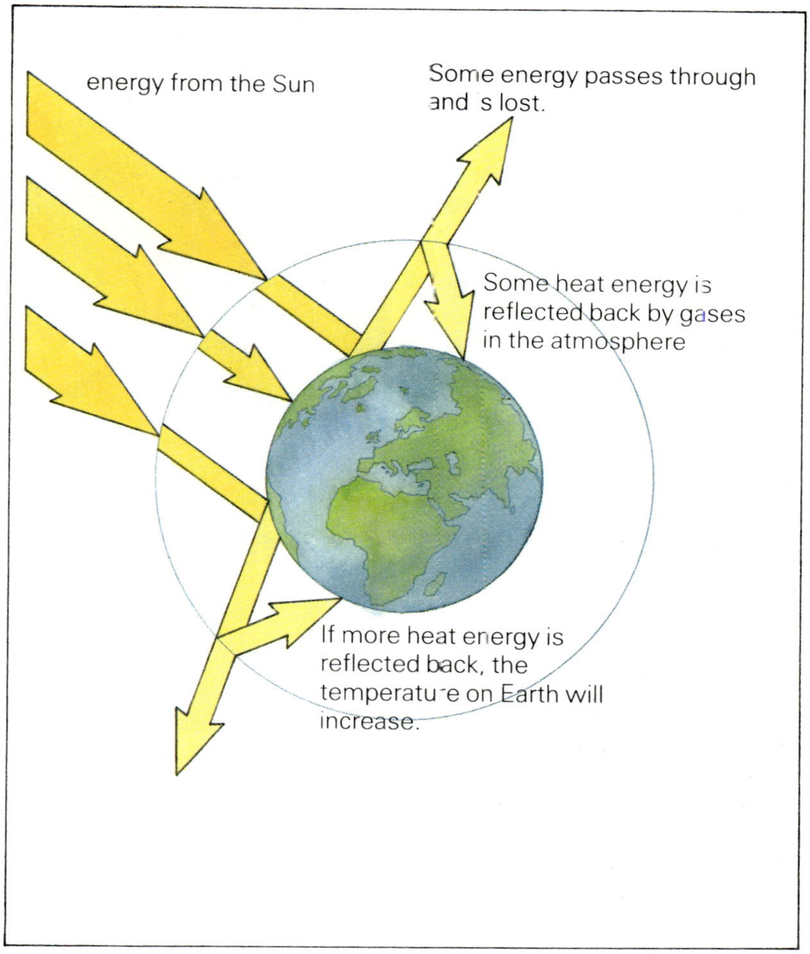

Global warming

People in developed countries have increased the 'infra-red trap' in many ways. **CFCs** (gases in aerosol cans) have been released into the atmosphere and are *very good* reflectors of infra-red rays. But it is thought that the main way has been the burning of fossil fuels. Over the past 100 years, developed countries have increased dramatically their use of fossil fuels – and the amount of carbon dioxide in the atmosphere has risen by 30%. Developing countries are now doing the same as they set up energy-consuming industries and use more cars and electrical appliances.

As the levels of carbon dioxide continue to rise, more and more heat will be reflected back and temperatures on the planet will rise. The effects of this global warming could include larger deserts, changes in climate and a rise in sea level.

A rise in global temperature of 1°C would cause the sea level to rise 20 m – and cities, towns and farmland would be under water.

1 **a** How efficient are most power stations?
b What other forms of energy does a power station produce besides electrical energy?

2 **a** What can happen when heat energy escapes into the environment?
b How can some of this 'waste' energy be used?

3 Throughout the history of the planet, energy has been changing from one form to another. The final result of *all* energy changes is heat energy. Why are energy changes causing such a problem now?

4 Why is the increase in carbon dioxide so dangerous to the people who live on this planet?

Radioactive pollution

The nuclear gamble

Nuclear power stations produce 'waste' heat energy but *not* carbon dioxide or acid gases. Using nuclear fuel, we can obtain electricity *without* adding to acid rain and global warming. But nuclear power stations do pose problems of a different kind.

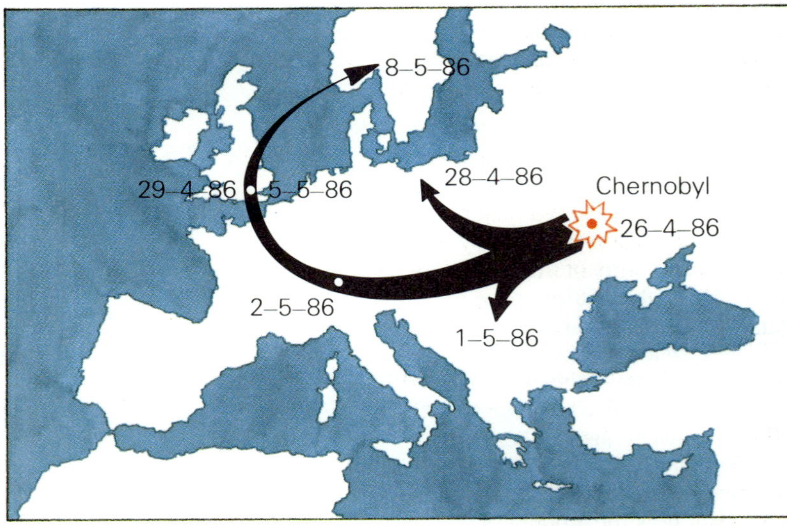

As well as severe damage in the area round Chernobyl, trails of radioactive pollution spread thousands of kilometres across Europe.

An explosion at the Chernobyl power station in 1986 released a cloud of radioactive materials into the atmosphere. As this cloud was blown over much of Europe, radioactive substances fell to the ground. In some areas, such as parts of northern England, rain brought down even more radioactive pollution. Radioactive materials in the soil can be absorbed by plants and then become concentrated in the animals that feed on plants, such as sheep and cows (*see 11.6*). The pollution from Chernobyl is still in our food system today.

Low-level radiation

Fission produces energy *and* radiation and radioactive daughters. Although nuclear power stations use many devices to *contain* the radioactive material, small amounts may seep out into the environment. The area around each nuclear power station is carefully monitored to make sure the levels of radiation are low and safe – but how low is safe?

The number of cases of leukaemia (a cancer which reduces the number of white blood cells in the body) is higher than normal in certain areas. Studies have linked these **leukaemia clusters** to radiation from the nuclear power industry. Other studies have suggested that natural radiation from rocks could also be linked with the disease.

Can you see a link between the clusters and radiation? Is the link equal in all places?

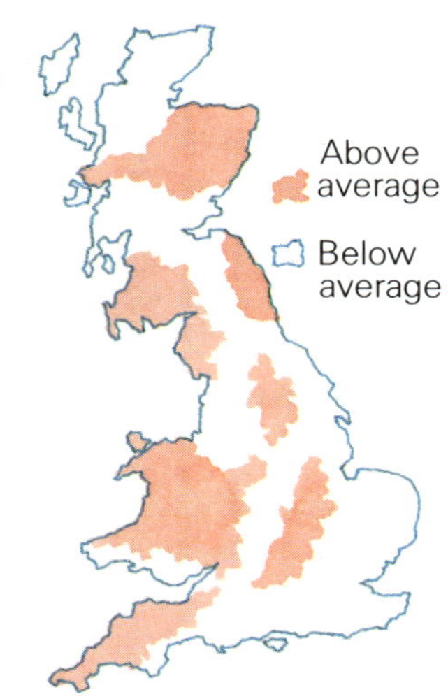

Natural radiation levels across the country

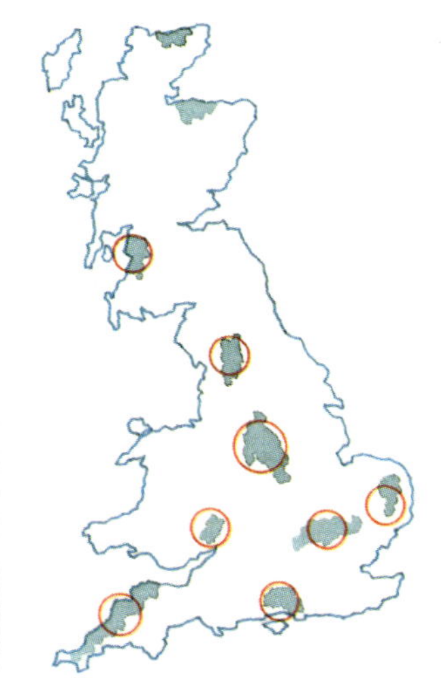

Leukaemia clusters

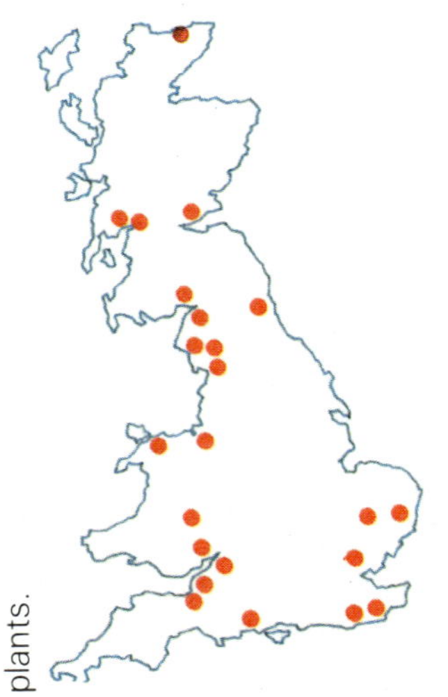

Nuclear power stations or reprocessing plants.

A lifetime of storage

The spent fuel from nuclear reactors is treated in a **reprocessing plant**, where valuable materials such as uranium and plutonium are separated off. The rest of the spent fuel is still highly radioactive and dangerous to living cells. This **radioactive waste** must be sealed and stored safely away from living organisms – but for how long?

The storage time for a radioactive material depends on its **half life**. This is the time taken for the material's activity to decrease by *half*. So the material may have to be stored for many half lives before its radioactivity decreases to a safe low level.

Waste, sealed in blocks . . .

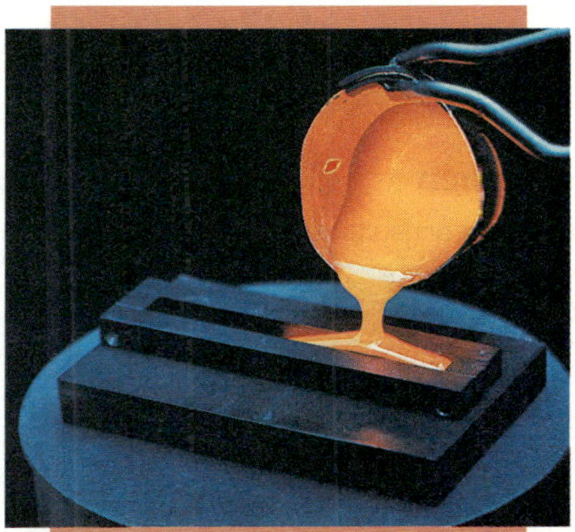

. . . packed in steel containers

Safe storage?

Radioactive waste from nuclear power stations contains a wide range of radioisotopes, each with a different half life (*see 11.6*). The waste may need to be sealed away for *at least* 10 000 years before its activity drops to 'safe' levels. How can this be done?

One way that is being tried is to mix the radioactive waste with glass in a sealed block. The blocks are then packed into steel containers, which are stored at the bottom of deep, disused mine shafts.

Will the radioactive waste be safely contained for 10 000 years?

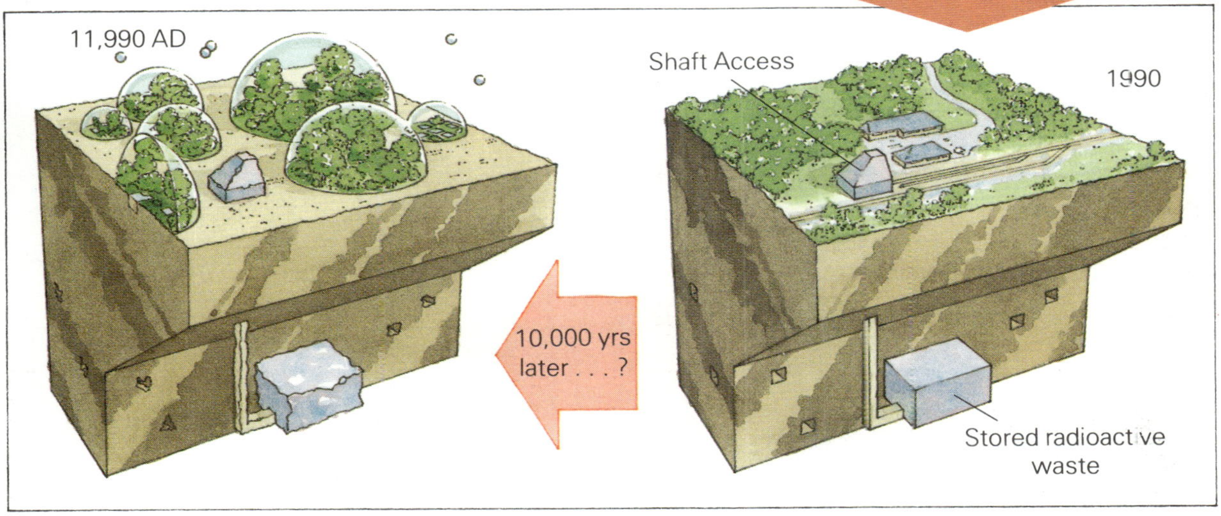

1 In what ways can nuclear power stations pollute the environment?

2 If you had to live near either a fossil fuel power station or a nuclear power station, which would you choose? Why?

3 Radioactive waste with a half life of 100 years has an activity of 100 000 counts per second. How long must it be stored before the activity has dropped to the 'safe' level of 100 counts per second?

4 Look at the method of storage shown above.
- **a** Why do you think a deep mine shaft is used?
- **b** How might the waste be disturbed? List as many ways as you can.
- **c** Can you think of a way to keep radioactive waste completely safe for 10 000 years?

5 Small amounts of radioactive waste are sometimes mixed with water and pumped into the sea.
- **a** How could this affect marine life?
- **b** How could the radioactive material in the waste reach you at home?

11.15 The great debate

Fossil fuels

Fossil fuel power station at Sheffield. The tall thin chimneys release acid gases.

Fossil fuels can be obtained easily.

Opencast mines may look ugly but they can be landscaped after use.

Fossil fuel power stations are cheaper to build, run and take apart than nuclear power stations.

They provide employment in mining, transport and power generation.

They produce acid gases but the amount of these gases can be reduced.

All the fossil fuels would eventually produce carbon dioxide gas anyway. Power stations just use the energy from that change.

Global warming will affect the climate and all living organisms. It will cause the sea level to rise, covering vast areas of farmland.

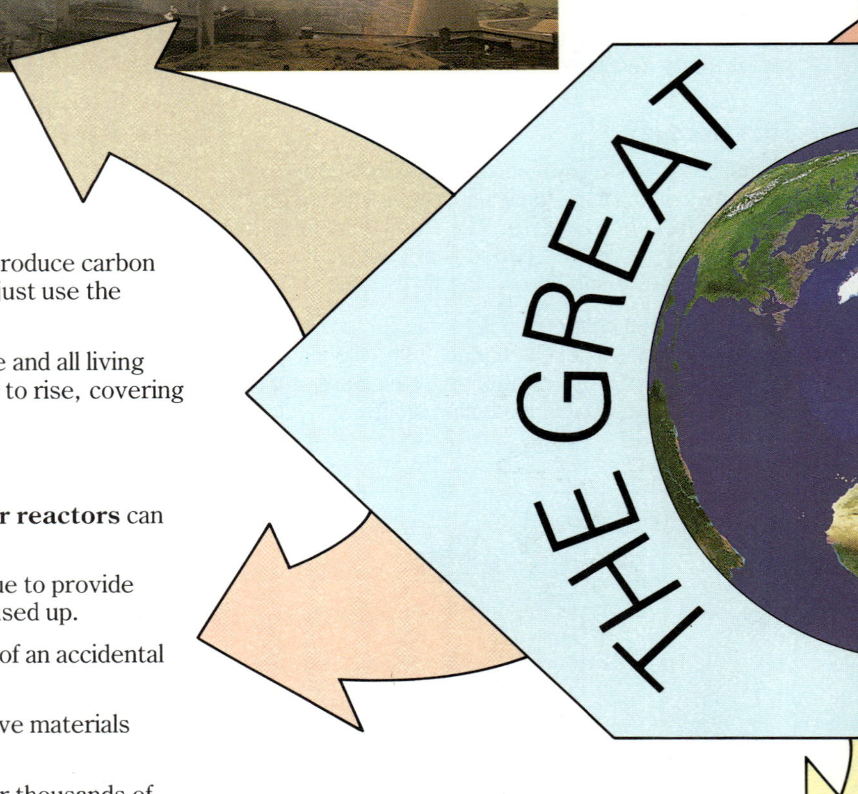

Nuclear fission

Nuclear reactors called **fast breeder reactors** can actually produce *more* nuclear fuel.

Nuclear power stations could continue to provide electricity long after fossil fuels are used up.

With all the safeguards, the chances of an accidental explosion are tiny.

Only very small amounts of radioactive materials escape into the environment.

Nuclear waste remains dangerous for thousands of years.

Radiation damages living cells.

The Hoover hydroelectric dam on the Colorado River.

Consider each side of the debate. Then draw up a plan for meeting our energy needs in the future. Back up your plan with arguments.

Other energy sources

Solar, wind and water power do not produce acid rain or global warming.

They are free and will continue for as long as we do.

A lot of money will be needed to fund research if we are to develop ways of exploiting these sources on a large scale before fossil fuels run out.

The Colorado river is eroding away the land below the Hoover Dam in the USA. The dam holds back silt that is used to replace lost soil.

Wind farms would have to occupy thousands of square kilometres of open countryside to supply as much energy as fossil fuel power stations.

Fusion reactors

Fusion reactors could provide unlimited amounts of clean energy from hydrogen, which is plentiful.

Fusion reactors are not even working yet.

Electricity powering the developed world – for how long?

The developed world

Electrical energy is needed for our manufacturing industries, heat, light and transport.

Hospitals, schools and the elderly need quick, versatile energy supplies.

We need to maintain the standard of living we have now and improve it.

The developing world

We need energy to provide the basic needs for millions of people.

To repay our international debts, we need energy to develop industry.

Why should we have to control our populations to limit our energy demand while the developed world continues to squander the planet's energy resources?

We should be able to enjoy the same standard of living as people in developed countries.

Developing countries should learn from the mistakes of the developed world, not copy it.

The planet Earth – how will the demand for energy affect the Earth's future, and ours?

A wind farm in California.

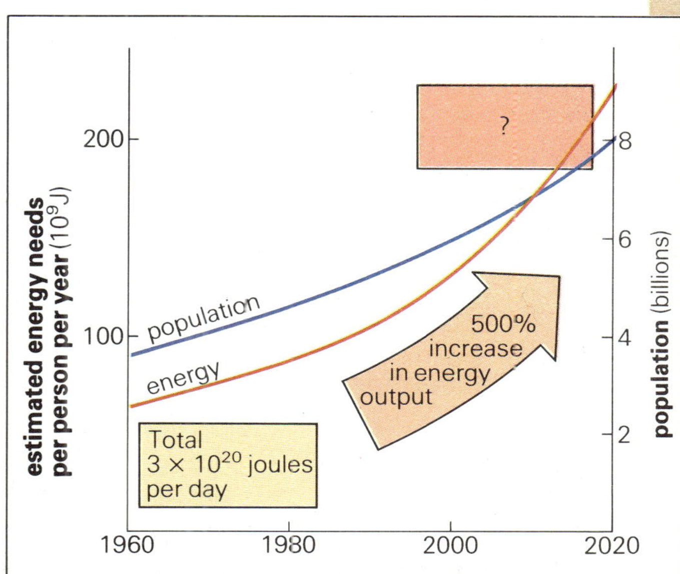

The more of us there are, the more energy we will need.

Index *(refers to spread numbers)*

For additional information, see the following modules:

1 Energy
6 Making the most of Machines
9 Chemical Patterns

Photo acknowledgements

These refer to the spread number (in italics), and where appropriate, the position on the page (lh = left-hand page, rh = right-hand page).

J. Allan Cash Ltd. *11.1* lh, top; Biophoto Associates *11.6*; Mary Evans Picture Library *11.8* lh; Holt Studios Ltd. *11.1* lh, bottom; ICCE Photolibrary (C. Agren) *11.13;* Ann Ronan Picture Library *11.2; 11.10;* Science Photo Library *11.3* (×2); *11.5; 11.7* lh; *11.8* rh; *11.9*; *11.13* rh; *11.14* (×2); *11.15* (×5) and *11.1* rh; St. Bartholomew's Hospital (Dept. of Medical Illustration) *11.7* rh;

Picture Research: Jennifer Johnson, Norman Franks

THE SCIENCES FOR GCSE

12 PLANET EARTH

Much of science deals with the small scale – atoms, genes and the like. Not all of science is small scale: the study of the **weather** covers the whole globe, the study of the **Earth** itself involves timescales of thousands, even millions of years; the study of **Solar System** and the **Universe** deals with almost unimaginable distance. Huge amounts of energy and forces are also involved in each area. This module helps to give you a manageable perspective on all apsects of the planet Earth.

Relevant National Curriculum Attainment Targets: Old ATs 5, 9, 16
New AT 3

12.1 Our planet – the Earth

The living Earth

Our planet is the third of nine planets orbiting the sun. It is the only planet *known* to have life and millions of plants and animals inhabit the lands and seas. The Earth carries all of us through space and provides us with the things we need to stay alive.

Conditions on Earth are constantly changing. Day and night, tides and seasons follow fairly short cycles.

Over vastly longer timescales, mountains are raised and worn away, and the huge continents drift slowly on the Earth's face. Now new changes are being caused by a fairly new life form: humans. More and more people are living on the Earth, stripping its resources and polluting the atmosphere. If we are not to destroy the planet – and ourselves – we need to learn more about the Earth in space and the natural ways in which it can change.

Oceans and clouds of water make the Earth appear blue and white from space.

The Earth's satellite

There is a gravitational attraction between the Sun and the Earth. This makes us orbit the Sun, together with our nearest neighbour, the **Moon**. The Earth and Moon also exert gravitational forces on each other, and move round each other. The Earth's pull is much the greater of the two forces because the mass of the Earth is 80 times more than that of the Moon. So we usually say that the Moon orbits the Earth and call the Moon a **satellite** of Earth.

From Earth, the Moon appears to wax (get bigger and more 'whole') and wane (get smaller). This is because the Moon does not emit any light, it only *reflects* light from the Sun. You see different amounts of the Moon's sunlit face as it orbits the Earth. These changing views of the sunlit face are called the **phases** of the Moon.

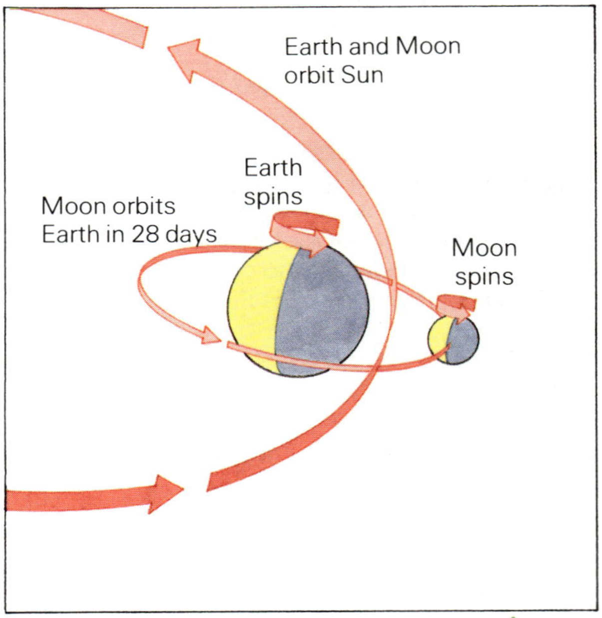

The Earth and Moon are constantly in motion.

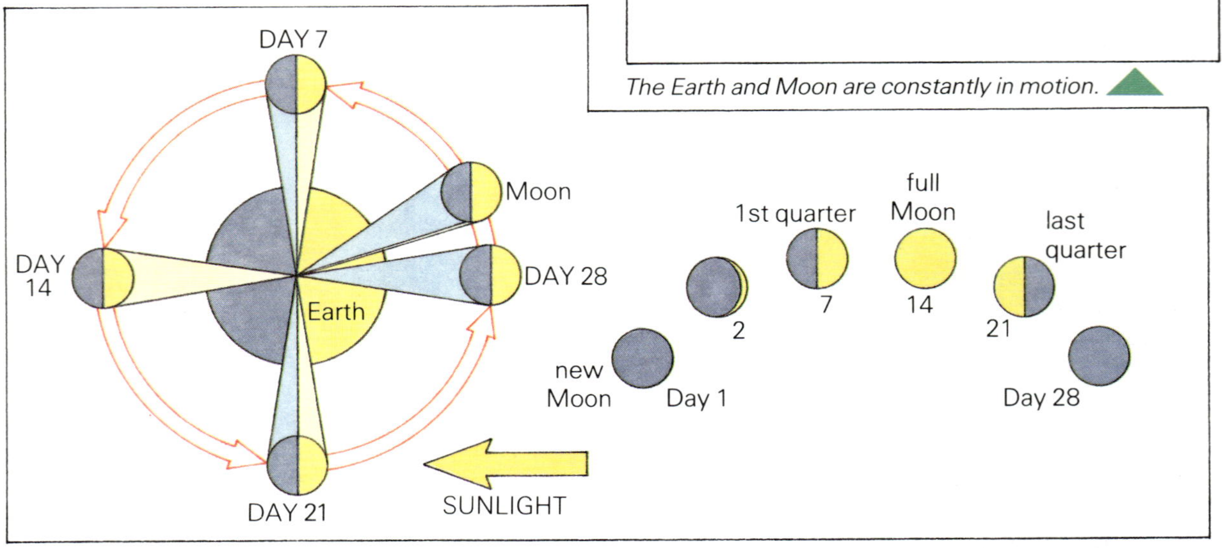

Half the Moon is always sunlit. . .

. . . but this is what you see from Earth.

Causing tides

The most obvious effect of the Moon's pull on the Earth is the **tides**. The Moon's gravitational pull on the Earth's surface is large, even raising the solid land by about 20 cm. The liquid oceans are lifted several metres forming two 'bulges' – one on either side of the Earth. The Earth spins, making a complete turn in 24 hours. This spin carries the coastline through the two bulges every day, resulting in two high tides a day.

Latitude and longitude

The Earth spins on its **axis** – an imaginary line passing *through* the Earth and the **geographic poles**. Other places on the Earth are described using imaginary lines passing *round* the surface.

Lines of longitude circle the Earth from north to south, passing through the poles. **Lines of latitude** circle the Earth from east to west. The longest line of latitude goes round the middle of the Earth; it is called the **equator**. Lines of latitude and longitude can be used to pinpoint any place on Earth.

The seasons

The Earth orbits the Sun in just over 365 days. If the Earth's axis was at *right angles* to the orbit, the Sun would appear in the same position in the sky at noon each day. This would mean that the number of daylight hours would always be the same. But you already know that there are *more* daylight hours in the summer than in winter. So the axis can't be at right angles to the orbit all the time. In fact, the axis is *tilted* at an angle of 23.5° to the vertical.

During our summer, northern latitudes are tilted towards the Sun bringing more sunlit hours. This means the Sun is more directly overhead and its rays are spread over a *smaller* area, increasing their effect. So we receive more of the Sun's energy in summer than in winter.

The Moon is one of the largest satellites in the solar system. This and its closeness to Earth make the Moon's gravitational pull on the Earth large.

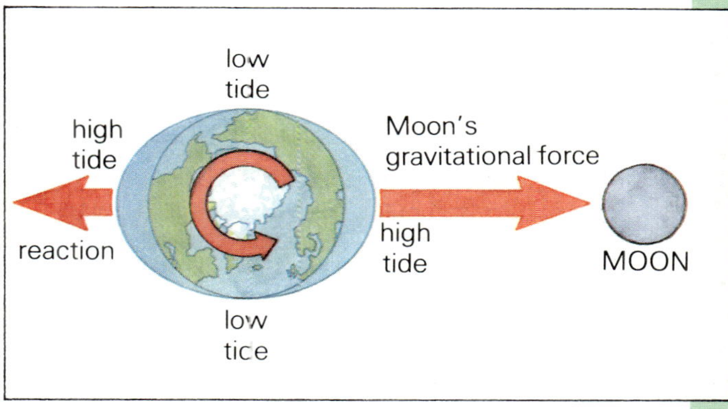

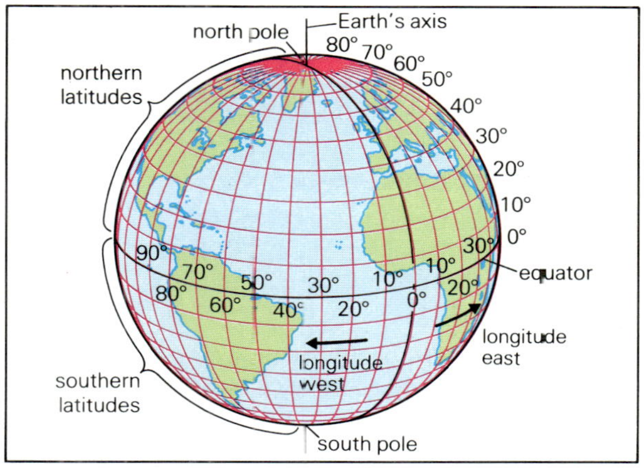

The Earth is divided into time zones 15° longitude wide. Every zone away from 0° indicates 1 hour difference from Greenwich Mean Time – either earlier or later, depending on the direction east or west.

Six months after our summer, the Earth has travelled to the other side of the Sun. Northern latitudes are tilted away from the Sun and we have our winter.

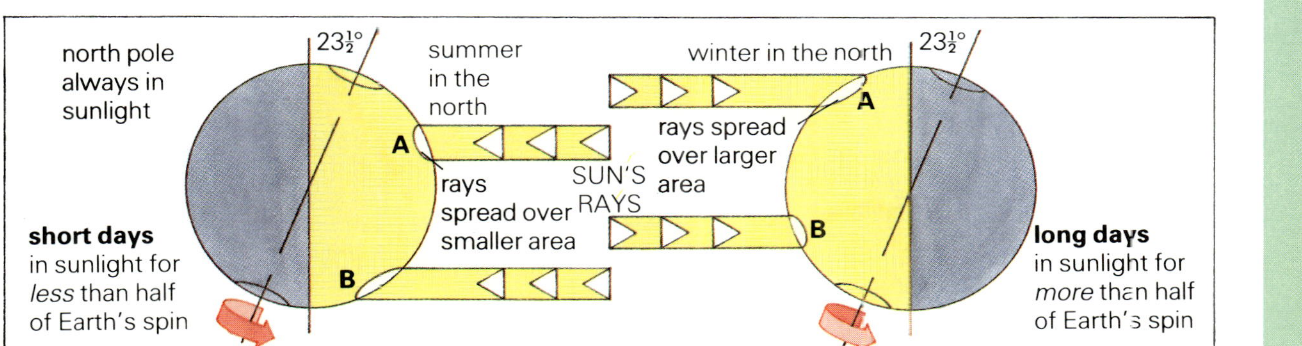

1 **a** When you see the Moon, why does it appear to be the largest natural object in the night sky?
b Explain why our view of the Moon changes on a monthly cycle.

2 In the middle of our Northern summer, how many daylight hours do you think there are –
a at the North Pole? **b** at the Equator?
c at the South Pole?

12.2 Bring on the clouds

The Earth's atmosphere

The Earth is surrounded by a thin transparent 'shell' gases held by the Earth's gravity. The shell is known as the **atmosphere** or, more commonly, as just 'air'.

You live at the bottom of this shell of air – indeed you could not live without it. The atmosphere is many kilometres thick – the whole shell of air has a mass of many million tonnes. The air near the ground is compressed by the weight of all the air above it. The weight causes the air to exert a pressure on everything around it. At sea level, this is equivalent to 1 kilogram pressing down (i.e. a force of 10 N) on each square centimetre.

This **air pressure** is usually measured in pascals (Pa = N/m^2) or millibars. At sea level, the air pressure is 1.013×10^5 Pa (1013 millibars).

At sea level, you have the weight of a vast column of air pressing on you.

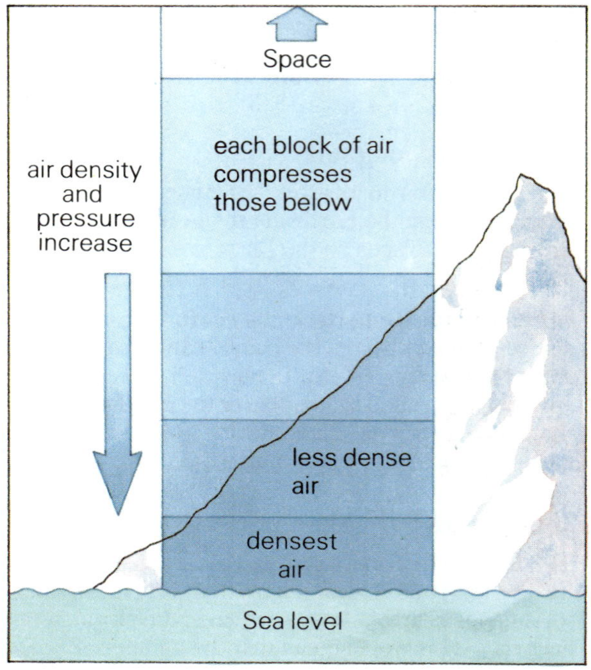

Exploring the atmosphere

People explore the atmosphere by sending up balloons and artificial satellites. These carry instruments that record, for example, the temperature and pressure at different heights.

Such investigations show that air pressure and density decrease with height as the weight of air above gets less.

At 150 kilometres high, air pressure and density are very low, and eventually the atmosphere merges into space. The temperature of the air also varies with height, but in a much less uniform way. The way the temperature changes with height is used to divide the atmosphere up into 'layers'.

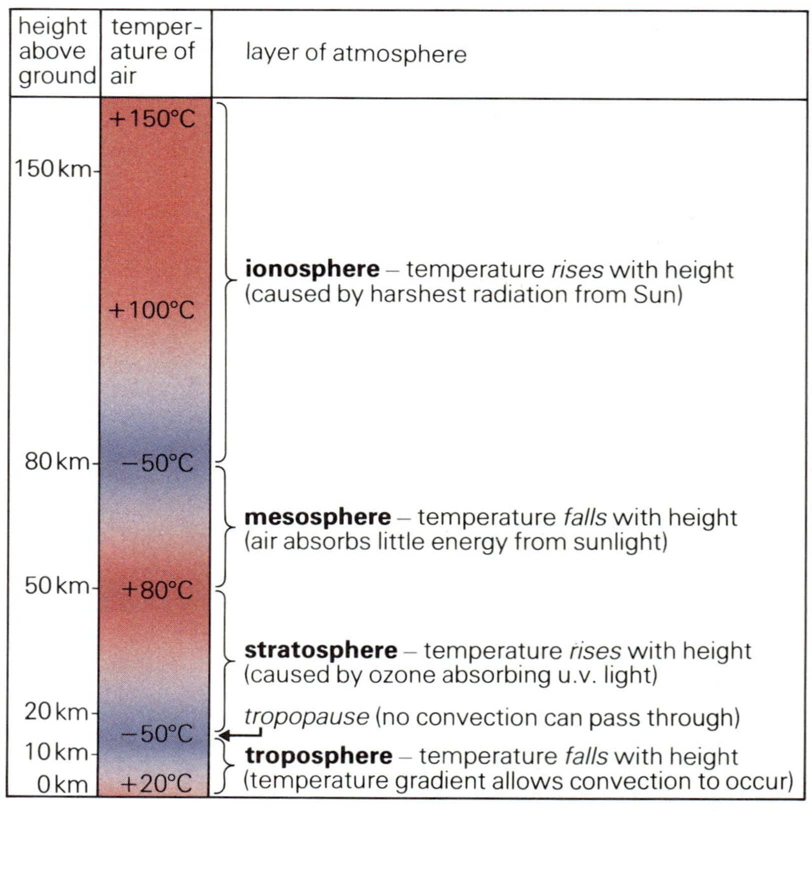

Layers of air

In the layer of air closest to the ground, the **troposphere**, the temperature decreases with height, dropping steadily by 6.5°C/km. This is why you can find ice forming at the equator – if you are at the top of very tall mountains!

Heating occurs in the **stratosphere** because a form of oxygen called **ozone** absorbs some of the energy in the Sun's ultraviolet rays.

The temperature falls in the **mesophere**, to rise again in the **ionosphere**, where other gases absorb energy from the Sun's rays.

Moisture in the air

Energy from the Sun warms the surface of the Earth, which heats the air near the ground. This warm air rises in a **convection current** up through the troposphere.

The rising warm air gradually loses heat energy to the surrounding cooler air. Water vapour in the warm air also loses heat until it condenses as tiny droplets of water, forming a mist or **cloud**. The temperature at which a mist forms is called the **dewpoint**. If the air is cooled further, the water droplets become so large they fall as **rain**.

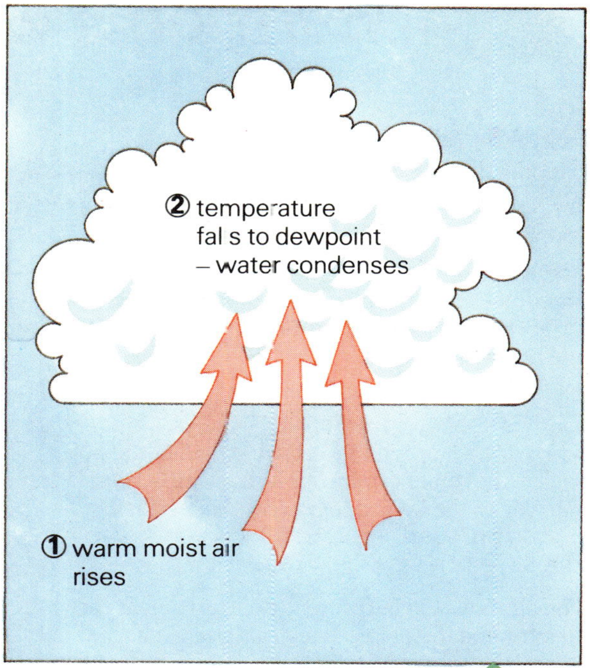

Invisible water vapour in the rising moist air condenses to form clouds.

The lid on the weather

Warm air rises in the troposphere because in this layer temperature *decreases* with height. But in the stratosphere, temperature *increases* with height. So convection currents cannot usually move from the troposphere into the stratosphere.

The cloud-carrying convection currents are trapped *beneath* the **tropopause**, which acts like a 'lid' on the weather. Only very violent convection currents, such as those from a volcano, can break through the tropopause and rise into the stratosphere.

Mountains in the rain

In this country, winds often blow from the west, bringing wet, warm air mainly from over the large area of Atlantic Ocean. These winds push the wet air up over any mountains in their path.

As the air rises the temperature may drop to the dewpoint. Then clouds will form and rain may fall over the mountains.

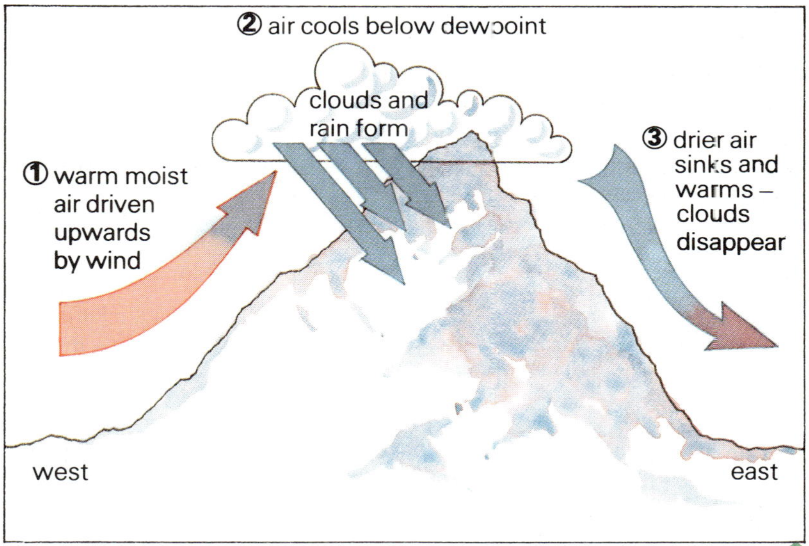

Mountains, as well as convection currents, can cause clouds to form.

Types of cloud

The shape of a cloud depends on *how* it is formed, the *height* at which it is formed and the *speed of the wind.*

Each shape or type of cloud is given a name. The fluffy, cotton-wool clouds are called **cumulus**, while layered clouds stretched out by the wind are known as **stratus**.

Cirro- is used to describe high clouds, and **alto-** is used for middle-level clouds. So, for example, alto-cumulus is a medium-level cumulus and cirro-stratus is a high-level stratus.

1. Why do people find it difficult to breathe at the top of high mountains?
2. What happens when the dewpoint temperature falls to ground level?
3. At any time, bases of clouds are all about the same height above the ground. Why?
4. Do winds from the east cause as much rain on the mountains in Britain as winds from the west? Give reasons for your answers.
5. Passenger aircraft fly in the stratosphere rather than the troposphere. Suggest reasons for this.

What's the weather like?

Driven by the Sun

Conditions in the atmosphere around you – the **weather** – may be wet or dry, hot or cold, sunny or cloudy. This will affect what you do, the clothes you wear and even the food you eat.

The weather can change rapidly. Accurate forecasts of the weather are important for many industries (such as ice-cream manufacturers), farmers and transport, particularly shipping. What causes the weather and its variations?

The weather systems of the world are powered by the Sun. Because the Earth is a sphere, the Sun's rays fall on a *smaller* area (and are more *concentrated*) around the equator than at the poles. This uneven heating causes movement of the air – the **winds**. Winds transfer energy from the warmer to the cooler regions of the Earth.

The Sun evaporates water from the oceans and seas. The rain that falls on you may have been evaporated here in the Caribbean Sea and carried to Britain by the wind.

The Earth's winds

The air moves in fairly steady patterns near the equator and the poles. Warm air rises in huge convection currents over the equator. It then falls back at latitudes of about 30°.

Air rushes across the surface towards the equator to replace the rising air. Similarly, the cold air above the poles falls and is replaced by warmer air drawn from lower latitudes. Between these two huge convection currents, no steady patterns form.

This is because high in the atmosphere very strong winds known as the **jet-stream** flow from west to east. These disturb the air, resulting in the unsettled weather we experience in the UK.

The great convection currents would flow north or south if the Earth were still. But the Earth keeps spinning to the east! Even if the air flows directly south, when you compare it to the point on the Earth where it started from, the air will have moved south *and* west.

Why should this be so? On any spinning sphere, the further the surface is from the axis, the faster it spins. So at the equator, the Earth spins *fastest*. North of the equator, air and Earth spin eastwards more *slowly*. As this air flows south to the faster-spinning equator, it can't 'keep up' with the eastward spin at the equator. When it reaches the equator, the Earth has spun round further. Compared with the point on the Earth where it started from, the air will have moved south *and* west.

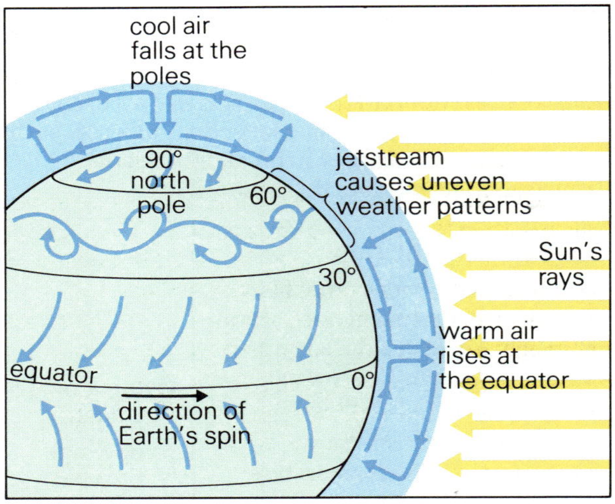

All the Earth's winds are deflected away from north–south by the Earth's spin.

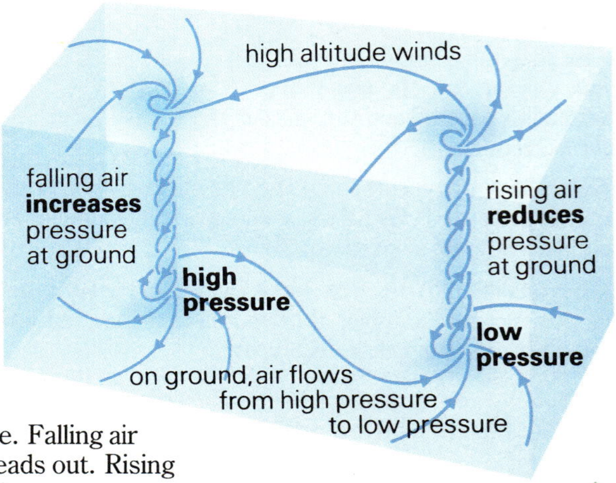

In the northern hemisphere, the winds flow anti-clockwise around low-pressure areas and clockwise around high-pressure areas.

Air pressure and wind

The rising and falling air causes differences in air pressure. Falling air produces a *high* pressure at ground level, and the air spreads out. Rising air leaves a *low* pressure at ground level and air is drawn in.

Air always moves from areas of high pressure to areas of low pressure creating winds. The spin of the Earth causes these winds to swirl or spiral around high and low-pressure areas.

Plotting the weather

Weather maps show where areas of high and low pressure are situated. They do this using **isobars** – lines joining places where the pressure at ground level is the same. Just as contour lines on ordinary maps indicate steep slopes – so if isobars are close together, the pressure differences in that area are great. The *closer* the isobars, the greater the pressure difference – and the *stronger* the winds.

As winds spiral in towards low-pressure areas, the air they carry may be warmer or cooler than the air it replaces. Where such a *change* of air is taking place is called a **front**.

Change makes rain

Warm air is less dense than cool air. When warm air is blown into replace cooler air, the warmer lighter air is pushed up and over the cooler heavier air. This is known as a **warm front**. When a **cold front** occurs, the cold air moving in is pushed *underneath* the existing warm air.

As the warm air is forced upwards, it cools, and moisture condenses out and falls as rain. Bad weather is associated with the changes that take place when fronts move. Once the original block of air has been completely replaced the weather is usually settled and fine. It is the *change* of air that causes rain.

Weather and climate

Although the weather can vary from day to day, over a number of years the weather of an area follows a pattern. The *average* weather of an area over many years is called its **climate**. The climate of an area affects people in many ways – particularly the food they can grow. Farmers in Britain plant crops and keep livestock suited to our temperate climate.

Until recently, only natural changes could affect the climate. For example, the Sun's energy fluctuates slightly over the years and this *may* result in fluctuations in climate. Now our industries are releasing carbon dioxide into the atmosphere, which is trapping more of the Sun's energy. This may lead to serious climate changes.

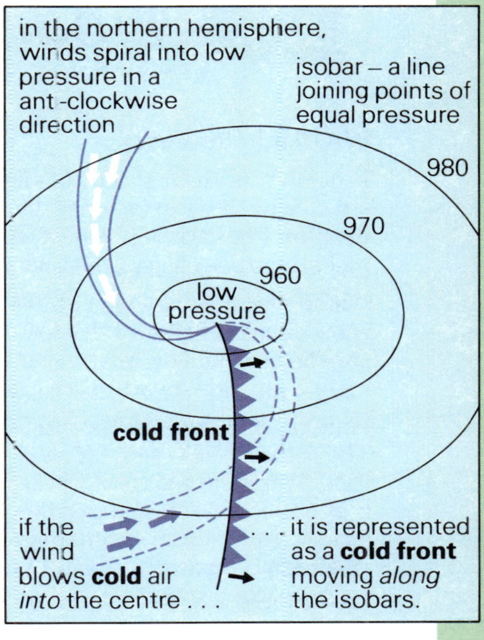

Low pressure areas are called cyclones and high pressure areas are anticyclones.

A warm front moving in brings rain – until the warm air has replaced the cold air.

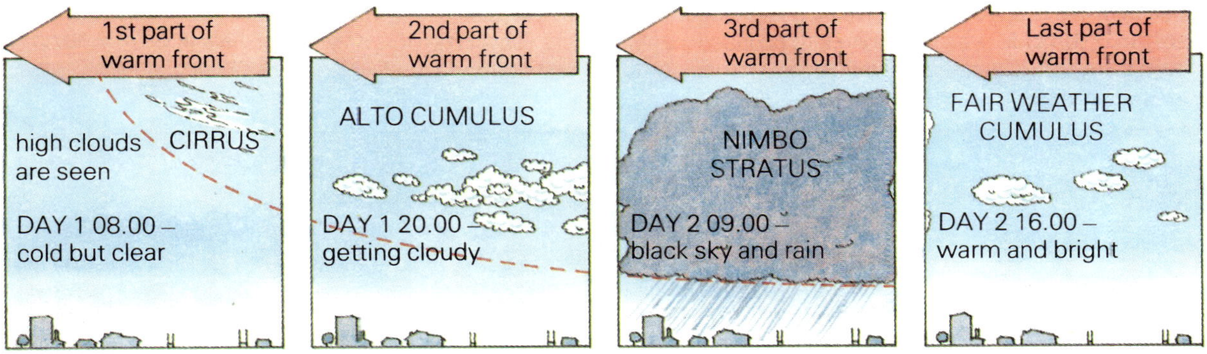

1 **a** Give four examples of industries which might need accurate forecasts of the weather.
b What provides energy to create the destructive winds in hurricanes?

2 All winds are named after the direction they blow *from*. Name the Earth's winds shown in the diagram on the opposite page.

3 In the northern hemisphere, water runs down the plughole in an anti-clockwise direction. Suggest why.

4 How does a front cause rain?

5 When a high-pressure area has its centre over Sweden, we get a heat wave in summer or a cold spell in winter. Suggest reasons why.

6 Carbon dioxide traps the Sun's energy through the '**greenhouse effect**'.
a Find out about the greenhouse effect.
b Predict how this might affect the climate in Britain and the food we can grow.

12.4 Eroding the rocks

Weatherbeaten rocks

From the day the first drop of rain hit the Earth's crust, **weathering** (wearing down of rocks) and **erosion** (the carrying away of weathered parts of rocks) started changing the landscape.

Water evaporated by the Sun eventually falls as rain, snow or hail. The water that falls on land may soak into the ground, flow as streams and rivers, freeze to ice or even form 'rivers' of ice called **glaciers**.

Water in all its forms is the main agent of weathering. The pounding sea can wear away the solid rock of cliffs. Water expands as it freezes, and if ice forms in rock crevices it can split the rock. These are examples of *physical* weathering. Rocks can also be weathered *chemically*, mainly by weak acids in the water reacting with the rock.

U-shaped valley carved by glacier – and containing *a glacier.*

Erosion transports away pieces of rock broken away by weathering. Often such rock is broken down further by other rocks as it is being carried away (e.g. in rivers).

Repeated weathering eventually breaks down rock into small particles of **sand** or **clay**. These particles gradually settle out as deposits on river-beds, banks and beaches.

Chemical attack

As rain falls, **carbon dioxide** in the air combines with the water to form a **weak acid**. Some of the substances in rocks, such as the calcium carbonate in **limestone**, dissolve in the slightly acidic rainwater. This happens gradually – for example, it has taken centuries for rain to eat away the faces of limestone statues on old cathedrals in Britain.

The process is speeded up by industrial pollutants, such as the gas **sulphur dioxide** which dissolves to produce sulphuric acid. This type of **acid rain** wears away more quickly limestone statues, buildings and natural rock faces.

In limestone areas, water transforms the landscape through chemical attack and the rubbing action of loosened stones carried along by the water.

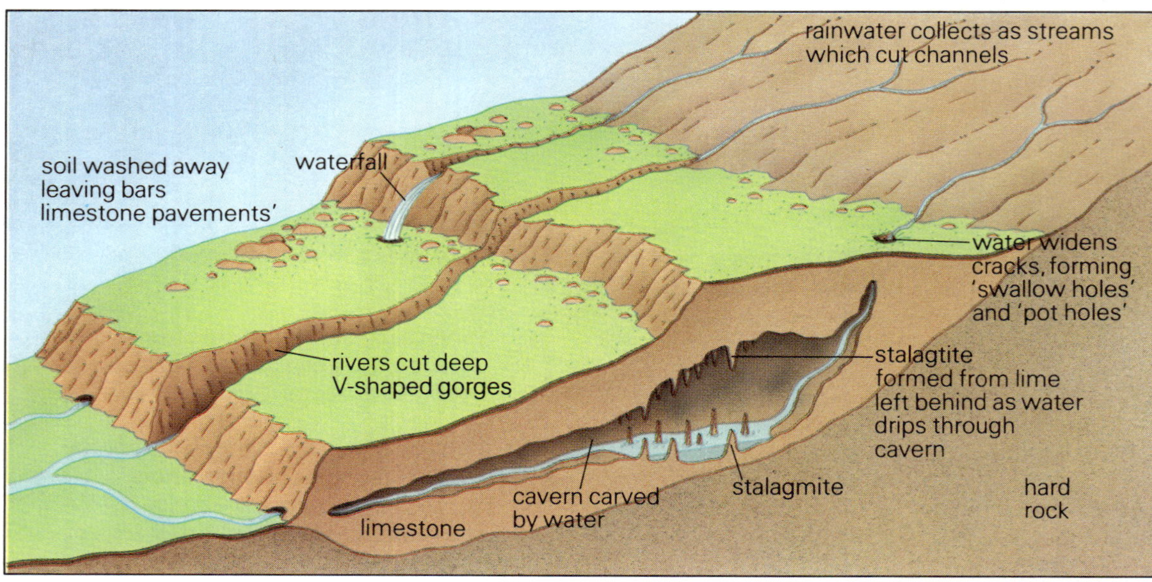

As a river flows from the hills to the sea, the slope of the river bed becomes gentler and the water flows more slowly.

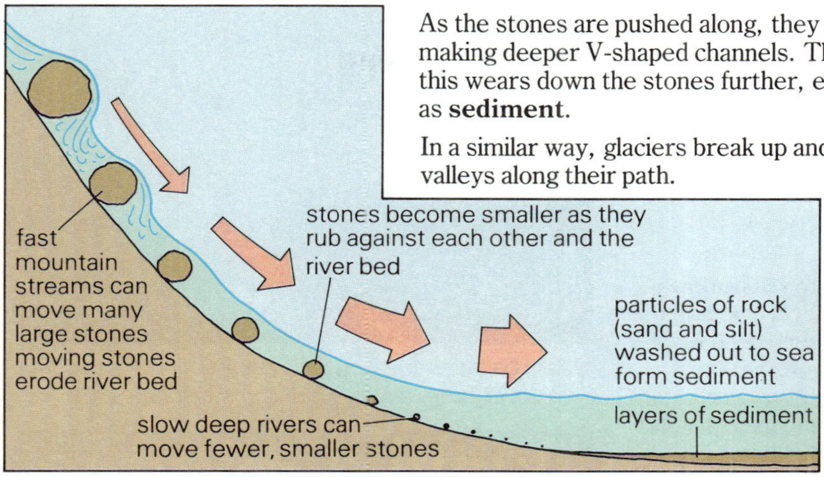

From the river to the sea

Rain collects on hills in streams which later combine to form rivers. Up in the hills, fast-moving waters sweep up the pieces of rock (stones) washed into them, including those loosened by chemical attack.

As the stones are pushed along, they scratch away at the rock below making deeper V-shaped channels. The moving stones hit each other and this wears down the stones further, eventually depositing tiny particles as **sediment**.

In a similar way, glaciers break up and transport rocks, carving **U**-shaped valleys along their path.

Any steep slope tends to be eroded by flowing water.

Other weatherers

Although water and ice are the main breakers of rocks, there are other weathering agents.

Rocks expand as they get hotter and contract as they cool. In desert areas with extremes of **temperature** between day and night, frequent expansion and contraction can *shatter* the rock. **Wind** carrying small particles of sand and grit can carve rocks, in the way that sandblasting is used to clean the faces of buildings.

Even **plants** can cause weathering – their roots grow into crevices in rocks, splitting the rocks apart.

Vanishing soil

Over thousands of years, weathering and erosion slowly change the landscape, and may expose valuable minerals. This also helps to produce a fertile layer covering the rocks – **topsoil**.

The tiny particles of clay, sand and other materials formed by weathering provide all the minerals plants need. The type and amount of plants that can grow depend partly on the quality and depth of the topsoil.

Plant roots, particularly the large root systems of trees, **bind** the find particles of soil together. When people clear away trees, rainwater or wind can carry the soil away leaving barren rock. The soil which took so long to form can be eroded in only a few years.

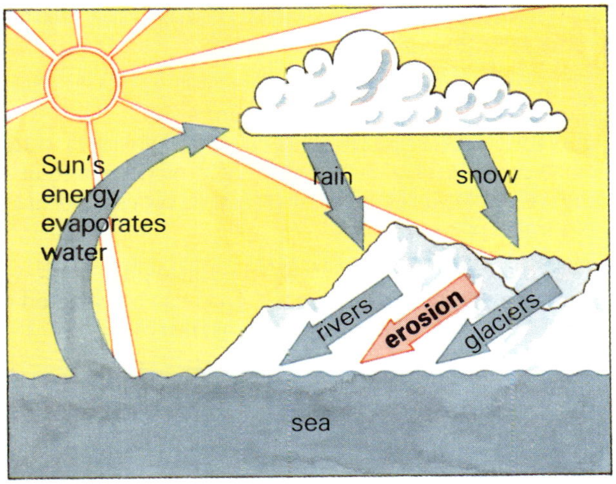

The Sun 'powers' erosion. The eroding water is recycled but the eroded rocks and soil move one way – downwards.

1 **a** Give two examples of physical weathering.
b In chemical weathering, what would happen if the rainwater became even more acid than it is now?

2 **a** The estuary of a river (where the river meets the sea) often **silts** up. Explain where the silt has come from.
b If you found a rock on the shore with sharp edges, what type of weathering might have caused them?

3 Farmers who want to grow crops on steep hillsides often build wide 'steps' or **terraces** in the hill. Suggest reasons for this.

4 Erosion and weathering have been moving soil and rocks downhill for millions of years. Suggest a hypothesis to explain why all the hills have not worn away.

Recycling rocks

Rock types

The Earth's crust is made up of many kinds of rock which differ in their hardness and other properties. The properties of rocks depend partly on *how* they were formed. Rocks are classified into three *groups* – **igneous**, **sedimentary** and **metamorphic** – according to their origin.

Igneous rocks were once molten rocks. Temperature increases with depth in the Earth. Below the crust, some rock melts to form **magma** (molten rock). This magma may be forced up into the crust, forming a **pluton** – or it may surface as **lava** from a volcano. On cooling, crystals grow in the magma – and it solidifies. The *type* and *size* of crystals in igneous rock depend how *quickly* the magma cools – and on the chemical composition of the magma.

Igneous rocks are very hard and some of the crystals they contain, such as diamonds, are the hardest materials of all.

Sedimentary rocks are formed from grains of eroded rock (silt, sand and so on) or the undecomposed parts of plants and animals. These sediments settle in horizontal layers, usually under water. The older layers, buried under newer layers, are slowly *compressed* into sedimentary rock. For example, mud is compressed into **mudstone**, and the remains of tiny shellfish form the white rock, **chalk**.

If a sedimentary rock continues to be buried *deeper* in the crust, it is subject to higher temperatures and pressures. Although the rock does not fully melt, later small crystals form on cooling. The great pressure of the weight of rock above causes the crystals to form in parallel planes or **bands**.

The *changed* rock is known as **metamorphic rock**. For example, sedimentary mudstone can be changed to metamorphic **slate**, and chalk to **marble**.

Metamorphic rocks are usually harder and more resistant to erosion than sedimentary rocks.

Using rocks

Rocks are quarried or mined for the **minerals** they contain, and also for use as **building materials**. The choice of rock for building depends on the properties of the rock and the cost of quarrying it. Harder rock is longer lasting, but it is more difficult (and so more expensive) to work.

Basalt contains small *crystals because it is formed from lava which cools* rapidly *on the surface of the Earth.*

Granite is formed by slow *cooling in a pluton, allowing* large *crystals to form.*

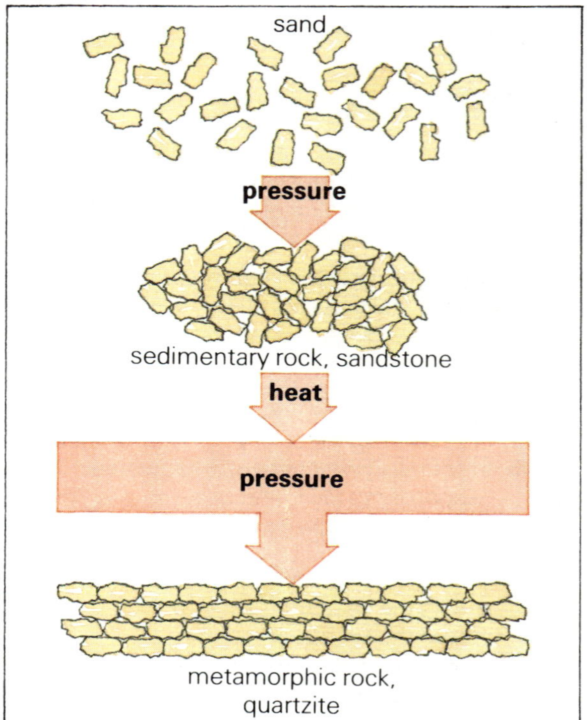

Deep in the crust, sedimentary sandstone changes to metamorphic quartzite.

Rock type	Relative properties			
	crush strength	impact strength	wear on tyres in dry	wear on tyres in wet
Flint (igneous)	9	24	24	26
Gabbro (igneous)	7	31	26	22
Schist (metamorphic)	14	15	20	16
Quartzite (metamorphic)	28	20	26	24
Sandstone (sedimentary)	9	16	24	12
Limestone (sedimentary)	2	0.5	18	1

This table shows some properties of rocks used to make roads. Compare the properties of sandstone and quartzite (metamorphic sandstone) and suggest reasons for the differences.

The rock cycle

Over millions of years, one rock type can gradually change into another.

The rock cycle shows sandstone being formed and recycled as sedimentary rock – Quartzite – (metamorphic rock) and some melts as magma. The rocks get cooler as the diagram moves from bottom to top.

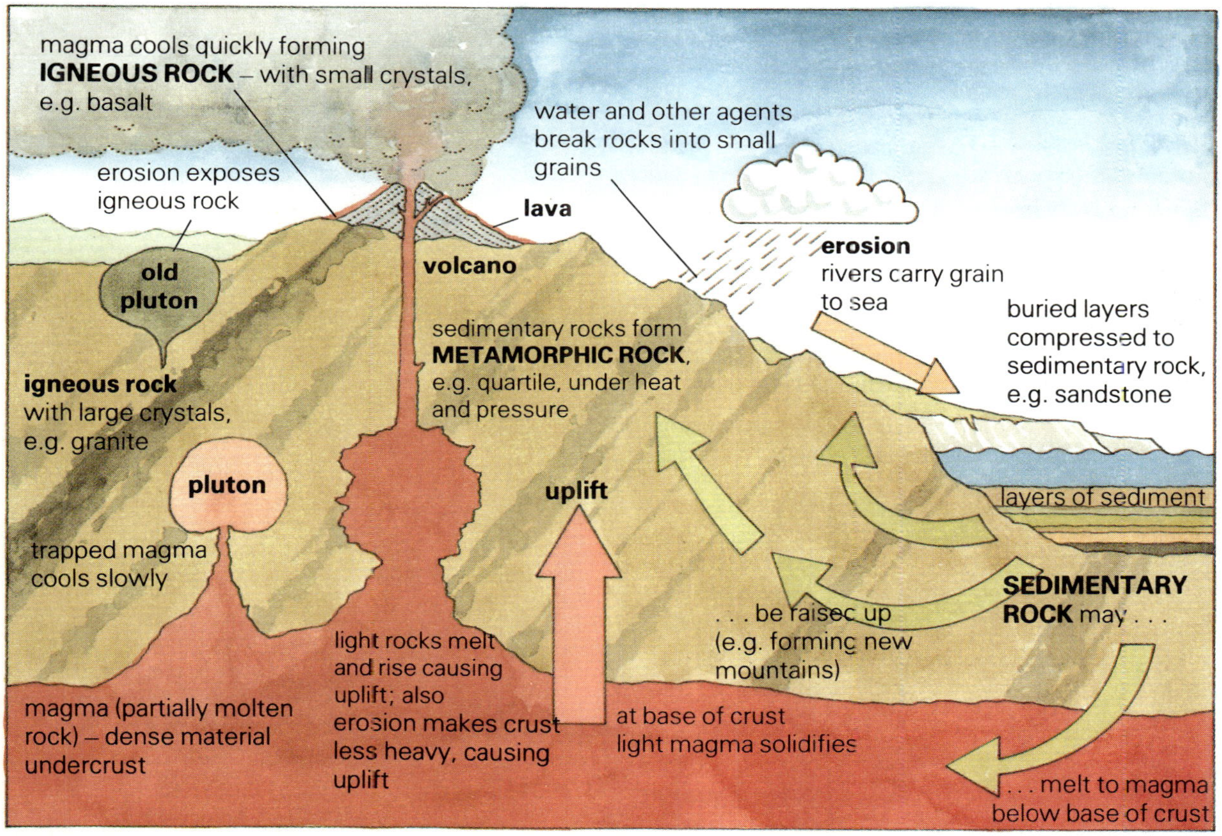

1 **a** What is a pluton?
b Would you expect to find larger crystals in lava or in a pluton?

2 Explain the following:
a Slate (a metamorphic rock) can easily be broken into thin sheets;
b Plugs of volcanic lava are often left standing as vertical columns.

3 Sedimentary rocks are recycled by nature in three ways. Describe the changes that take place during each of these.

4 **a** Display the information in the table above in a way that highlights the different properties of the rocks used for roads.
b Which of the three main types of rock:
i) cause least wear on tyres in the dry;
ii) are the hardest to crush;
iii) the hardest to crack;
c A road-maker wants a surface that will resist accidental damage and give good road-holding in the wet, yet will not be too damaging to tyres in the dry. Suggest a mixture of rocks for the road-maker to use.

12.6 The restless Earth

Below the surface

According to the rock cycle theory (*see 12.5*), partially molten magma will form in certain places below the crust. How did scientists gather evidence for this theory?

We live on the surface of the crust and it seems firm and calm. Yet the evidence of activity below the surface is only too apparent in some parts of the world – areas with volcanoes and earthquakes.

Volcanoes change the landscape forming hills (also known as volcanoes), plateaux and depressions.

Volcanoes

Deep in the crust, rocks are pushed down by the weight of rocks above. The higher temperatures further down in the Earth melt the lower rocks and they form partially molten magma. This magma is less dense than surrounding rocks and so rises up towards the crust. The pressure of surrounding rocks, and from gases in the magma, forces it to rise up through any areas of weakness in the crust. If the area of weakness reaches to the surface, a volcano is born! A **volcano** is an opening or vent through which magma reaches the surface.

Gases trapped in the magma eject it from the volcano as **lava**. Depending on the pressure of the gases, this may be a gentle or violent process. During an explosive **eruption**, hot ash and rocks may fall over a wide area causing serious damage and loss of life.

Other evidence of Earth movements – earthquakes – can have even more catastrophic effects.

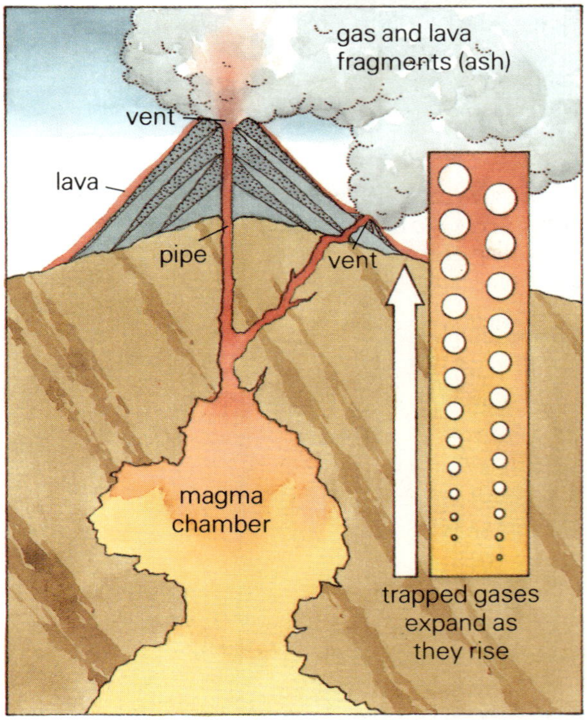

Some volcanoes build up a layered core of lava and ash.

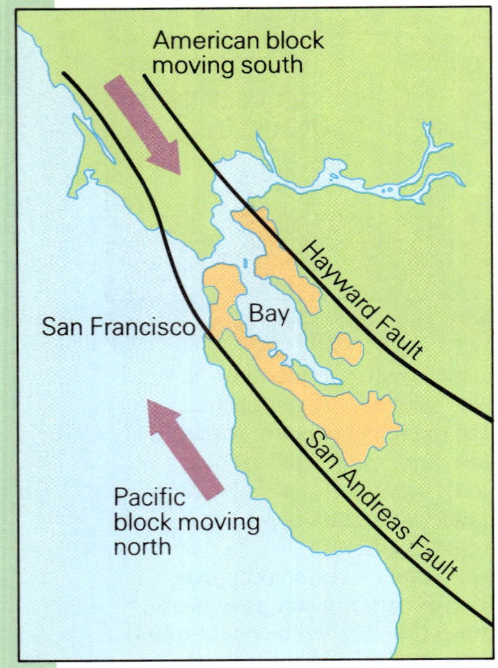

Would you live in San Francisco?

Earthquakes

During the evening rush-hour on 17 October 1989, an earthquake hit San Francisco. Over 300 people died as bridges, motorway and buildings collapsed. Ever since the great San Francisco quake of 1906 people had been waiting for 'the big one' – but although it was expected, it wasn't accurately predicted.

San Francisco lies on the *San Andreas fault* – a place where two great pieces of the Earth's crust are trying to move in opposite directions. The friction between the two blocks holds them together. But when the pressure below them becomes too great, they move past each other.

Frequently, a block slips a few metres resulting in smaller tremors. But during this recent quake, slippage occured over a 56 km length of the fault, releasing as much energy as an atomic bomb explosion!

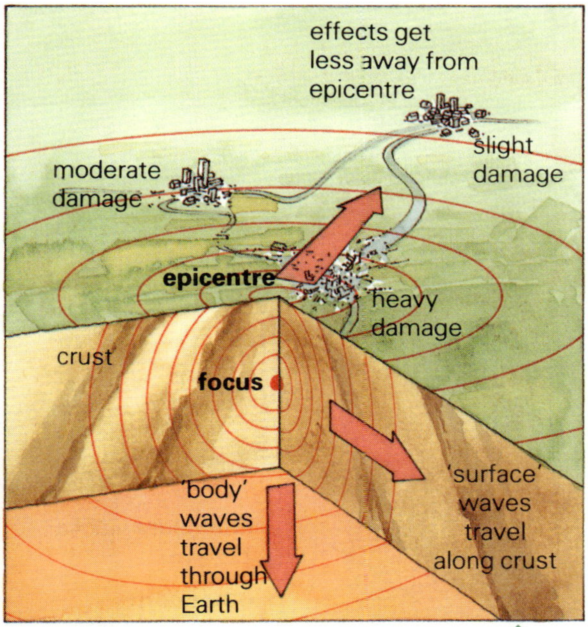

During a major earthquake, the surface waves cause extensive damage.

Predicting disaster

Before a volcanic eruption, there is increased activity in smaller vents and the temperature in the volcano rises. These signs may be detected by special satellites orbiting the Earth.

As a result, volcanic eruptions *can* often be predicted. When Mount St. Helens erupted in 1980 everyone except the photographers and scientists had been evacuated! Unfortunately, earthquakes are more difficult to predict. They may be preceded by small tremors – or none at all. Any shock waves are detected by **seismometers** at stations all round the world.

Locating earthquakes

Body waves travel faster along a more direct route than surface waves. So there is a time interval between the arrival of body and surface waves at a seismometer station. This time interval, and others, indicate the *distance* from the station to the epicentre.

The distance of the epicentre from at least three stations can be used to locate the epicentre.

Shock waves

The point where the slippage occurs between the blocks is the **focus** of the earthquake. This may be close to the surface or deep underground. The point on the surface directly above the focus is called the **epicentre**. The movement sends **shock waves** along the crust (**surface** waves) and through the Earth (**body** waves).

The damage an earthquake can cause depends on the energy released. This is measured on the **Richter scale** – named after the scientist who first classified the effect of earthquakes. You would scarcely notice an earthquake measuring 2 on the Richter scale. Anything over 7 is a major earthquake capable of destroying buildings. Each year throughout the world about 20 earthquakes 'score' more than 7 on the Richter scale.

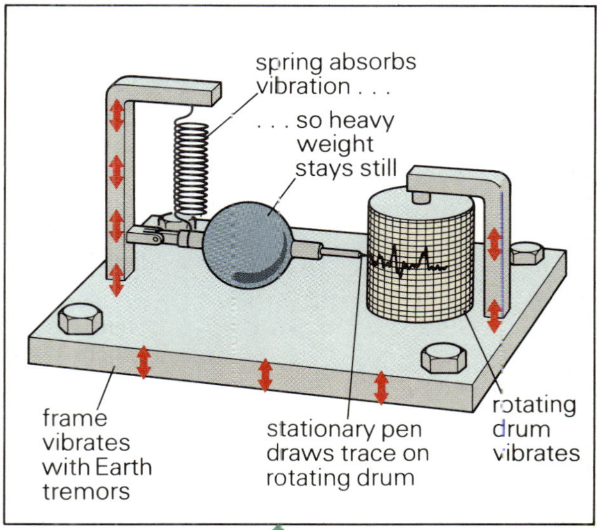

A simple seismometer

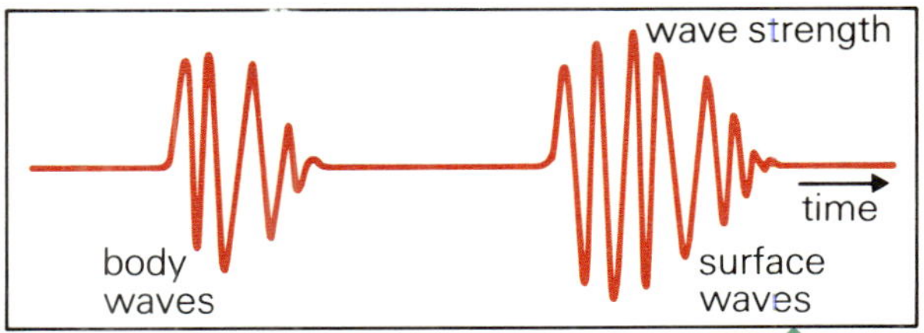

*Shock waves recorded by a seismometer – a **seismograph**. The larger the time interval between certain waves, the further away the epicentre.*

1 How do volcanoes and earthquakes provide evidence for the rock cycle theory?

2
- **a** What pushes lava out of a volcano?
- **b** Cooling lava can plug the vent of a volcano, making it appear inactive What could happen if magma continues to be forced up to the base of the plug?

3 Explain the difference between the focus of an earthquake and its epicentre.

4
- **a** How can shock waves be used to direct aid to earthquake disasters?
- **b** In 1988 in Armenia, Russia 25 000 people were killed by an earthquake measuring 6.9 on the Richter Scale. Compare this with the San Francisco quake and suggest reasons why fewer people died in the Californian one.

The inside story

Revealing the Earth's structure

We can observe the Earth's atmosphere and surface, and people have drilled or mined about 13 km down in the crust. But the centre of the Earth is about 6370 km down. How can we find out what the inside of the Earth is like? Although there is no *direct* information, the shock waves of earthquakes (and underground explosions) reveal clues about the Earth's structure.

Shock waves, like many other waves, can be bent or *refracted*. They travel at different speeds in materials of different density, and the waves are refracted as they pass from one material into another.

By detecting the body waves that have passed through the Earth, a picture of the inside of the Earth can be built up. This suggests that the Earth is made up of layers of different density. The waves also reveal the **state** of the layers – whether they are solid or liquid.

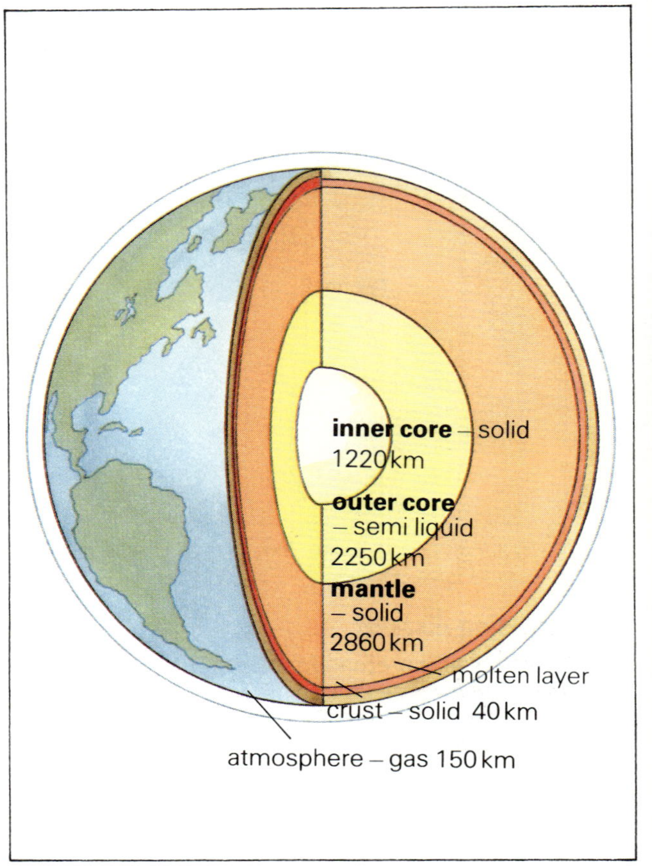

The layered Earth

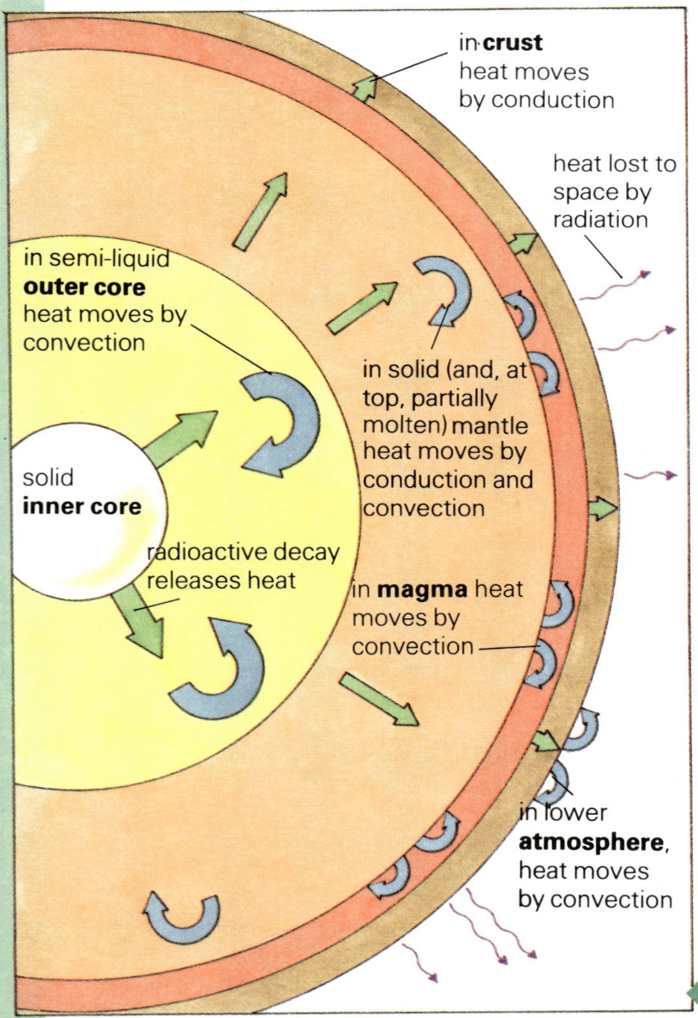

Hotting up

If you go down a very deep mine you find that temperature increases with depth in the Earth. Near the surface, the temperature rises between 10 and 20°C for every kilometre you go down. This change in temperature shows that much heat is released from deep inside the Earth.

There is no way of measuring temperatures below the deepest mine, so scientists make various assumptions. For example, they assume that the rate of heat loss is greater through the crust than lower in the Earth. This leads them to suggest that the temperature at the centre is about 5000°C.

Since heat is being lost from the Earth, it should be cooling down – but the rate of heat loss near the surface remains steady. So the Earth must be *producing* heat to make up for this loss. One hypothesis suggests that this heat is provided by natural radioactive materials decaying near the centre of the Earth.

Heat is transferred from the centre of the Earth to space by conduction, convection and radiation.

YOU CAN READ MORE ABOUT RADIOACTIVE DECAY ON SPREADS 11.4 AND 11.5.

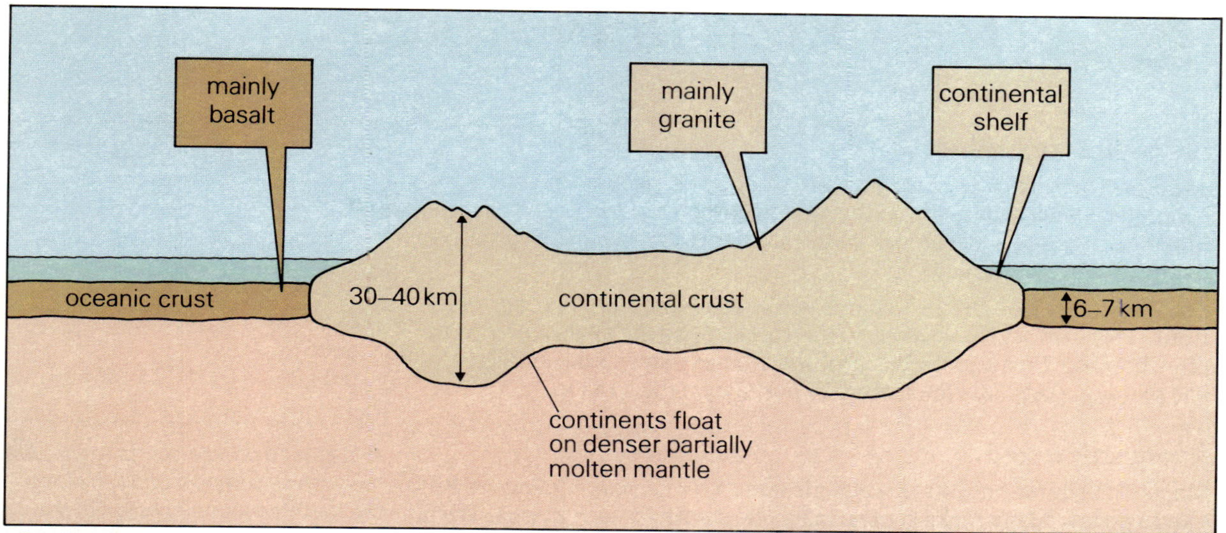

The light continents 'float' on the denser partially molten mantle – like an iceberg on water.

The floating crust

The **crust** is the lightest (least dense) layer of the Earth. *Under the continents* the crust is made up of light rocks such as **granite.** Somewhat denser rocks such as **basalt** occur mainly in the much thinner crust *beneath the oceans.*

Under the light rocks of the crust are the much denser rocks of the **mantle.** *Between* the crust and mantle is a region of *partially molten* mantle. This semi-solid layer is like 'gooey toffee' and it seems to allow the crust to 'float' on the mantle.

The outer and inner core

As shock waves pass through the Earth, they are strongly refracted about 2900 km below the surface. This is the boundary between the mantle and the densest part of the Earth – the **core**.

One kind of shock wave will not travel through a liquid. This wave does not appear to *enter* the core. So the ***outer* core** is probably liquid. Scientists reckon that the outer core contains molten iron and nickel, mixed with a lighter element (silicon or sulphur).

The *other* shock waves that can travel *through* the core speed up and are refracted as they do so. This indicates that there is an even denser layer at the centre of the Earth – this is the solid ***inner* core,** which is thought to be made up of a mixture of solid iron and nickel.

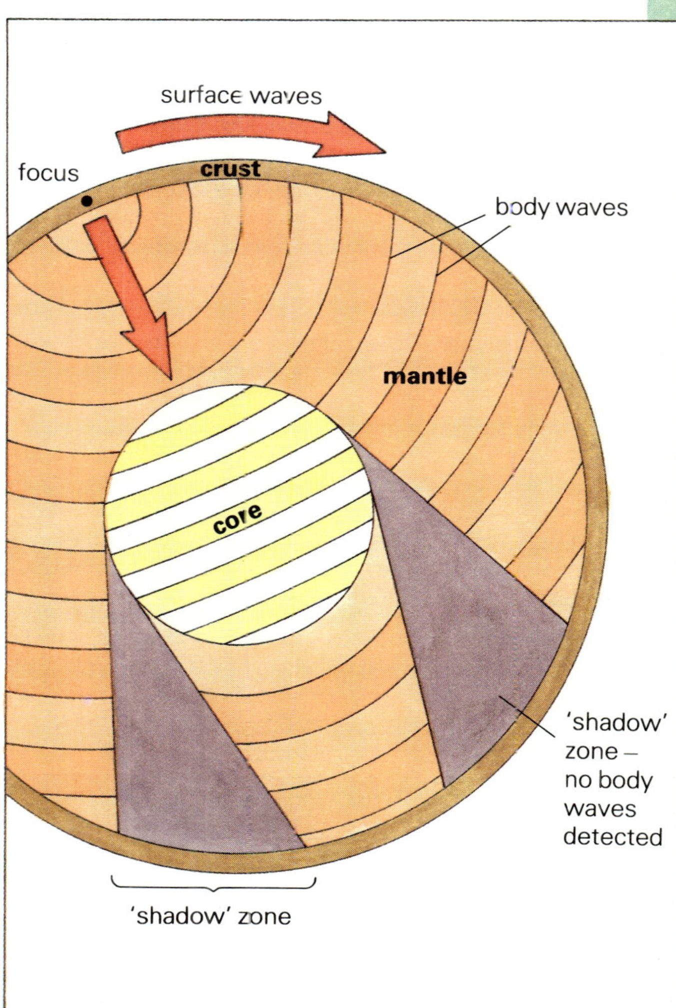

The dense core acts rather like a giant lens, 'focusing' the body waves that pass through it – and creating 'shadow' zones where no body waves can be detected.

1 How do shock waves help reveal the Earth's structure?

2 Explain why the Earth has not cooled down to a solid lump.

3 The average density of the Earth is 5.5 g/cm^3, while that of the rocks in the crust is 2.7 g/cm^3. What does this tell you about the centre of the planet?

12.8 The record in the rocks

The Earth's magnetism

The Earth acts like a huge magnet with **magnetic poles** currently a few hundred kilometres away from the *geographic* poles of the Earth's axis. Movements in the liquid metals in the outer core are thought to produce the Earth's magnetic field.

Any magnetic material free to move will lie along the Earth's **magnetic field**. This field acts at an *angle* to the surface, and the angle *varies* from place to place. So magnetic material will lie at an angle to the surface – and this angle indicates the material's position on the surface.

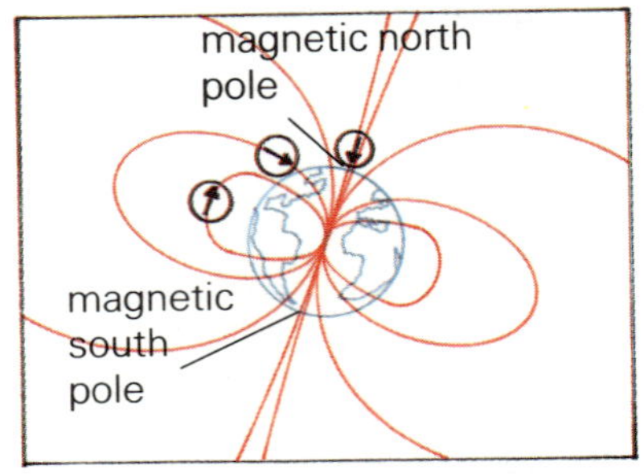

A magnetic needle points to the magnetic north pole and lies along the Earth's magnetic field. As the compass needle shows, the field is parallel to the Earth's surface at the equator but is straight down at the poles.

A magnetic record

Magnetic material only stays magnetic up to a temperature known as its **Curie point**. Many rocks contain magnetic materials such as iron. When a rock melts to magma below the crust, its temperature rises above the Curie point for iron and its magnetism is destroyed. If the magma is then pushed back up into the crust, it cools.

Any iron crystals in the solidifying rock become magnetised by the Earth's field. The crystals lie in the direction of the magnetic field *at that place*. So the crystals 'record' where the rock was on the Earth's surface when the rock last solidified.

Earth movements may later shift the rock to a different place – but if the rock doesn't melt again, the rock's magnetic record can reveal its original position.

The cooling iron crystals set along the Earth's magnetic field.

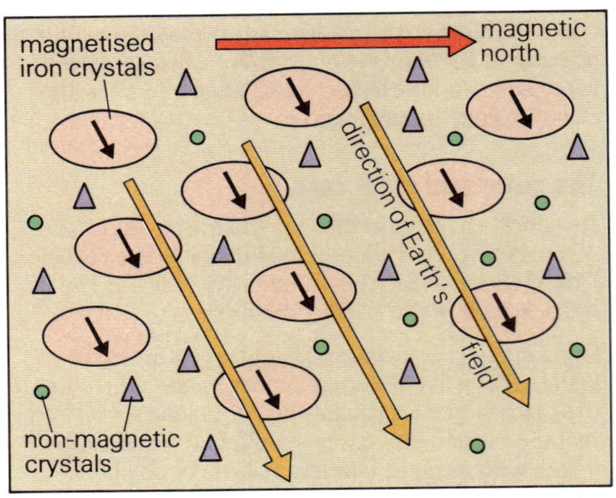

A magnetic diary

Investigations of the magnetic records in rocks have shown that the Earth's magnetic field is not fixed. The magnetic poles are even *reversed* from time to time – and the magnetic 'north' pole then lies in the geographical south! These changes mean that the magnetic record in a rock also depends on *when* the rock was formed. Rocks with similar magnetic records may have been formed at the same time. Dating one of these rocks by the methods opposite then suggests a date for all of them!

These three blocks of rock, broken by faults, now lie alongside one another – did they always? The rock type and thickness of the layers are the same in each block. But what does the magnetic record tell you about when the blocks were formed?

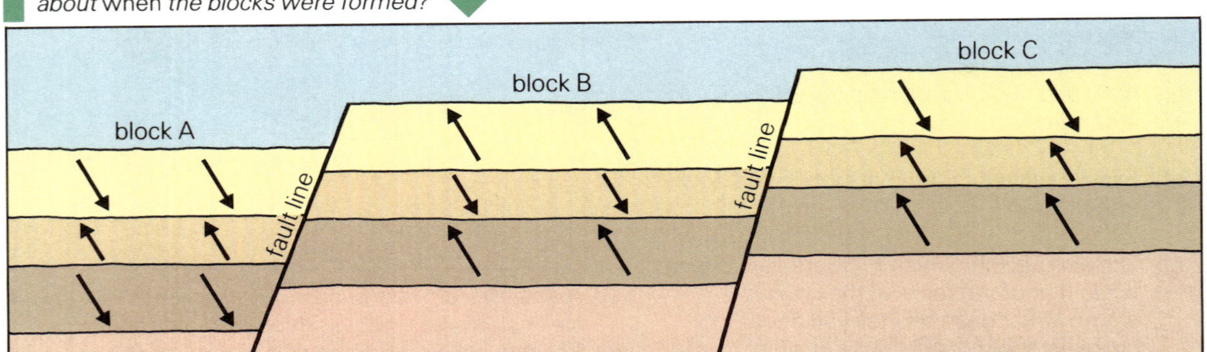

YOU CAN READ MORE ABOUT THE EARTH'S MAGNETISM ON SPREAD 11.5.

Radioactive dating

Many rocks contain **radioisotopes** and these provide a more accurate way of dating rocks. As a radioisotope (or 'parent') decays, its atoms change into the atoms of a different isotope (the 'daughter').

The time for *half* the atoms to decay is always the same for a particular radioisotope and is known as its **halflife**. The decay of radioisotopes in a rock can be used to estimate its age.

For example, suppose someone tried to cut down their consumption of chocolates by each day only eating *half* the chocolates still left in a box. The 'half-life of the chocolates' would be one day. If they left the *wrappers* behind (the 'daughters' of the chocolates), the ratio of sweets to wrappers would show you how long the 'diet' had lasted.

In the same way, the halflife and ratio of parent to daughter atoms in a rock can be used to date the rock. The remains of living things less than 10 000 years old can also be dated by looking for an active radioisotope called **carbon 14**.

Past life

Sedimentary rocks sometimes contain **fossils** – the remains of plants and animals which lived long ago. To form a fossil, the animal or plant must be buried quickly under sediment – and the sediment must harden to rock. Usually only the *hard* parts of animals and plants are preserved such as bones, shells and bark.

Animals and plants have evolved (changed) over time. Say a certain type of fossil is found in a band of rock which is easily dated. Then in another area, an *identical* fossil is found in another *undated* band of rock. The chances are that the two bands of rock were formed at roughly similar times.

*Carbon 14 has a half life of 5700 years, and can be used to date plant and animal remains up to 10 000 years old. This is called **radiocarbon dating**.*

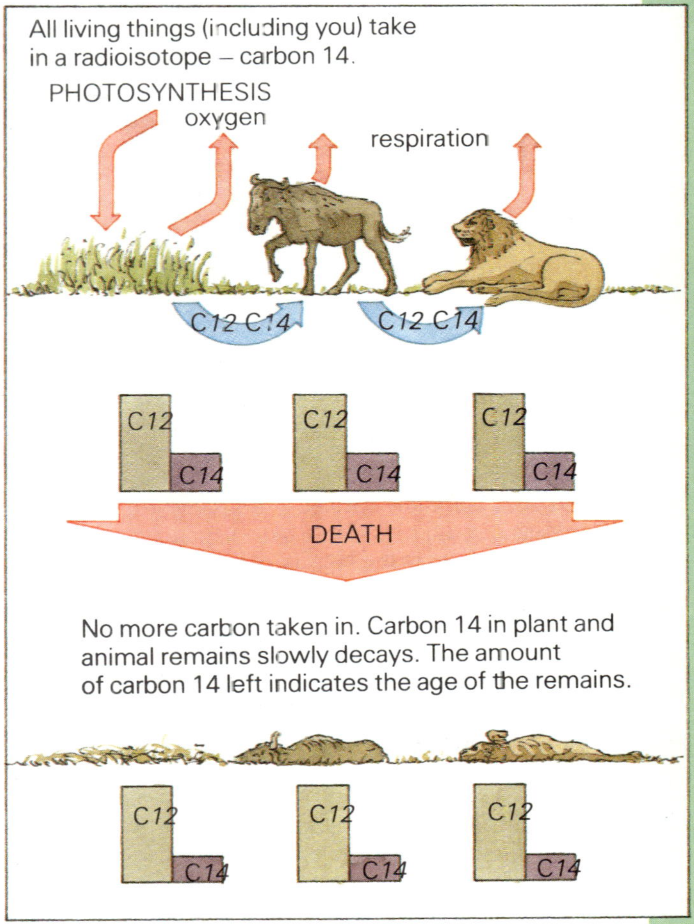

Only a tiny proportion of the countless animals and plants that have lived were preserved as fossils

1 At present, a compass needle points roughly north, towards the magnetic north pole. Would this always have been the case in the past? Explain your answer.

2 Why are the strongest magnetic records found mainly in iron-bearing *igneous* rocks?

3 Explain whether you could use the radisotope carbon 14 to date:
- **a** a flint axe-head
- **b** the fossil of a dinosaur
- **c** an Egyptian wood carving.

YOU CAN READ MORE ABOUT RADIOISOTOPES AND THEIR DECAY ON SPREAD 11.4.

The evolving world

The fossil record

Dating rocks (*see 12.8*) also suggests the age of any fossils contained – and they, in turn, can be used to date other rocks. This is because life slowly changes or **evolves** over time. A particular fossil only occurs in rocks of a certain age – and any rocks containing it must be that age. For example, rocks containing intricately shaped graptolites must be *older* than rocks containing simpler-shaped graptolites. The millions of fossils discovered allow rocks to be dated easily. They also provide a **fossil record** of life on Earth.

Life evolves in response to changing conditions on the Earth. To survive, animals and plants must adapt to new conditions. Those that fail to do so die out or become **extinct**, while those better suited flourish. The fossil record shows when new creatures evolved and others became extinct. Fossils and other evidence in the rocks have been used to draw up a chart of events in the history of the Earth (*see opposite*). Among the most important events affecting life were the changes in atmosphere and climate.

Fossils of the delicate skeletons of graptolites show that these sea animals became simpler in shape over time.

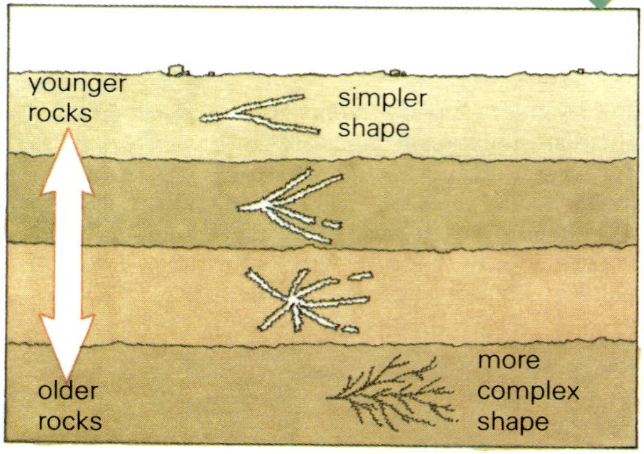

The evolving atmosphere

The atmosphere of the hot early Earth contained many gases, including steam. As the Earth slowly cooled, water condensed and collected in seas. These absorbed other gases from the air and chemicals from the land to form the 'chemical soup' in which life began. About 3500 million years ago, there was carbon dioxide and other gases in the atmosphere but no free (uncombined) oxygen.

Then the first life – plants – began *taking in* carbon dioxide and *releasing* oxygen during **photosynthesis**. Oxygen reacts easily and so little of this oxygen remained uncombined. It was at least another 2500 million years before there was enough free oxygen for **aerobic respiration** – and animals evolved. Some free oxygen also collected as **ozone**. This absorbs the Sun's ultraviolet rays which would be harmful to life on land. The ozone in the atmosphere allowed life to move on to land. As plants cloaked the bare rock, more and more oxygen was released, and eventually the air became similar to that we breathe today.

The early atmosphere changed greatly as oceans formed.

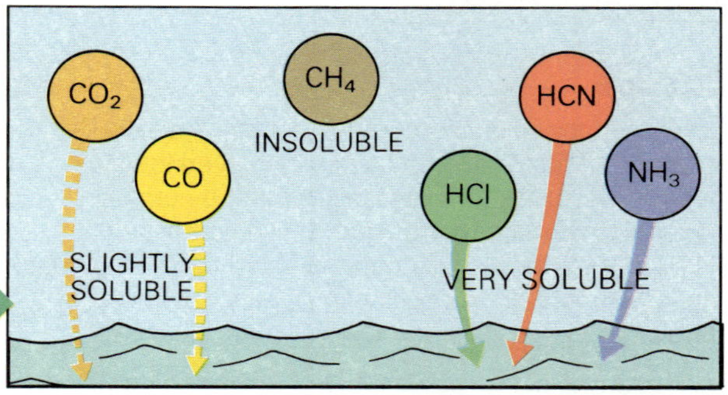

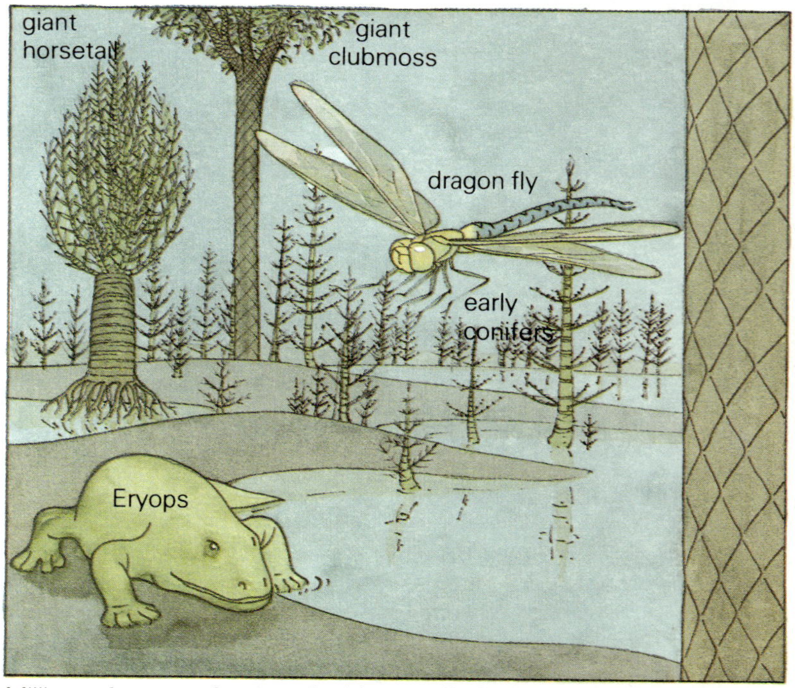

Millions of tonnes of carbon dioxide were 'locked up' in the hot, swampy carboniferous forests – which eventually became the coal we burn today.

Climatic change

The animals and plants that evolved and flourished at a particular time must have been well suited to the climate in that place at that time. So the fossil record gives clues about past climates.

For example, sedimentary rocks formed in the early Cretaceous period contain many shellfish fossils. This suggests there were many shallow warm seas at the time, since shellfish favour these conditions. There have been large variations in climate during **geological time** (the time since the formation of the Earth). These have caused 'population explosions' and extinctions – many such changes are evident in the fossil record.

Geological time

Ideas about events up to 570 million years ago are backed up by scant evidence in the rocks.

By about 570 million years ago, creatures with hard parts had evolved, and these left far more fossils in the rocks. The fossil record for that last 570 million years contains so much information that this time is divided into **eras** and **periods**.

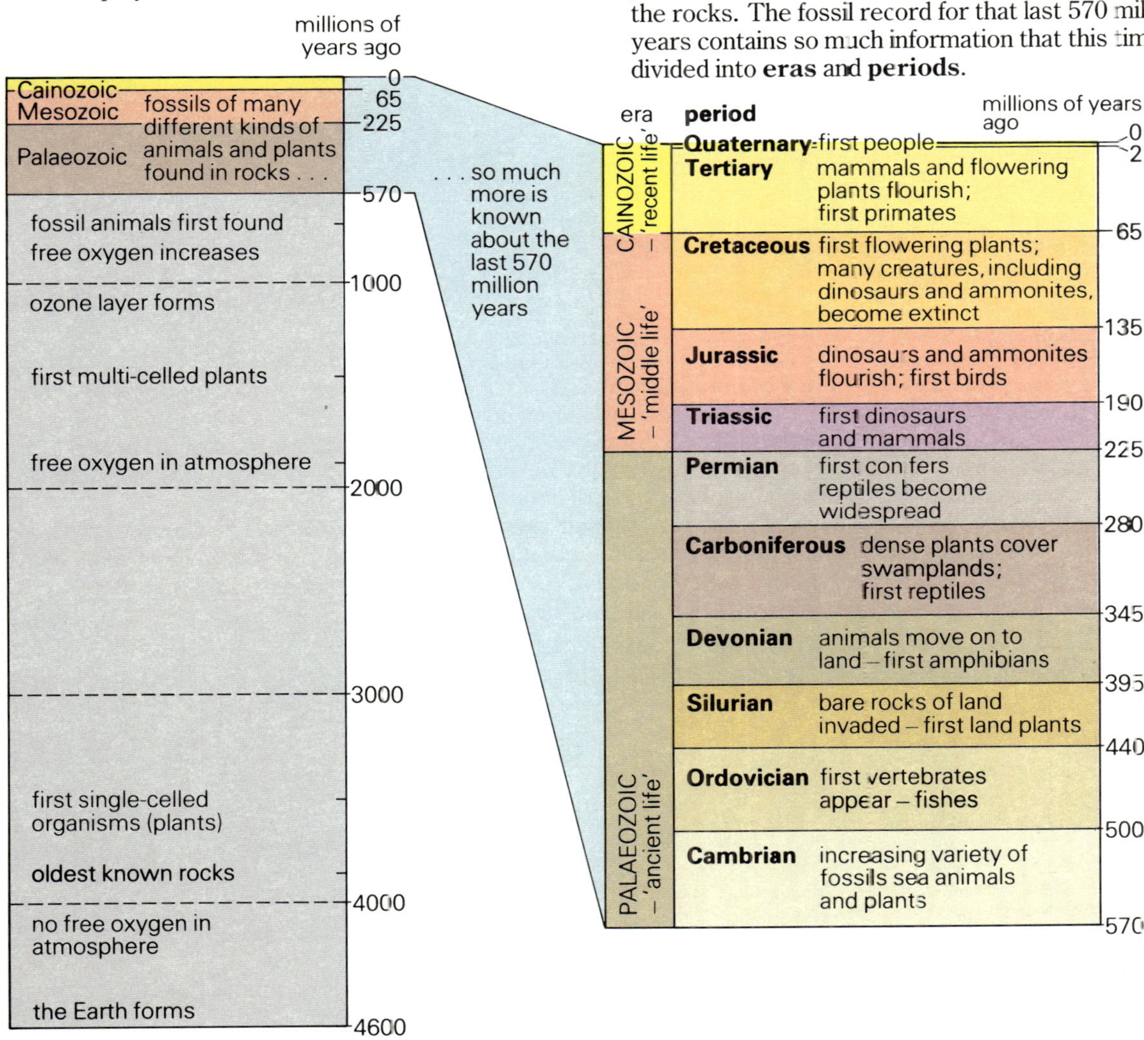

1 Fossils can be used to date rocks. What else can fossils tell us?

2 List some ways in which:
- **a** changes in the atmosphere affected the evolution of life
- **b** living things changed the atmosphere.

3 Suggest reasons why:
- **a** plants had to develop before animals
- **b** plants had to move on the land before animals could
- **c** mammals did not flourish until 65 million years ago.

12.10 The Earth's changing face

The continental jigsaw

At the beginning of this century, people believed that the position of the continents never changed. But some were intrigued by the fact that the shapes of South America and Africa fitted together like the pieces of a jigsaw. The German scientist, Wegener, thought this fit was too close to be just chance. He suspected that the continents were *not* fixed – and that South America and Africa had been connected and then drifted apart. He looked for evidence in the rocks that the two continents had once been joined.

Fossil evidence

When land masses are joined, animals and plants can spread freely between them – and the same animals and plants are found on both. When land masses are separated, their animals and plants are *isolated* and evolve *differently*. Yet fossils of the same animals and plants are found on widely separated continents. Wegener claimed these fossils were evidence that the continents were once joined.

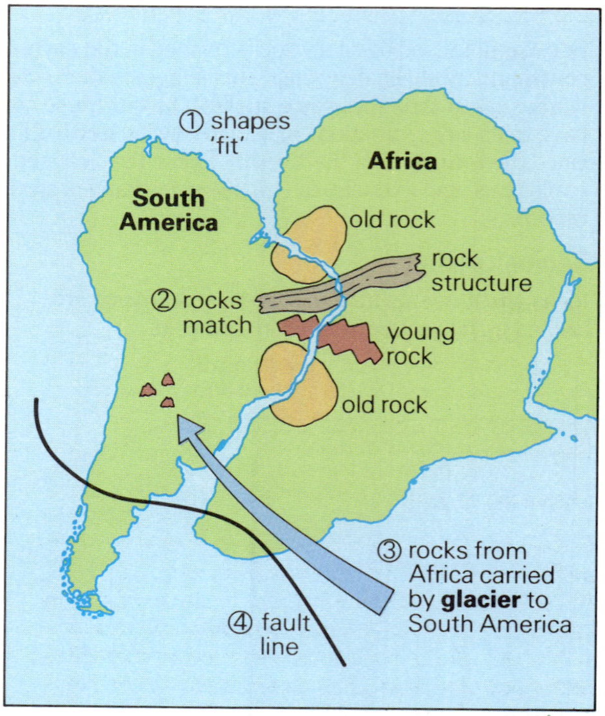

This diagram shows some of the evidence linking Africa and South America. Do you think the two continents were once joined?

Drifting continents?

In 1912, Wegener proposed his **theory of continental drift**. He presented a lot of evidence but could not explain *how* the continents were moved sideways. Most scientists found the idea of drifting continents incredible, and the theory was rejected for decades. But in time new techniques, such as radioactive dating and 'reading' the magnetic record in the rocks, provided further evidence. Investigators found signs that *other* continents have been joined in the past. Eventually, scientists had to accept the theory. It is now thought that continents have come together and drifted apart many times since they formed.

Some of the fossil animals and plants found on the two continents. What does this fossil evidence tell you?

South America	Glossopteris 	Mesosaurus 	Tyrannosaurus 	no fossil horses found in South America 	llama 
Africa	Glossopteris 	Mesosaurus 	Allosaurus 	Mesohippus early horse 	camel 
period of millions of years ago	Carboniferous	Permian	Cretaceous	Tertiary	Quaternary

Evidence

There are several pieces of evidence which indicate that South America and Africa were joined:

- **shapes** 'fit'
- **fossils** of certain ages match
- **rocks** of certain ages match:
  - *chemical analysis* shows rock material matches
  - *dating* (e.g. radioactive) shows rocks same age
  - *magnetic record* shows rocks formed at similar time in similar place
- **faults** continue across both continents
- **climatic records** match:
  - e.g. both have U-shaped valleys formed as *glaciers* moved across continents which were joined

Changing patterns

Fossils and other evidence suggest that some 500 million years ago, Africa, South America, India, Australia and Antarctica formed one huge land mass known as **Gondwanaland.** By about 250 million years ago, *all* the continents were joined together in the 'super continent', **Pangaea.** The drift of the continents about the surface caused changes in the continents' climates. Land that was over the equator could drift towards a pole and become covered in ice. Fossil palm trees have been discovered under London, showing that at one time Britain had a tropical climate.

The spreading ocean

By 1960, the theory of continental drift was accepted but a problem remained – what force could move the vast continents round the face of the Earth? Then some clues were found – under the ocean! North and South America are now separated from Europe and Africa by the Atlantic Ocean. Down the middle of this ocean runs a ridge. Scientists discovered that magma wells up along this ridge and cools to form layers of rock on either side. As more magma wells up, older rock layers are pushed further apart – and the ocean *spreads*. The rate of '**ocean-floor spreading**' can be found by measuring and dating the rock layers. As the Atlantic grows larger, America is moving away from Europe at a rate of about 2 cm a year.

About 200 million years ago, Pangaea began to split up – and the continents slowly drifted to their present positions.

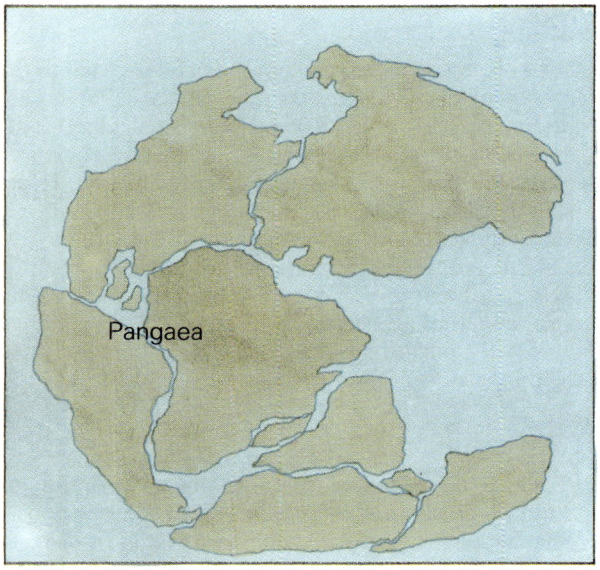

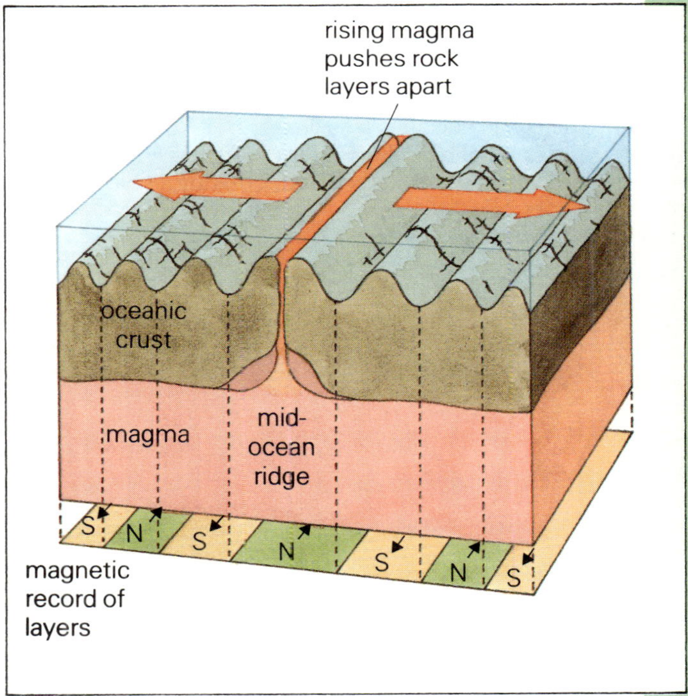

What evidence is there about the rock layers being pushed apart?

1 Look at the diagram comparing fossils found in Africa and South America. During which ages do you think the continents were:
a joined?
b drifting apart?

2 Scientists found Wegener's ideas very difficult to accept. Suggest two reasons for this.

3 Coal and animal fossils have been found under the ice sheets that cover Antarctica. Explain how this is possible.

4 Marsupials (pouched mammals, such as the kangaroo) were once widespread. Now they are mainly found in Australia. Suggest why.

12.11 Plate tectonics

Moving the pieces

Ocean-floor spreading and other discoveries led to the **theory of plate tectonics**. According to this theory, the Earth's crust is cracked up into a small number of gigantic pieces called **plates**. These plates are not fixed; they '*float*' on the partially molten mantle. Heat from the centre of the Earth rises in strong convection currents through the mantle and these currents are thought to cause cracks through weak spots in the crust. The convection currents force hot magma up to the surface. As magma wells up through the crack it pushes apart the crust on either side – and the huge plates are moved sideways.

Convection currents cause cracks in continental crust . . .

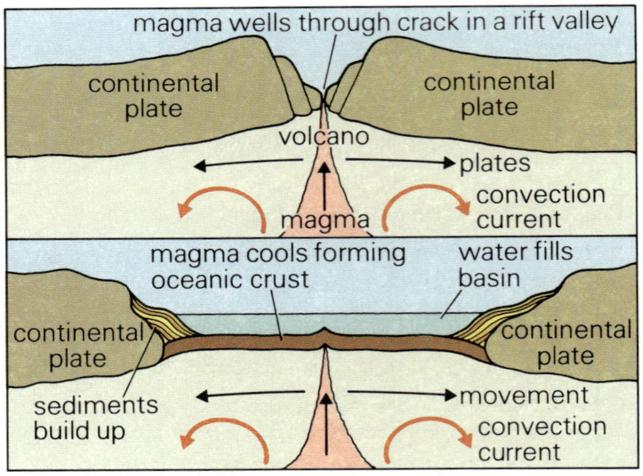

. . . an ocean is born and continents 'drift'.

Colliding plates

Plates are being pushed apart in some parts of the world – so they must be *colliding* in other places. What happens when plates collide depends on the density of their crust. Oceanic crust is much denser than continental crust. When the two collide, the oceanic crust is pushed *beneath* the continental crust, forming a coastal **mountain range** and a deep **trench** in the ocean floor. The rock pushed down melts and becomes less dense, so it floats up towards the crust. This light magma can be forced up through any weaknesses in the crust, creating a volcano or a series of volcanoes.

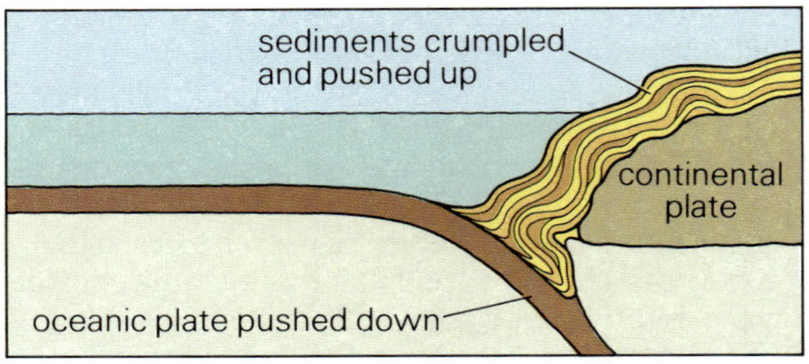

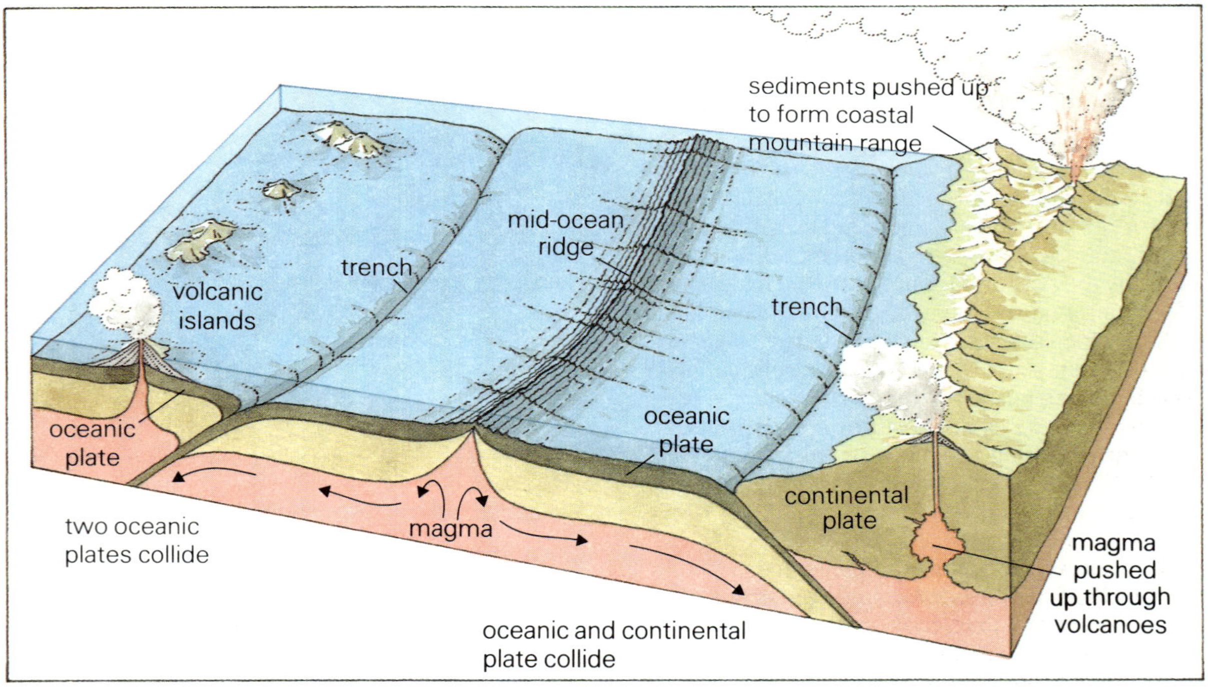

When oceanic plates collide, one is pushed beneath the other. Sediment scraped off the surface of the descending plate may be forced up, forming an ***island arc****. Light magma welling up makes this arc of islands volcanic.*

Folding rock

Only oceanic plates are forced down and 'recycled'. When the thick continental plates move together, neither is pushed below the other. But the collision can cause the sedimentary rock between the plates to buckle up into **fold mountains**. The Alps and the Pyrenees mountain ranges were formed in this way. The Himalayas were created when two great continental plates squeezed the oceanic crust between them up into mountains.

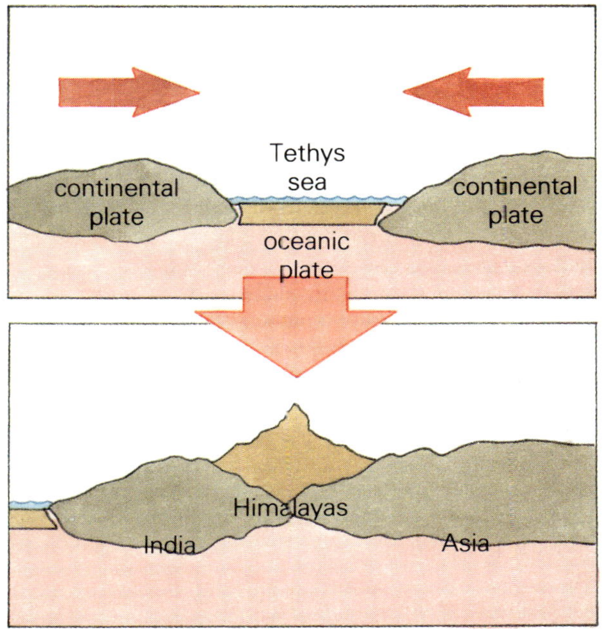

A great theory to fit the evidence!

Before the theory of plate tectonics was proposed, many points about the Earth puzzled scientists. What causes the continents to drift? Why do mountains tend to stretch in long curved chains? Why do volcanoes and earthquakes usually occur only in certain long, narrow areas of the world? The theory was quickly accepted because plate tectonics explains these and many other questions. Mountain building and volcanoes occur at **plate boundaries** between colliding plates. The energy released when plates move gives rise to earthquakes.

Most volcanic and earthquake activity occurs where the plates collide.

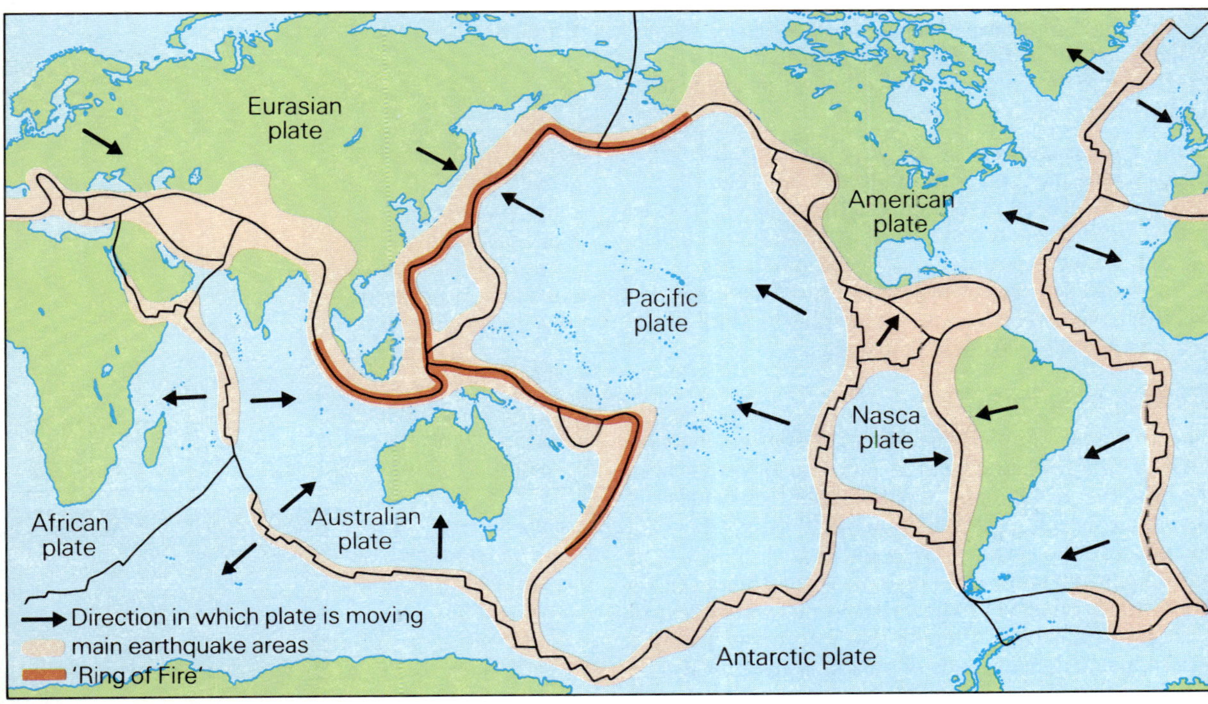

1 Look at the map above, showing the plates.

a Why do earthquakes occur mainly along plate boundaries?

b The Rocky Mountains and the Andes run down the west coast of North and South America. Suggest reasons for this. Would you expect them to be fold or volcanic mountains?

c Why do you think the area marked in red is called 'Ring of Fire'?

d Would you expect to find a deep ocean trench near the mid-Atlantic ridge? Explain your answers.

2 What causes the plates and their movement?

3 Why might you find fossil fish on Mount Everest (in the Himalayas)?

The Earth and Venus

Planetary twins?

Venus is our closest planetary neighbour. The Earth and Venus, along with the other planets and the Sun, are thought to have condensed from the same cloud of matter about 4600 million years ago. Formed (relatively) close together, at the same time from similar materials, the two planets were probably planetary 'twins' at birth. How similar are the 'twins' now?

Compared with Earth

Some details of a planet can be estimated by observing it from Earth. Comparing this information with what we know about the Earth gives clues to conditions on the planet. For example, the Earth's atmosphere is held by gravity. As gases in the atmosphere are heated by the Sun, they move faster. *Light* atoms, such as hydrogen, may become hot enough to move at the **escape velocity** (the velocity needed to escape the planet's gravity) and stream off into space. So a planet's atmosphere depends on its gravity and temperature. Small, hot Mercury is likely to have very little atmosphere compared with the Earth, while the cooler, massive Jupiter probably has a much denser atmosphere.

Venus's mass and gravity are very similar to the Earth's. The most obvious difference between these two planets is their distance from the Sun. Venus is so much closer that it receives nearly twice as much of the Sun's energy per unit area as the Earth. So temperatures on Venus will be higher. What effect will this have had on Venus's atmosphere? Until a few decades ago, people could only guess.

Viewing from Earth

Like all the planets (and the Moon), Venus can only be seen by light reflected from its sunlit face. Venus is the brightest of all the planets because thick clouds envelop it, which reflect the Sun's light very well – and obscure the surface. Even the largest optical telescopes just show close-ups of swirling layers of cloud. Early observers knew that Venus would be hotter than Earth and thought that water was boiling off producing dense clouds of steam. Some people imagined that Venus had a hot damp surface covered with swamp plants – like the Earth during Carboniferous times.

Through Venus's clouds . . .

Such fantasies were destroyed in the 1960s when a series of **space probes** started visiting Venus. The probes carried instruments controlled by computer. These instruments analysed the atmosphere and found that it contains mainly carbon dioxide – and virtually no water. Capsules sent down to the surface were crushed by an atmospheric pressure *90 times* that on Earth!

How long is Venus's 'day'?
How long is Venusian 'year'?

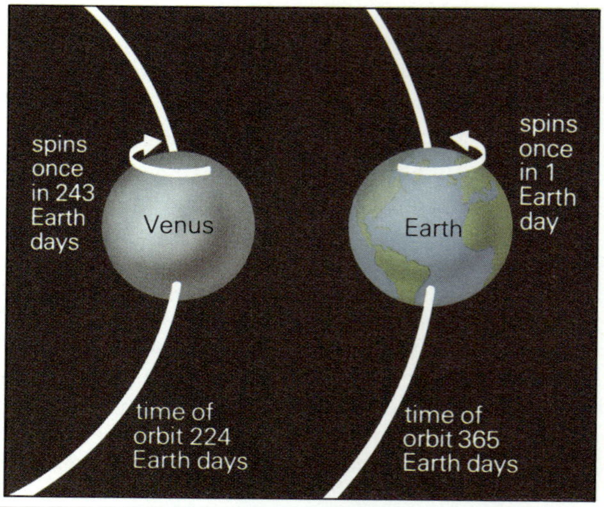

(compared with Earth's)	Earth	Venus
mass	1	0.82
diameter (km)	12756	12104
density (kg/m^3)	5517	5250
gravity (compared with Earth's)	1	0.903
escape velocity (km/s)	11.2	10.4
average distance from Sun (million km)	150	108
surface temperature	22°C	?
atmosphere	mainly nitrogen and oxygen	?
atmospheric pressure at ground (compared with Earth's)	1	?

Like the Moon, Venus has ***phases****. This shows a 'full' Venus.*

. . . to the surface

Sturdier capsules managed to operate on the surface – for a short while. These photographed the surface and took rock samples. The **surface temperature** was found to be 465°C – so hot that the rocks probably glow red in the dark. More information was provided by a probe which orbited Venus, mapping the surface using **radar**. Radio waves can pass through the thick clouds and revealed a long rift valley, small mountains and volcanoes. No-one knows what the inside of Venus is like but it is thought to be similar to the Earth's (*see 12.7*).

Venus looks inviting . . . but the swirling clouds are sulphuric acid, and acid drips through an atmosphere rent by lightning.

How did the twins become so different?

Over the past 4600 million years, the Earth has developed into a 'blue and white planet' teeming with life. Venus probably started off with the same amount of water, but never became cool enough for the water to condense. It is thought that in the hot atmosphere, water (H_2O) split into hydrogen (H) and oxygen (O). Hot light hydrogen atoms have been reaching escape velocity and leaking away into space ever since – leaving Venus virtually waterless. The heavy carbon dioxide molecules remained and trapped the Sun's heat by the **greenhouse effect**. This could have heated the rocks so they gave off *more* carbon dioxide which trapped *more* heat, and so on. Such a 'runaway' greenhouse effect is thought to have caused Venus's present high temperature. The weight of the carbon dioxide (which is heavier than air) produces the high atmospheric pressure.

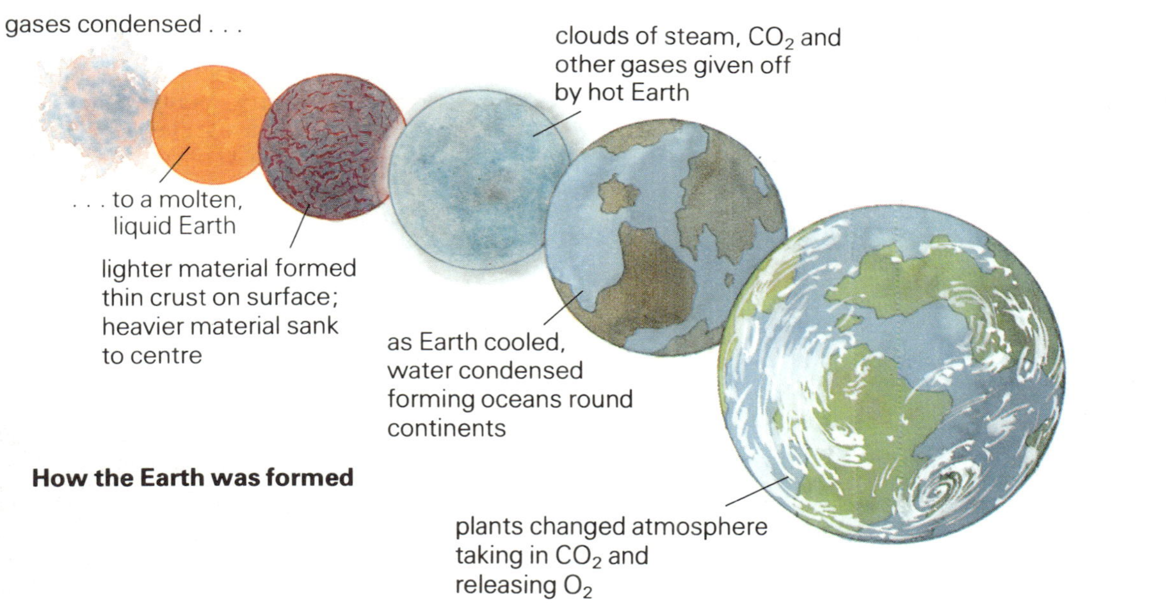

How the Earth was formed

1 Why were Venus and the Earth expected to be similar?

2 **a** Copy and complete the table opposite comparing the Earth and Venus.
b Divide the table up to show similarities and differences.

3 What factors affect a planet's atmosphere?

4 Suggest why:
a The rocks on Venus's surface are sharp-edged.
b The surface of Venus is hotter than that of Mercury (which is even closer to the Sun)
c No life like the Earth's evolved on Venus.

The solar system

Orbiting the Sun

The Earth and Venus are members of a family of planets that move in nearly circular orbits round the Sun, held by the Sun's gravity. The system stretches from Mercury (about 60 million km from the Sun) to Pluto (about 6000 million km away).

Little is known about tiny, distant Pluto, but it seems to be very different from the rest of the family. It has a strange orbit, which is not in the same plane as the other planets, and sometimes brings it closer to the Sun than Neptune. Lumps of dust and ice resembling huge 'dirty snow-balls' also orbit the Sun. These **comets** travel along strange elongated orbits which are often outside the plane of the planets.

The solar system. The sizes of the planets are roughly to scale but their distances from the Sun are not – if you look at the distances below you'll see why.

Planetary facts	Mercury	Venus	Earth	Mars	Jupiter	Saturn	Uranus	Neptune	Pluto
distance from Sun (million km)	58.8	108	150	228	778	1427	2869	4496	5880
diameter (km)	4880	12104	12756	6790	143360	120320	52480	49920	3200?
mass (compared with Earth's)	0.06	0.82	1	0.11	318	95	15	17	0.003?
density (kg/m^3)	5430	5250	5517	3900	1330	700	1270	1700	1100?
escape velocity (km/s)	4.3	10.4	11.2	5.0	60	35	22	24	1.2?
time of orbit (Earth years)	0.24	0.6	1	1.9	11.9	29.5	84	165	248
time of spin (Earth days)	58	243	1	1.02	0.41	0.45	0.72	0.63	?

A desert scene on Earth? No, this is the surface of Mars! Find out how deserts were formed on Earth – and you might be able to guess at how this Martian desert was formed.

The inner planets

The four planets closest to the Sun – **Mercury**, **Venus**, **Earth** and **Mars** – have quite *high* densities and so must contain fairly *heavy* materials.

The first out from the Sun, *Mercury* is the smallest of the inner planets and has virtually no atmosphere. During its long 'day', its sunlit face heats up to 430°C, while its dark side cools to −170°C.

Beyond Venus and the Earth lies the least dense of the inner planets, *Mars*. Its surface can be seen from Earth and early observers thought the planet looked similar to Earth – and could be inhabited by Martians. It does have volcanoes, rift valleys and polar 'ice' caps but, as far as we know, no Martians. The atmosphere of Mars is very thin (mainly carbon dioxide). Its surface temperature never rises above 0°C and the little water left there is ice. Beyond Mars, a belt of small pieces of rock known as **asteroids** orbit the Sun.

The gas giants

The next four planets – **Jupiter**, **Saturn**, **Uranus** and **Neptune** – have *low* densities indicating that they are made of *light* materials. Each is likely to contain mainly hydrogen, increasing in pressure to the centre, where there is probably a small solid core. A probe trying to land on the 'surface' of a gas giant would just sink through gas to liquid until it was crushed by the high pressure. Although they contain light material, these planets are so huge that they have large masses.

Their very thick atmospheres contain substances such as methane (CH_4) and ammonia (NH_3) – rich in the hydrogen that is lost by small planets. The gas giants are very cold because they receive little energy from the distant Sun. Yet Jupiter and Saturn have convection currents in their atmospheres causing strong winds – up to 1500 km/hr on Saturn! It is thought that these two planets must have a source of internal energy that powers their weather.

Pieces of ice and rock form a ring round Saturn, just as asteroids form a ring round the Sun.

The birth of the solar system

All the planets (apart from Pluto) move round the Sun very regularly, in the same *plane* and in the same *direction* – the direction of the Sun's spin. Why is this? And why are the inner planets denser than the gas giants? There are many theories to explain how the solar system was formed but, to be accepted, a theory must answer these and other questions. The theory shown here explains *some* questions and is widely accepted. The planets orbit in the same way because they were formed *at the same time* as the Sun. The gravity at the centre of the cloud would have been higher than at the edge. So heavy materials could have pulled in to form the inner planets near the Sun, but light materials would have stayed further out, forming the gas giants.

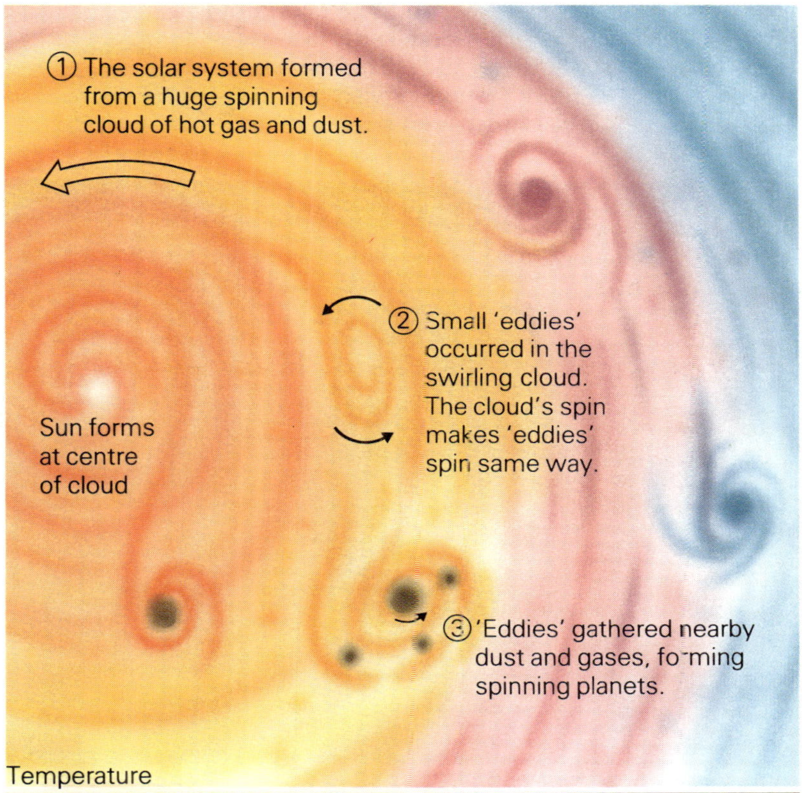

Temperature	Very high	High	Medium	Very low
Effect of: a Sun's gravity –		Heavy elements pulled in	Light elements not pulled in, move out from centre	
b falling temp –		Heavy elements soon condense out	Light elements . . . . . . some condense as gases get cold	. . . solidify when far from Sun
Planets formed		Dense, solid core not much gas	Small core, huge liquid gas layers	Large ice-like cores, some gas

1 Some people think that Pluto was not formed along with the rest of the planets but is a captured comet. What evidence is there to support this theory?

2 Suggest why:
- **a** the temperature on Mercury varies so much between day and night
- **b** probes found no traces of life on Mars
- **c** Jupiter has a very dense atmosphere
- **d** the gas giants contain mainly light materials.

Star gazing

A star is born

The solar system formed from a cloud of matter that was mainly hydrogen – the most common element in the universe. Most of this cloud was pulled by gravity into a swirling ball at the centre. The temperature and pressure at the centre of the ball increased as hydrogen particles were drawn closer and closer together – until the hydrogen started *fusing* to form helium. This **nuclear fusion** reaction released energy and the Sun began to shine. All stars produce energy by nuclear fusion. The Earth only receives a tiny fraction of the Sun's energy – just enough to make conditions on Earth right for life. The Sun continues to provide all the energy which is locked up in food and all the energy to power the weather. The Sun was also the original source of the energy which is released from fossil fuels when used in transport and power stations.

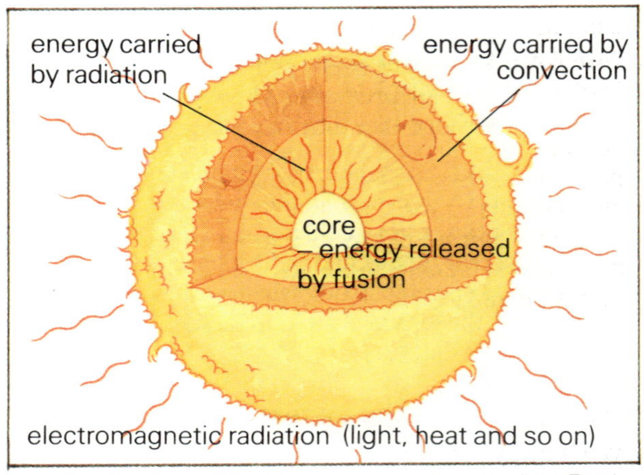

The tiny fraction of the Sun's energy that reaches Earth has travelled as radiation across 150 million km of space!

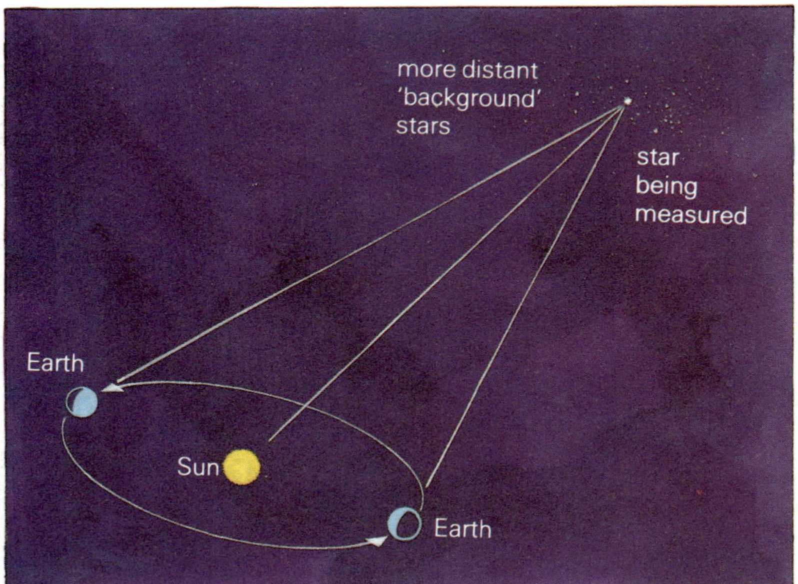

The position in the sky of a nearby *star can be measured against a background of more distant stars. By measuring the star's position at six-monthly intervals – from* opposite *ends of the Earth's orbit – the distance to the nearby star can be calculated.*

Star distances

When the Sun sets, you can see countless other stars in the night sky. The distances to some ***nearby*** stars can be calculated by viewing them from different points in the Earth's orbit. Even these nearby stars are an enormous number of kilometres away – for example, the nearest, Proxima Centauri, is over 40 billion km away! So a special unit is used for star distances – the **light year**. This is the distance that light travels in a year and is about 9.5 billion km. Proxima Centauri is 4.25 light years away, while the brightest star in the sky, Sirius, is 8.7 light years distant.

Size and colour

Through a telescope, you can see that there appear to be different colours and sizes of stars. Of course, a star will look smaller the further away it is. But if astronomers know the distance to a star and how big it *appears* to be, they can work out the star's *actual* size. Such calculations have shown that there is a huge range of star sizes. Stars also differ in colour, and the colour of a star gives a guide to its **surface temperature**. Just as heated metal glows dull red, then yellow, then white and finally blue, cooler stars appear dull red while the hottest stars look blue. Our sun is a medium-sized yellow star. Betelgeuse in Orion is a red giant star – large enough to take in the Sun and all the inner planets.

The light from stars

Much more can be found out about a star by passing its light through a prism to form a **spectrum**. This shows the colours or **wavelengths** of light received from the star. A star's spectrum is always crossed by dark lines. Gases round the star *absorb* some wavelengths of light leaving these dark lines. Each element absorbs *particular* wavelengths of light, creating its own pattern of dark lines – and this pattern acts as a 'code' for the element. By studying a star's spectrum carefully, astronomers can work out the star's **composition** – what elements the star is made up of. A star's spectrum also reveals whether a star is moving towards or away from us.

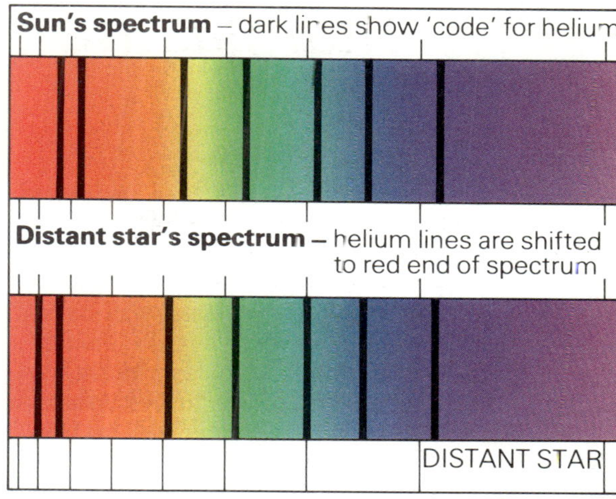

The **red shift** in the distant star's helium lines shows that this star is moving away from us. A shift of lines towards the blue end (a **blue shift**) would indicate that a star is moving towards us.

Star groups

Telescopes can gather light from very distant sources, millions of light years away. These sources are not single stars but groups or **galaxies** of stars, held together by gravity. The Sun is also part of a galaxy, known as the **Milky Way**. This contains thousands of millions of stars. The nearest galaxy to us, Andromeda, is about 2 million light years away.

The death of a star

The stars in the sky seem unchanging, but each is converting hydrogen to helium in its core and its hydrogen will eventually run out. Then other fusion reactions will occur, such as helium fusing to carbon. What happens next depends partly on the size of the star. Our medium-sized Sun will slowly cool and swell. The red giant Sun will expand out perhaps as far as Mercury's orbit – but not for another few thousand million years! Then the Sun will gradually shrink to a cold lump of matter.

Some very large stars have a more spectacular end – they explode in a **supernova**. This releases enormous amounts of energy and atoms smash together to form heavier elements. A supernova is like a 'factory of the elements'. The solar system is thought to have formed soon after a supernova explosion. The heavier elements in the Earth and the other planets were probably created by this supernova.

On a clear night (away from city lights) you can see a milky band of light stretching across the sky – the Milky Way.

1 The speed of light is 300 000 km/s. How long does it take the Sun's light to reach:
a the Earth, 150 million km away?
b Pluto, 5880 million km away?

2 Space probes have been sent to investigate other planets but not other stars. Suggest reasons for this.

3 **a** There are six stars nearer to the Sun than Sirius, yet Sirius is the brightest star in the night sky. What could you guess about the nearer stars?
b The second brightest star, Canopus, is over 100 light years away. It is yellowish in colour. What could you guess about the size of Canopus?

4 The dark lines in a star's spectrum are called absorption lines. Explain why.

5 Write a brief description of what you think might happen to Earth as the Sun expands out to take in Mercury.

12.15 The expanding universe

A flat Earth?

If you had no information from telescopes and probes, and no knowledge of forces such as gravity, would it occur to you that the Earth is a spinning sphere moving at about 30 km/s round the Sun? Naturally enough, early people assumed the Earth was still and that the Sun and Moon orbited it. They also thought the world was flat, because they could *see* that it was. Sailors on a long journey could have noticed unfamiliar stars rising above the horizon and guessed that the Earth is round – but none did as far as we know! About 500 BC, some Greeks started arguing that the Earth is a sphere – the Sun and Moon were clearly spheres so why should the Earth be different? Slowly people came to accept that the Earth is not flat, but for another 2,000 years the Earth remained the 'centre of the universe'.

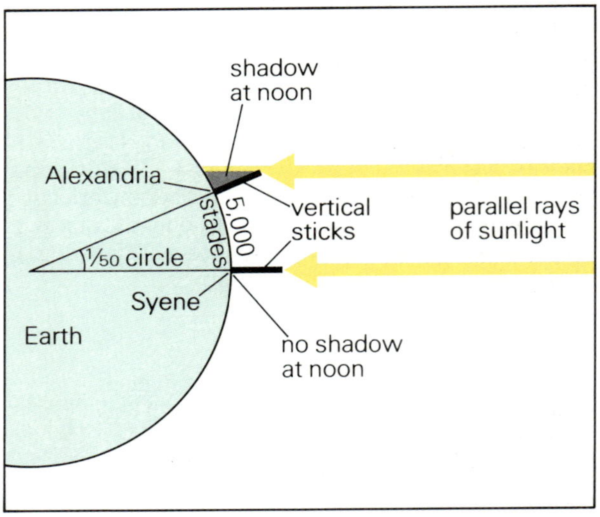

Eratosthemos used these shadows to calculate that the Earth's radius was 6400 km.

Right shape, wrong place – the Greeks vision of the Earth in space.

The centre of the universe?

The planets were thought to orbit the Earth along with the Sun and Moon. From Earth, the planets seem to move steadily, then go backwards for a short distance before continuing on. Astronomers found it very dificult to explain these complicated orbits. Then in the 1500s, Copernicus and others realised that the motion of the planets was very simple – they moved in regular orbits *round the Sun*. After the invention of the telescope (in about 1600) astronomers could observe the planets much more closely. Soon most astronomers thought that the Earth and other planets moved round the Sun – and the Sun became the 'centre of the universe'.

The Hubble telescope orbits above the Earth's atmosphere – and so has a clearer view of space.

Observing space

As telescopes got bigger and better our 'universe' grew in size. Three more planets, Uranus, Neptune and Pluto, were observed past Saturn. Light from more distant sources revealed information about stars and galaxies. Some sources emit little or no light but do give out radiowaves, and these are detected using **radio-telescopes**. The most distant and perhaps the strangest objects discovered are star-like (quasi-stellar) objects known as **quasars**. These emit vast amounts of energy in the form of light, radiowaves or both.

On the sidelines

From their observations, astronomers think we are about two-thirds of the way out from the centre of the Milky Way. This is a fairly large but otherwise ordinary flat spiral galaxy. The Milky Way rotates as it moves through space with our Local Group of galaxies. This contains nearly 30 galaxies, held together by gravity. There are many groups of galaxies between us and the furthest observed sources, quasars. Some quasars are more than 5,000 million light years away – so their energy we detect must have been emitted over 5,000 million years ago. This means that we are observing them as they were before the solar system was formed!

Rushing apart

The vast number of galaxies which have been observed differ in many ways but they all have one thing in common. The spectrum of light from every galaxy shows a **red shift** (*see 12.14*) and the further away the galaxy, the greater the red shift. This means that every galaxy is moving away from every other galaxy and that those furthest away are moving fastest. Why should this be? To try to explain it, some scientists suggested the **big bang theory**. According to this at some time in the past (about 15000 million years ago) all the matter in the universe was concentrated at one point. An explosion, the '**big bang**', forced the matter to rush apart and galaxies slowly formed from this expanding matter. The galaxies are still rushing apart.

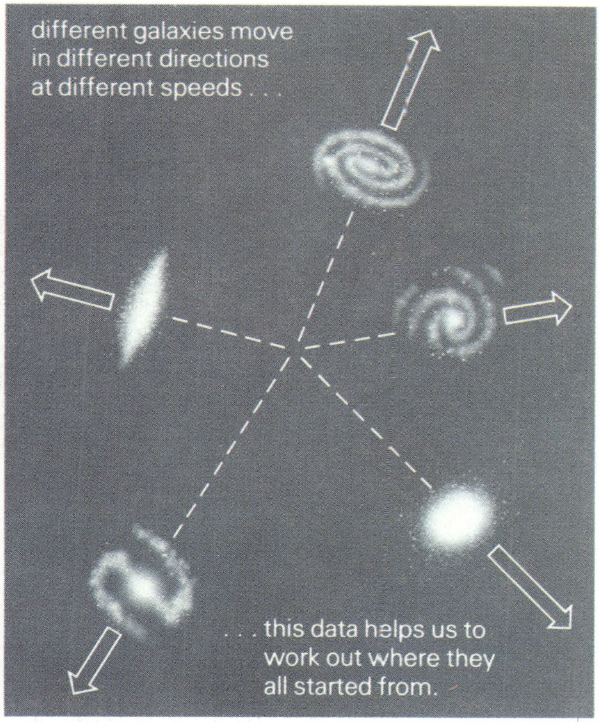

'Plotting back' along galaxies movement – is this the site of the ***Big Bang****?*

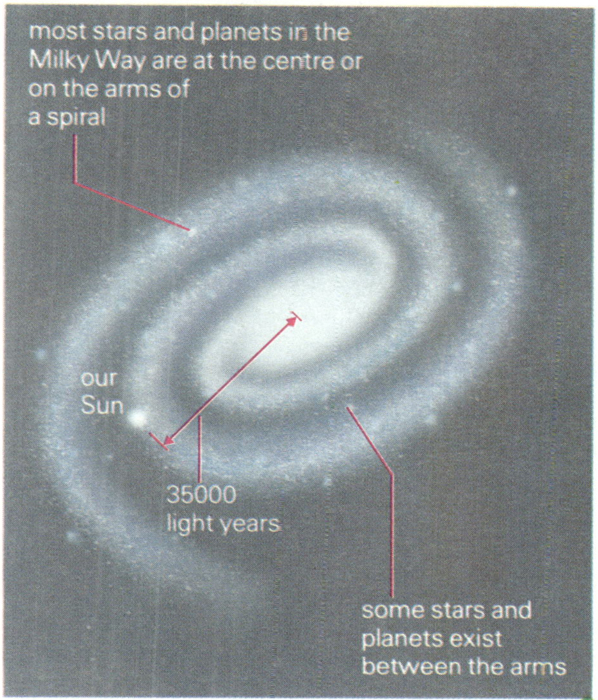

Imagine this diagram on the penalty spot of a football pitch in the centre of, say, Birmingham. The centre of the pitch represents the centre of the universe, and the edge of the universe would be on the city outskirts – 15 km away!

The mysteries of space

In only 500 years our idea of the 'universe' has grown from a small number of objects orbiting the Earth to inflinite space containing countless galaxies. In the process, some questions have been answered but many mysteries remain. One of the greatest of these is: do any other stars have planets like Earth? Astronomers think that some nearby stars may have planets and that there could be millions of stars in our galaxy with planetary systems. If so has life, like the Earth's, evolved anywhere else? Or are we the only 'living Earth in space'?

1. Sailors see the mountain tops of an island before they see its shore. Why is this?
2. How did the telescope change people's ideas about the universe?
3. Through a large telescope, you can see light from a star that no longer exists. Explain how this is possible
4. Some people think we should spend far more time and resources searching for another planet like Earth. Others think we should conserve our resources and concentrate on repairing the damage we have caused on Earth. What do *you* think? Write a short article giving your views.

Index *(refers to spread numbers)*

For additional information, see the following modules:

1 Energy
4 Environments

Photo acknowledgements

These refer to the spread number (in italics), and where appropriate, the position on the page (lh = left-hand page, rh = right-hand page).

J. Allan Cash Ltd. *12.1; 12.3; 12.4* rh; G.S.F. Picture Library (Dr. B. Booth) *12.5* (×2); *12.6;* H. Jalland *12.4* lh; Ann Ronan Picture Library *12.15* lh, top; Science Photo Library *12.12* (×2); *12.13* (×2); *12.14*; *12.15* lh, bottom.

Picture Research: Jennifer Johnson, Norman Franks